EMPOWERED MILLIONAIRE

EMPOWERED MILLIONAIRE

by J. Martin Kohe and Judith Williamson

Two books combined in one volume
Your Greatest Power
&
How to Become a Mental Millionaire

An Approved Publication of The Napoleon Hill Foundation

Published 2019 by Gildan Media LLC
aka G&D Media
www.GandDmedia.com

EMPOWERED MILLIONAIRE. Copyright 2012, 2019 The Napoleon Hill Foundation. *Your Greatest Power*, Original Edition Copyright 1953, Revised Edition Copyright 2004, The Napoleon Hill Foundation; *How to Become a Mental Millionaire* Copyright 2005, The Napoleon Hill Foundation

No part of this book may be used, reproduced or transmitted in any manner whatsoever, by any means (electronic, photocopying, recording, or otherwise), without the prior written permission of the author, except in the case of brief quotations embodied in critical articles and reviews. No liability is assumed with respect to the use of the information contained within. Although every precaution has been taken, the author and publisher assume no liability for errors or omissions. Neither is any liability assumed for damages resulting from the use of the information contained herein.

Front Cover design by David Rheinhardt of Pyrographx

Interior design by Meghan Day Healey of Story Horse, LLC

Library of Congress Cataloging-in-Publication Data is available upon request

ISBN: 978-1-7225-0112-9

10 9 8 7 6 5 4 3 2 1

Empowered Millionaire is the first time ever combined edition of two corresponding works—*Your Greatest Power and How to Become a Mental Millionaire* by J. Martin Kohe and Judith Williamson. By placing these motivational works in the same volume readers can enjoy the big message that Kohe delivers in less than thirty minutes, and then immediately begin to apply the dynamic lesson in daily life by practicing the examples set in *How to Become a Mental Millionaire*. This double edition offers a real one–two punch for getting to the heart of the matter. The main thought to bear in mind as you work through this material is that first you gain the knowledge, and secondly you are taught how to apply it.

This book is so easy to follow and put into practice that you will immediately feel more powerful and in control just by reading it! It is a terrific little book that is dynamic and forceful and promises to render you a real service for the investment of your time in reading it. As W. Clement Stone advises, "Do it now," and don't wait another minute in getting started on the road to your personalized success.

Contents

The Choice is Yours
An Introduction by W. Clement Stone... 11

Your Greatest Power

Your Right to Choose
A Preface by Don Green... 17
Discovering It... 19
Choosing Wealth.. 29
Choosing Conditions.. 35
Choosing Your Personality.. 41
Choosing Happiness.. 51
Hidden Treasure.. 65

How to Become a Mental Millionaire

Preface by Judith Williamson... 75
Introduction by Judith Williamson... 78

Lesson 1
Power of Mental Pictures... 83

Lesson 2
Power of Self-Confidence... 94

Lesson 3
  The Secret of Dealing with People.. 114

Lesson 4
  How to Get Ahead Financially... 135

Lesson 5
  Psychology of Trouble... 154

Lesson 6
  How to Control Your Nerves... 159

Lesson 7
  Power of the Imagination.. 166

Lesson 8
  New Psychology of Success.. 178

Lesson 9
  Secret of Happiness, The Power of Joy................................. 189

Lesson 10
  Power of Mind Over Body.. 205

Lesson 11
  Secret of Good Health.. 218

Lesson 12
  Secret of Youth... 231

Lesson 13
  The Secret of Dealing with Children..................................... 241

Lesson 14
  Power of Creation.. 254

Lesson 15
  How to Get What You Want—Part 1...................................... 267

Lesson 16
  How to Get What You Want—Part 2...................................... 280

Lesson 17
How to Solve Your Problems 289

Lesson 18
Solving the Mystery of "Why Are We Here?" 296

Lesson 19
How to Become a Mental Millionaire 309

Lesson 20
Power of Grace 322

Appendix 1
Our Human Barometer 337

Appendix 2
The Secret of Dealing with Trouble 362

Appendix 3
Mental Millionaire Progress Report 390

The Choice Is Yours

An Introduction by W. Clement Stone

Powers . . . you have them, but you may not choose to use them. For some are so obvious you don't recognize them. Thus you may not intentionally choose to use what J. Martin Kohe discovered to be your greatest power . . . power you, and every boy and girl, man and woman, possess.

Peace of mind . . . happiness . . . physical, mental and moral health . . . success and wealth . . . have come to those who have read *Your Greatest Power*, authored by J. Martin Kohe, and deliberately used the secret which it reveals.

Hundreds of thousands of lives . . . perhaps millions . . . have been changed for the better because of Mr. Kohe. For he was the publisher and distributor of inspirational self-help books. Examples: *Think and Grow Rich* and *Law of Success*. During his lifetime he kept striving for the knowledge that would help him and others become better persons and lead truly successful lives. Because he searched so diligently, he made the discovery which he reveals in his book *Your Greatest Power*.

As President of Combined Insurance Company of America and its subsidiaries, I have been amazed to find how great a motivating influence this little book has had on the lives of our sales representatives and office personnel.

As President of The Chicago Boys Clubs I have used *Your Greatest Power* to awaken the teenager to his power voluntarily to control himself and find the true riches of life as well as success in school, sports and the activities in which he wishes to excel.

As an associate of Bill Sands, the author of *My Shadow Ran Fast*, I have seen the power in *Your Greatest Power* inspire prisoners in The 7th Step Foundation program intentionally and successfully strive to rehabilitate themselves.

As director of several organizations interested in mental health, I have observed that *Your Great Power* has given hope to the emotionally disturbed and the alcoholic.

Your Greatest Power is exciting and easy to read. Its charm is in its simplicity; its strength in its sincerity. But most of all, it inspires and moves you to desirable action. Your life too can be changed for the better when you voluntarily choose to use your greatest power.

W. Clement Stone

"Millions of people go through life expecting a battle at every turn," J. Martin Kohe wrote, "simply because they fail to recognize their greatest power." And he spoke from experience. As an author, lecturer, and psychologist, he travelled across the country helping people to solve their problems. His personal appearances helped thousands face up to their problems and do something about them. But even more important, he left behind books like this that will help others for years to come. For once you discover *Your Greatest Power*, you will never forget it! J. Martin Kohe has given you a lifelong guide to greater happiness and fulfillment.

Your Greatest Power is a book with a big message. It contains a message that applies to anyone, regardless of age, position, or status. Married couples have used it to add many happy hours to their lives. The peace of mind it provides has saved many needless doctor bills. Businessmen have learned to overcome unfavorable economic conditions. Employers have bought hundreds of copies for their workers. Seldom has such a little book had such a big effect on so many people!

Your Greatest Power

Your Right to Choose

A Preface By Don M. Green

We all have choices to make on a daily basis, and the sum total of these choices defines our station in life. Our choices determine if we are a part of society's ills or an instrument in the solutions that will help make the world a better place in which to live.

J. Martin Kohe, the author of *Your Greatest Power*, reveals the secret that will help you find peace of mind, happiness, good health and success.

Millions of lives have been improved by the reading and application of inspirational self-help books. Kohe distributed *Think and Grow Rich* and *Law of Success* in an effort to obtain knowledge that would help him and others become better persons and lead successful lives. More knowledge for self improvement is revealed in this great book.

Don't let the small size of this book fool you. *Your Greatest Power* is a valuable motivational book for those willing to read, study and apply the message. The choice is yours.

Your Greatest Power is an easy-to-read book that can help prepare you for a better life—a life that most people dream about but never realize.

DON M. GREEN
Executive Director
The Napoleon Hill Foundation

Discovering It

You are the possessor of a great and wonderful power. This power, when properly applied, will bring confidence instead of timidity, calmness instead of confusion, poise instead of restlessness, and peace of mind in place of a heartache.

Millions of people are complaining about their lot, disgusted with life . . . and the way things are going, not realizing that there is a power which they possess which will permit them to take a new lease on life. Once you recognize this power and begin to use it, you can change your entire life and make it the way you would like to have it. A life that was filled with sorrow can be a life filled with joy. Failure can be turned into success. Where poverty once gripped an individual's life, it can be changed to prosperity. Timidity can be turned into confidence. A life of disappointment can become a life of interesting experiences and pleasant associations. Fear can be changed to freedom.

Too many times, as life goes on, a person may have a number of reverses, he may have run into a series of difficulties, he may even have had a number of various troubles to contend with. Before long he adopts the attitude that life is difficult, that life is a battle, that the cards are stacked against him . . . so what's the use . . . "you can't win." Then this same individual settles back and is convinced that no matter what you do is "no good." Beaten in his own desire to win in life, he finally turns to his children, hoping that with them it will be different. Sometimes, this is a way out, and sometimes the children fall into the same way of life as the parent. Many times the individual comes to the conclusion that there is only one way out, and he finally comes to the end of life through his own hand . . . suicide.

Yet, all this time, the individual fails to discover this great power that will change his life. He doesn't recognize it . . . he doesn't even know it exists . . . he sees millions of others struggling the way he is and decides that THIS IS LIFE.

Raimundo DeOvies tells a story that, when the great library of Alexandria was burned, one book was saved. But it was not a valuable book; and so a poor man, who could read a little, bought it for a few coppers. It was not very interesting; yet there was a most interesting thing in it! It was a thin strip of vellum on which was written the secret of the "Touchstone."

The touchstone was a small pebble that could turn any common metal into pure gold. The writing explained that it was on the shores of the Black Sea, lying among thousands and thousands of other pebbles which looked exactly like it. But the secret was this. The real stone would feel warm, while ordinary pebbles are cold. So the man sold his few belongings, bought some simple supplies, camped on the seashore, and began testing pebbles. This was his plan.

He knew that if he picked up ordinary pebbles and threw them down again because they were cold, he might pick up the same pebble hundreds of times. So, when he felt one that was cold, he threw it into the sea. He spent a whole day doing this and there were none of them the touchstone. Then he spent a week, a month, a year, three years; but he did not find the touchstone. Yet he went on and on this way. Pick up a pebble. It's cold. Throw it into the sea. And so on and on. But one morning he picked up a pebble and it was warm . . . he threw it into the sea. He had formed the "habit" of throwing them into the sea. He had gotten so into the habit of throwing them into the sea, that when the ONE HE WANTED CAME ALONG . . . HE STILL THREW IT AWAY.

Oh! How many times have we contacted this GREAT POWER and did not recognize it? How many times have we had THIS GREAT POWER right in our hands and we threw it away, because we did not recognize it? How often have we seen it before our very eyes? How many times have we seen THIS GREAT POWER demonstrated right before us? Yet, we did not see it with all its possibilities, with all its wonder-working effects. That is the reason we have devoted this entire treatise to THIS GREAT POWER . . . THE GREATEST POWER THAT MAN POSSESSES!

Conwell, in his book, "Acres of Diamonds," tells about a farmer who was a very happy farmer. His farm was all paid off. He had a very lovely family. Each year he managed to save some money from his plantings. He wasn't short of anything to make his life worthwhile and happy. However, one day a traveler came along and said to the farmer, "If you will find a place where water runs over white sand, there you will find diamonds. Your daughter will be richer than any princess, your son will be richer than any prince, and you will have all the wealth that you could possibly imagine." That night this farmer did not sleep . . . for the first time in many months. He rolled and tossed and turned. Finally when dawn broke he decided he would sell his farm and go out and search for diamonds. This he did. He put his family in with one of the neighbors, took his money and went all over the world searching for diamonds. Finally, when he came down to his last few cents, thoroughly disgusted with himself and what he had done, he committed suicide. In the meantime, the traveler returned to the farm. He walked into the house, looked up on the mantelpiece, and exclaimed, "Did the original owner of the farm return?" The new owner said, "No, he did not." The traveler said, "He must have, why those stones up there on the mantelpiece are diamonds." "Oh! no," exclaimed the new owner of the farm, "that's impossible . . . I found those stones out in the backyard." The traveler again assured the new owner, "Yes, those are diamonds." That is the way the Kimberley Diamond Mines in Africa were founded.

Certainly, you see the point in the story. We search all over the world looking for diamonds and still, there they are right in our own back yards. We search all through our lives for THAT POWER which will make our lives complete, but most people never find it. Yet, it is right before us. All we have to do is recognize it and start to use it. It's here.

Before we tell you what this GREAT POWER is, we want you to know about another story that took place in Africa. There was an explorer who went into the wilds of Africa. He took a number of trinkets along with him for the natives. Among some of the things that he took with him were two full-size mirrors. He placed these two mirrors against two different trees, and then sat down to talk to some of his men about the exploration. Then the explorer noticed that a savage approached the mirror with a spear in his hand. As he looked into the mirror, he saw his reflection. He began to jab his opponent in the mirror as though it were a real savage, going through all the motions of killing him. Of course, he broke the mirror into bits. In the meantime, the explorer walked over to the savage and asked him why he smashed the mirror. The native replied, "He go kill me. I kill him first." The explorer explained to the savage that that was not the purpose of the mirror, and then led the savage over to the second mirror. He explained to him. "Look, the mirror is an object whereby you may see if your hair is combed straight, to see if the paint on your face is proper, to see how chesty you are, and see how muscular you are." The savage replied, "Oh! me no know."

So it is with so many millions of people. They go through life fighting it. They expect a battle at every turn and that is the way it turns out. They expect to have enemies, and they certainly do. They expect to have one difficulty after another, and that is exactly the way it happens. "If it isn't one thing, it's another ... there is always something" ... and that is the way it has been and will continue to be for millions of people who fail to recognize this GREAT POWER. This GREAT POWER that could completely change the world remains as hidden as the diamonds from the farmer who had them in his own back yard. Millions of people will continue to live plain, ordinary, miserable lives because this GREAT POWER escapes them and they never have been able to catch up with it. YOU CAN'T FIGHT LIFE. You have tried it. Millions have tried it and have failed. Then what is the answer? THE ANSWER IS THAT WE MUST UNDERSTAND LIFE . . . IF WE WISH TO MAKE THE MOST OF IT.

The amazing part about this power is that anyone and everyone can use it. It doesn't require any special training or education. It isn't a power that requires any special aptitudes to make it work successfully. It isn't a power that anyone has any special claims to, nor does it require wealth or prestige to make it work. It is a power that everyone is given at birth, whether he be rich or poor, successful or unsuccessful, whether he be born on the right side of the tracks or not. The sooner we recognize this power, the quicker we get on the main road and stay there. The more of us who will get on the main road and stay there, the more hope will spring in the hearts of others to follow this healthy pattern of life.

Millions of people fail to realize that when they go into a shoe store, they may choose to buy a pair of black shoes or they may choose to buy a pair of brown shoes; that when they go into a clothing store, they choose to buy a light garment or they choose to buy a dark garment; that when they turn on the radio, they may choose to tune in one station or they may choose to tune in another station; that when they go into an ice cream parlor, they may choose to buy a chocolate sundae or a pineapple soda; that when they go to the movies, they may choose to go to a neighborhood movie or they may choose to go to a downtown movie. Yes, it is true, if you CHOOSE, when you go on a vacation, to go to the seashore instead of going to the mountains, that YOU MADE THIS CHOICE. When you buy a car YOU CHOOSE to buy a car of one particular make or YOU CHOOSE to buy a car of another manufacturer. In other words, THE GREATEST POWER THAT A PERSON POSSESSES IS . . .

THE POWER TO CHOOSE.

Yes, you have this power, regardless of your religious beliefs. You choose the shoes, the car, the radio program, the picture show, the vacation, the mate. You have this power. There was nothing outside of yourself to force you to make the decision that you did. You did it, because you made this choice. You made this choice because YOU WANTED IT SO. If the choice was bad, then, of course, we want something or someone to blame. So, some people will say, "It was God's Will." But was it? You are probably familiar with the old saying "God helps those that help themselves." Regardless of what we believe regarding God, God does give each and every man and woman the right TO HELP HIMSELF . . . OR IN OTHER WORDS, THE RIGHT TO CHOOSE.

Henry Drummond in his book "The Greatest Thing in the World" tells a story of a little boy who was very sick. The boy was going to die. The parents were very much upset about it, and yet, there was nothing the doctors could do. One day an elderly, religious man walked into the house and noticed how depressed everyone was. He asked why they were so downhearted. He was told that their little son was very sick and they expected the little fellow to die. The religious man asked where the boy was and he was told which bedroom to go to. The elderly religious man walked into the bedroom, put his hand on the little fellow's head and said, "My boy, GOD LOVES YOU, don't you know that?" and walked out of the room, then shortly afterward left the home. After he had gone, the little fellow who was sick and was going to die, jumped out of bed, ran all over the house shouting, "God loves me . . . GOD LOVES ME." He no longer was sick, but a well, strong and healthy boy.

Here is a perfect illustration of what happens when a person CHOOSES to believe that God loves him. No doubt, the little fellow had done something which was wrong . . . certainly not anything punishable by death . . . but he evidently thought that God was punishing him. But once he made the realization that GOD LOVED HIM, he was no longer sick. The little fellow made use of that GREAT POWER . . . THE POWER TO CHOOSE. It gave him life. It saved the family much sorrow and heartache.

Too many people have the very bad habit of telling their children that God will punish them if they do something wrong. The child is filled with fear . . . the fear of God. He chooses to be afraid of God. The child goes into adult life . . . still with this fear. Is it any wonder that the average person's life is a shadow of what real living could be? He, in turn, does the same thing with his children. And so, century after century, this fear is perpetuated by parents who fail to understand that THE POWER TO CHOOSE can change their lives. If telling the child that God will punish him would prevent the evil doing, it would be all right . . . but look around and you will see that it has not turned the trick. On the other hand, if we would realize *that the wrong doing itself carries with it its own punishment,* then we will CHOOSE what is right. Because we will then know that it isn't God that is going to punish us, but it is our own BAD CHOOSING that carries the punishment with it. If we make the right choice in the first place, what can go wrong?

For example, a woman who had a very lovely son was constantly in the habit of telling her little boy that if he did not do what was right, God would punish him. The result was that the little fellow was always having colds. The mother was beside herself; she didn't know what to do. Then she learned that you don't say that to a child. You tell a child that God loves him. She explained this to the child, with the result that the child no longer had any colds. The mother was amazed and astounded. Here you can see as long as the mother CHOSE to tell her youngster that God would punish him, he was filled with colds ... when she CHOSE to tell her son that GOD LOVES YOU, the change came about. WHAT BROUGHT ABOUT THE CHANGE? Did God make the change? It was the mother, who in CHOOSING THE RIGHT IDEA OF PRESENTING GOD changed her child's life and her own.

We must, therefore, realize that there is NOTHING OUTSIDE OF OURSELVES to hurt us. GOD DOESN'T HURT US. GOD LOVES US. THEREFORE, WHAT CAN HURT US ... *ONLY OUR OWN BAD CHOOSING.*

If we choose to eat so much that we make ourselves sick, who is to blame? If we choose to drive our cars so fast that we cannot control them, who is to blame? If we choose to allow ourselves to have nasty, disagreeable personalities, who is to blame? If we try to become the "richest man in the cemetery" and make ourselves invalids, who is to blame? If we have failed to learn how to live, whom shall we blame? God? Oh, no! not any more. GOD LOVES YOU. He doesn't hurt anybody. We hurt ourselves through the bad use of this GREAT POWER that God gave us ... THE POWER TO CHOOSE.

Choosing Wealth

Millions of people are seeking wealth. They would like to be able to say to themselves, "Now, I don't have to worry about money anymore." They would love to be free from money worries. So they scheme, plan and try many different ways to help themselves financially and nothing seems to work. The result is that they become discouraged, and decide that they are not the ones who will achieve this enviable position. They tried everything but changing their thoughts—the one thing that would make the difference.

Some time ago we came in contact with a man who was having all kinds of financial trouble. His wife complained that she was afraid to go to the door, because the only people who came to the door were bill collectors. It was a very discouraging situation. We gave this family a book that we thought would help them improve their thinking. The wife looked at the book and said, "I wouldn't read that stuff... there is nothing to it." The husband said, "I'll read it, leave it here." The result was that the man began to think differently. He showed a new spirit for living. Within a year's time, they moved into a better neighborhood; they bought a whole houseful of new furniture; he even made a down payment on a new car.

We did not give the man any money. Certainly money would have helped him, but it would only have been a temporary lift. What we did do was to start the man on the right road of CHOOSING HIS THOUGHTS FOR IMPROVING HIS FINANCIAL STATUS. That is what we need, if we are going to improve our financial positions. If we do not change our thinking, we can never hope to change our financial positions. What most of us fail to realize is that A TOOTH GROWS FROM THE INSIDE OUT. So, we must change our inner thoughts . . . as we change our inner thoughts about our financial positions, the outward change is bound to come about. So LET US CHOOSE GOOD, HEALTHY THOUGHTS ABOUT MONEY AND FINANCES.

By using this GREAT POWER TO CHOOSE in the right direction, you are bound to improve your financial station. But too many people through their own failure to use this great power have made themselves slaves to the very thing they have wanted to avoid. There was a young man for whom life had been quite a struggle. He had been unemployed for quite a length of time. He finally obtained employment that was by no means anything to be proud of. Yet, this same young man, who was married and had a youngster, had the nerve to say, "I don't want to be rich." He was trying to set aside a few pennies every day so that his son would be able to go to college some day. This man was wise enough to choose to set aside a little money for his son's education. To say that it was a struggle is putting it mildly. He refused to go to a downtown movie, instead preferred to go to a neighborhood show, in order to save a quarter. He refused to go to a better type restaurant because it would cost more money. When he went to the legitimate theater, he would buy balcony seats, instead of orchestra, because that was all that he could afford. When he bought a car, he bought the most economical kind of car. He was unable to take his family on a vacation, because he couldn't afford to do it. This man had the nerve to choose to say, "I don't want to be rich."

Is it any wonder that millions of people are steeped in poverty? NOT REALIZING IT, THEY CHOOSE TO REMAIN POOR. THEY FAIL TO RECOGNIZE THIS GREAT POWER. No one can be blamed for being economical. Many people must be thrifty or they would not get along at all. But these same people could be making use of this GREAT POWER TO CHOOSE. They could start to fill their minds with the better things of life. Instead, we hear day after day people saying, "I would like that, but I can't afford it." "I can't afford it." "I can't afford it." It's true, BUT DON'T SAY IT. As long as you continue to say "I CAN'T AFFORD IT" . . . *you will go all through your life* with "I CAN'T AFFORD IT." CHOOSE A BETTER THOUGHT. Say, "I'll buy it. I'll get it." When you build up the thought that you will get it, that you will buy it, you build up the thought of expectancy. YOU BUILD UP YOUR HOPE. NEVER DESTROY YOUR HOPE. When you destroy your hope, then you have created for yourself a life of difficulty and disappointment.

A young man who didn't have a dollar to his name said, "One of these days, I am going to Europe." A friend sitting by started to laugh and said, "Look who's talking." Twenty years later the man and his wife went to Europe. The man did not say, "I want to go to Europe and I suppose I never will be able to afford it." He had the hope. The hope gave him spirit. The spirit moved him to do things so that he would be able to go to Europe. When you say "I can't afford it" ... everything stops. The hope is gone ... the mind becomes dulled ... the spirit is gone ... then WE CHOOSE to believe that nothing can be done about it. THIS GREAT POWER ... THE POWER TO CHOOSE will give you the necessary hope, the necessary spirit, the necessary courage to carry on and GET THE THINGS FROM LIFE THAT YOU REALLY WANT.

Allen in his little book "As a Man Thinketh" says that "Thoughts are Things." We like to change it to read THOUGHTS BECOME THINGS. The telephone was a thought in the mind of Bell before it became a telephone. The harvester was a thought in the mind of McCormick before it became a harvester. The electric bulb was a thought in the mind of Edison before it became an electric bulb. John D. Rockefeller, when he didn't have a dime to his name, said, "Some day I am going to become a millionaire." AND HE DID. So you must realize that the things that you want out of life are thoughts first before they become things. Our financial condition is a thought first, and then a reality. If we want to change our financial picture, we must first CHANGE OUR THOUGHT. If we CHOOSE TO CHANGE OUR INNER THOUGHTS ... our outer conditions must change. THAT'S THE LAW. When you choose thoughts of "I can't afford it" ... "I'll never get it" ... "I am one of the blessed poor" ... you are blocking the pathway to YOUR GOOD. CHOOSE YOUR THOUGHTS ... YOU CAN ...

CHANGE YOUR THOUGHTS . . . YOU CAN . . . use your imagination in the beginning, if necessary. You will never regret it. Things will begin to happen for you, changes will come into your life, such as you never believed possible. YOU WILL TRULY GAIN A NEW LEASE ON LIFE.

It is surprising how many times THIS GREAT POWER . . . THE POWER TO CHOOSE . . . if used correctly could make a person's life what he wants it to be. One young man had a very unusual experience. He found that every time he saved up to seventy dollars, something would happen. He would have an accident . . . some unforeseen difficulty would arise . . . HE JUST COULDN'T SAVE OVER SEVENTY DOLLARS. This man will go through life with this problem and difficulty, unless he uses this GREAT POWER . . . THE POWER TO CHOOSE and starts to think differently.

Another man found that every time he had a little money in the bank . . . something would happen so that he JUST COULDN'T KEEP IT for any length of time. He went through his whole life with this thought . . . he could have just as easily used his GREAT POWER . . . THE POWER TO CHOOSE . . . and changed this thought destroyer.

One young man was a jack-of-all-trades. He was able to do many things well. Although he was successful in everything that he did, nevertheless, he never made any money. People could not understand why. He was ambitious. He was likable. He had a pleasing personality, but financially, he struggled year after year. Finally this young man had it pointed out to him just what his trouble was. He constantly made the statement, "I can do everything well but make money." Once he began to realize that his big trouble was simply a bad choice of thought . . . things began to change. Instead of saying, "I can do everything well but make money," he began to say, "I can do everything well, including making money." Within a few years' time this man's financial condition changed. He really and truly started to make money. He began to get ahead financially, until today, people say that he is a rich man. This man could have gone through his whole life doing many things well, but never making any money. As soon as he realized that he was CHOOSING THE WRONG THOUGHT, and did something about changing that thought, then his financial condition turned for the better. THE POWER TO CHOOSE brings about a much better and effective money-making power.

Choosing Conditions

Anyone with a little common sense knows that you cannot control conditions. Unless, of course, you happen to become the head of your government, and maybe then you would be able to control them.

But for most of us, we must agree that we cannot control conditions. This is true. So, what can we do? We can control our thoughts ... and by controlling our thoughts ... by USING THIS GREATEST POWER ... THE POWER TO CHOOSE ... we are INDIRECTLY ABLE TO CONTROL CONDITIONS. The most common illustration is in time of war. A young man is called into the service. Here he has no choice. He must go and serve his country. He is brought to camp. Here he is trained. He is prepared for action. All during this time HE HAD NO CHOICE as to what his officers made him do. He had to comply with their demands. BUT HE STILL HAD THE POWER TO CHOOSE HIS OWN THOUGHTS. If he chose the thought that he would not come out alive, that he would be crippled ... it wouldn't be a surprise that this is exactly what happened. We know that on the other hand, that a person or soldier can protect himself through his own POWER TO CHOOSE. F. L. Rawson, noted engineer, and one of England's greatest scientists, in his book, "Life Understood," gives account of a British regiment under control of Colonel Whittlesey, which served in the World War for more than four years without losing a man. This unparalleled record was made possible by means of active cooperation of officers and men in memorizing and repeating regularly the words of the 91st Psalm which has been called the Psalm of Protection. This is an extreme case of the POWER TO CHOOSE, but remember it is the GREATEST POWER THAT MAN POSSESSES.

We all know that there are good times and bad times. Some people can't even make a living in good times, let alone in bad times, mainly because they have failed to use THIS GREATEST POWER ... THE POWER TO CHOOSE. When bad times come along, most people sit back, fill themselves with discouragement and wait for the government to do something about it. Others will use this GREATEST POWER ... THE POWER TO CHOOSE ... and will make a success even in bad times. Many of our greatest businesses have been started and built in "so-called" bad times. Why? Because the founders of the business refused to believe in bad times ... they went ahead anyway ... and succeeded. In bad times, there are many times the number of advantages which good times do not allow. Less money is needed to start and keep the business going, help is easier to get and cheaper, competition is not so alert ... and more than anything else, there are so many discouraged people that the PERSON WITH A LITTLE COURAGE doesn't have to battle so hard.

There was a man who was in business during one of the "bad time" periods. He felt that the reason he was not doing so well was due to the bad times. He felt that unless conditions improved, there would be no opportunity for him to improve. Then during the very heart of the bad time period, he went into a certain shopping district. He noticed that there were two butchers within 10 stores of one another. One was as busy as he could be. People were standing three and four deep to be waited on. The other butcher hardly had a customer. Here is a problem. Bad times exist. Yet within the very same neighborhood there are two butchers, one who doesn't even know there is such a thing as bad times, and the other one is barely making a living. The young business man decided to investigate. He went into the store where the people were standing waiting for service, and as he did, the store owner said, "How do you do?" in a very pleasing and courteous manner, "I am busy, but I will be with you in a few minutes." He was gentle and kind with each and every customer. He was helpful and serviceable to people. He made suggestions to his customers, but at no time argued with them. The purchase was made. Then several days later, the young business man went to the other store. The proprietor growled, "What is it you want?" Instead of giving the young man the meat he wanted, this butcher attempted to force upon him the meat the butcher thought he ought to have. He was not pleasant at all, and was interested only in his immediate welfare. Here you can quickly recognize THE POWER TO CHOOSE.

The one butcher chose to believe that business was bad, due to the bad times, and that was the way it worked out for him. He was not a courteous and reasonable person with his customers. Furthermore, he even preferred to take his "bad business" out on the very people who came in to patronize him. The other butcher chose to believe that business was up to him. It was up to him to be fair and reasonable. It was up to him to be courteous and helpful. He didn't know what bad times were. He chose correctly. The man with little to do chose incorrectly. This ability TO RECOGNIZE THIS GREATEST POWER... THE POWER TO CHOOSE... makes it possible for a person to get the most out of life, while the other person not recognizing this power makes life a burden. THE POWER TO CHOOSE helps one to increase his money-making ability.

The young business man, after noticing the difference between the two butchers, went to his office the next day and started to work. HE CHOSE TO BELIEVE IT WAS UP TO HIM... not to the times or the government. He started to advertise, he made special sales, he made necessary changes for the times, he modified his prices, and before long he was busy again... business was good again... he was making money again. CONDITIONS HAD NOT CHANGED. BUT HE DID. Through this GREATEST POWER... THE POWER TO CHOOSE... instead of closing his doors, his business was once more on its feet... he had changed... even though the times had not.

In the field of employment, we have a similar situation. Let us take two employees and compare them and see how THE POWER TO CHOOSE AFFECTS EACH PERSON. One always chooses to be to work on time. He chooses to follow instructions. He chooses to do his work the very best that he knows how. He chooses to offer suggestions which may help the business. He chooses to do certain little odds and ends which may not be in his keeping with the position for which he was hired. He chooses to work a few minutes, or even an hour over-time if necessary. He chooses to study the business, even taking special courses after working hours to improve himself and the services of the company. This man, through his simple POWER TO CHOOSE, makes himself a successful employee who is bound to make progress. He makes himself so valuable to his employer, that his employer goes out of his way, if necessary, to keep this person employed.

Now let us take a look at the other kind of employee. He chooses to come to work at a time suitable to himself. He chooses to argue with his employer and his fellow-workers about certain things which have to be done. He refuses to work a few minutes or an hour overtime. He chooses to go outside of the business and talk against his company. He chooses to do only as much work as he is paid for. He chooses to spend his time in foolish entertainment and ungainly activities. He chooses to feel that the time outside of working hours belongs to him and he may do with it as he pleases. He chooses to refuse to look into the future, or to prepare himself for the future.

When bad times come around, the second man will be the first one let out. He will blame the times. He starts to complain bitterly because he lost his job. He will rant against his government, calling the heads of his government all kinds of nasty names. He will blame everybody but himself. His family and associates suffer along with him. He chooses to let the days and years go by. He finally finds himself in a home for the aged, which is kept up by the state. Why?

If there were only some way that people could be made to realize that THIS GREATEST POWER . . . THE POWER TO CHOOSE . . . and choose correctly *EXISTS WITHIN THEIR OWN MINDS,* that they could carry out the plans of their own choice and really live the way they may have dreamed of living. It is easy enough to blame conditions; it is easy enough to blame relatives; it is easy enough to blame the government; it is easy enough to blame anybody and everybody and everything, if ONE CHOOSES TO DO SO. But, any person who truly recognizes this GREATEST POWER . . . THE POWER TO CHOOSE . . . begins to make progress, not only in his business life, but also in his social, family and personal life. He begins to realize that he is the one THAT IS DOING THE CHOOSING and that friends, although they mean well, cannot do his choosing for him, nor can his relatives. Consequently, he develops real self-confidence based upon his own ability, upon his own actions, and upon his own initiative. No longer does he depend upon conditions. No longer does he depend upon some figure of imagination, but instead, he depends upon himself; the results begin to tell right from the beginning of his realization. *This realization seems so difficult because hundreds of thoughts are racing through our minds at such speed that we fail to recognize this simple yet amazing POWER TO CHOOSE.*

Choosing Your Personality

One of the greatest problems in life is the problem of personality. Personalities seem to be clashing constantly. Many of our troubles and difficulties come about because people cannot get along with one another. Homes are broken up, friendships are destroyed, employment problems by the hundreds arise because of a clash of personalities . . . and even wars are engaged in because of different nations failing to see eye to eye.

Here again, the GREATEST POWER man possesses . . . THE POWER TO CHOOSE . . . plays a most important part. Stop to think about it . . . you can choose to be friendly, or you can choose to be unfriendly. You can choose to be helpful, or you can choose to refuse to help. You can choose to be cooperative, or you can choose to be stubborn. You can choose to get excited, or you can choose to be calm. You can choose to lose your temper, or you can choose to overlook the matter which would ordinarily cause you to be upset. You can choose to be lovable, or you can choose to be bitter. You can choose to smile, or you can choose to walk around with a long face. You can choose to be trusting, or you can choose to distrust everyone you meet. You can choose to believe that "everybody is against you," or you can choose to believe that everybody likes you. You can choose to be neat and clean, or you can choose to be careless and slovenly. You can choose to be lazy, or you can choose to be ambitious. Stop to think about it AGAIN. Don't you do your own choosing? YOU CERTAINLY DO. Here is one of the best cases on record.

Benjamin Franklin came to the strange awakening that he was constantly losing friends. He began to realize that he was constantly arguing with people. HE JUST COULDN'T GET ALONG WITH PEOPLE. One day, around New Year's Day, when New Year's resolutions are generally made, he sat down and made a list of all his nasty personality characteristics. He listed them one by one. He arranged them, putting the most harmful trait at the top of the list, down to the least harmful. Then he decided that he would eliminate these nasty personality characteristics one by one. Each time that he found that he had successfully eliminated one, he would cross it off the list, until he had cleaned up the entire list. He developed one of the finest personalities in America. Everybody looked up to him and admired him. When the colonies needed help from France, they sent Franklin. The French liked Franklin so well that they gave him what he asked for. TODAY IN ALMOST ALL YOUR BOOKS ON PERSONALITY BUILDING, THE NAME OF BENJAMIN FRANKLIN is cited as the most outstanding case of personality development.

Suppose on the other hand, Franklin had CHOSEN to go through life without doing anything about his personality. Suppose Franklin had done what millions of people are doing today . . . using their personalities just as it was given to them by nature and their parents. Suppose that Franklin continued his argumentative ways . . . he never would have succeeded in getting the French to help the colonies, and the entire history of the United States would have been changed. ONE PERSONALITY made a great difference to a nation. And yet, millions of people are walking around and saying, "What can I do about it?" How do you know? How do you know what YOU might be able to do as the years go by. Lincoln said, "I will prepare myself and some day my time will come."

AND IT DID. HE CHOSE TO BELIEVE in preparedness. AT LEAST WE WILL MAKE LIFE REASONABLE AND ENJOYABLE FOR THOSE AROUND US. AT LEAST WE WILL NOT BE RESPONSIBLE FOR BRINGING UNNECESSARY TROUBLE TO THOSE ABOUT US.

How many times does one member of a family make life miserable for everybody else in the family? How often does an unreasonable father or maybe even a mother make all the other members of the family wish that they had never been born into that family? One person can destroy or make an entire family miserable. YET, THIS SAME PERSON, BY USING THE GREATEST POWER GIVEN TO MAN . . . THE POWER TO CHOOSE . . . COULD HAVE MADE A BEAUTIFUL LIFE FOR THOSE AROUND HIM AND ESPECIALLY THE MEMBERS OF HIS OWN IMMEDIATE FAMILY. If each one of us would make his own family life a pleasant and enjoyable experience, THE WHOLE WORLD COULD BE CHANGED IN A VERY SHORT TIME.

One problem that faces many people as they go through life is the loss of a beloved one. So many people, after losing a mother, father, brother, or a close friend or relative, become so upset that life to them becomes meaningless. "What is there to live for now?" they ask. All over the world there are thousands upon thousands of people who walk through the streets and through the balance of their lives "living corpses." Failing to realize that they possess this GREATEST POWER . . . THE POWER TO CHOOSE . . . they continue their lives choosing to be a burden to themselves and everyone around them. You cannot blame these people, for their loss was great. The shock may have been very sudden, for apparently no reason. They are unable to analyze why it had to happen. Sometimes it is not easy to analyze why it happened. But whether we can analyze it or not, the important job on hand now is what to do with the balance of life that remains to the one left behind.

We feel that the best way to answer this great question is through a story that we came across some time ago. A young college football star lost his mother the week before the "big game." The coach didn't know what to do. He had never had an experience like this before. He finally decided that he would leave it up to the young star himself. If the boy decided to play, that would be fine with the coach. However, if the young man decided that the shock was too great and that he would decide not to play, then the coach would abide by his decision. The day of the game came. The team ran out on the field. The young star was with them. The team proceeded to go through with their practice signals, while the young football star went over to the stands. He stood there. About twelve rows up in the stand there was an empty seat. It was draped in black. The young man stood there . . . looked at the empty seat draped in black and said, "Mother, I am playing this game for you." He then went into the game and helped his team to victory.

Here is a splendid illustration of the POWER TO CHOOSE. This young man could have sat down and started to cry. He could have made himself the subject of sympathy from all his fellow teammates. He could have made them all feel so sorry that the entire team would have been affected and the game would have been lost. But he chose for the benefit of all. He benefited, his team benefited, and surely, his mother wherever she was, was really proud of her son. He was playing the WAY SHE WOULD HAVE WANTED HIM TO. That is the answer. After the beloved one has passed on, what can we do about it? Go on living THE WAY THEY WOULD WANT US TO LIVE. MAKE THEM PROUD OF US WHEREVER THEY ARE. True, we cannot control conditions . . . but we can control our POWER TO CHOOSE. In controlling our POWER TO CHOOSE, we can make life interesting and worthwhile to ourselves and everyone else around us.

We look at all the problems of life and they seem insurmountable. We look around and we wonder if life will ever be worthwhile. Some people will go so far as to say that the world is getting worse instead of better. The world will start getting better the very minute WE CHOOSE TO MAKE IT BETTER. Do not wait for the other fellow to start improving the world. Do not wait for your neighbor to start improving himself . . . YOU START. If each one of us will start to CHOOSE TO IMPROVE HIMSELF, WE CAN

CHANGE OUR OWN LITTLE WORLDS, THE LITTLE WORLD THAT EACH AND EVERYONE OF US LIVE IN. THAT'S THE MOST IMPORTANT ONE FOR US. *THAT IS THE ONE WE CAN DO SOMETHING ABOUT.* Each one of us may have five or a hundred and five people that we can come in contact with. If we have a pleasant and helpful influence on these five or one hundred and five, our influence on them will be for the better . . . they in turn will influence others in a similar manner . . . it won't take as long as you might think to change this world to be a BETTER PLACE TO LIVE IN.

Some time ago we saw an article in the paper about a certain street that was to be made into a boulevard by the governmental authorities. The plans were all made and everybody sat back and waited for the powers that be to start to make the necessary improvements. It was going to be a "million dollar boulevard." But something happened. The government officials found it impossible to go ahead with the plans and the idea was tabled. One man who lived on the boulevard CHOSE TO DO SOMETHING ABOUT IT. He decided that if the government officials were not going to beautify the boulevard, the least he could do was to beautify his own front yard. This he did. It was one of the most attractive places on the boulevard. His neighbor saw what he did and the neighbor began to beautify his place; this continued with each neighbor, until the entire boulevard looked like the "million dollar boulevard." WHO DID IT? Actually, ONE MAN. HE CHOSE TO START AND EVERYBODY ELSE FOLLOWED. Don't say that you can't change the world. YOU CAN CHANGE YOUR LITTLE WORLD . . . and that's the one that counts. YOU CHOOSE TO THINK THAT YOU CAN CHANGE IT ... THE NEXT FELLOW WILL GET THE IDEA AND IT WILL BE DONE ... AND YOU CAN BE THE VERY PERSON TO START IT IN YOUR OWN HOME, JOB, COMMUNITY, OR EVEN IN YOUR COUNTRY.

Practically every personality problem could be solved if we would ONLY CHOOSE TO FOLLOW one simple little suggestion. So many husbands and wives are living miserable family lives because of various disagreements. Millions of people working on jobs are having their hands full because of many different forms of disagreements. Even nations find themselves at war because of unsettled disagreements. If these people involved would use this GREATEST POWER GIVEN TO MAN ... THE POWER TO CHOOSE ... we would find ourselves in an altogether different style of living. Many, many years ago a wise old philosopher said,

"IF WE MUST DISAGREE ...
LET US DISAGREE WITHOUT
BEING DISAGREEABLE."

If we would realize as individuals, if we would realize as husbands and wives, that two people living together are bound to have differences of opinion ... that it is perfectly alright to disagree ... BUT WITHOUT BEING DISAGREEABLE ... THE ENTIRE NATIONAL PICTURE OF MARRIAGE WOULD CHANGE OVERNIGHT. Marriage could be so much more enjoyable. Home life could be so much more worthwhile. The influence on the children would be tremendous. The divorce rate would be cut so deeply, it would be unbelievable.

The great difference of opinion in the minds of employees is such that millions of people are unhappy in their work. Many times, these people find that they like the work, they like the pay, they enjoy the surroundings, but THEY CANNOT GET ALONG WITH CERTAIN PEOPLE. Thousands are constantly changing jobs, because of differences of opinions. If these people would use this GREATEST POWER . . . THE POWER TO CHOOSE . . . and disagree without being disagreeable . . . they would find themselves much happier, much more enjoyably engaged in their work, and much freer and easier with the people they come in contact with. It would be a great burden off their shoulders, because instead of fighting people and conditions, they would be more alerted to understanding others and their opinions.

Most of us have had the experience of going through one or two wars or even more. We have observed that it is one thing to win a war and another thing to win the peace. It is most interesting when you think about it, that the very nation you defeat in war, you must, after the war, feed and clothe, help the conquered nation to its feet again, give her financial aid so that her economy will be self-sustaining. To what end? One never knows. To start another conflict? To recreate the very thing you sought to destroy? Will the nations of the world some day use this GREATEST POWER . . . THE POWER TO CHOOSE . . . and save themselves these great catastrophes? Will the nations of the world some day CHOOSE TO DISAGREE WITHOUT BEING DISAGREEABLE? Let us hope they will. THEY CAN. Just as we can use this GREAT-

EST POWER... THE POWER TO CHOOSE... to make our own individual lives worthwhile and enjoyable; just as we can use this POWER TO CHOOSE to make our family lives agreeable and happy, so can the nations of the world make the family of nations, one GREAT BIG HAPPY FAMILY. Sounds too wonderful? WE HAVE THE POWER... WE CAN, IF WE CHOOSE TO.

How can one be so sure? Go to a symphony sometime, or watch a great symphony orchestra on the television. What do you see? A hundred men or more playing one great musical selection. Notice a little more and you will see many, many different kinds of instruments, each making its own sound and contributing its own bit to the entire musical selection. Different instruments, yes... but disagreeing... not at all. Each player plays for the good of all. No conflicts... all in harmony. Each player desires to make the selection the most brilliant piece of music ever played. Each man gains pleasure in making this great production possible. Each man's pride swells as he notices the great musical selection draw to its close.

Analyze this great symphonic orchestra a little closer and what do you find. Each man chose to play in the orchestra. Each man chose to play the particular instrument that he was using. Each man chose to harmonize with the other players. Each man chose to do the best that he knew how. He chose to follow the conductor, as he directed them through the selection.

SO CAN WE. We have been given this power. We have been given this GREATEST POWER... THE POWER TO CHOOSE... by the GREAT CONDUCTOR. THE GREAT CONDUCTOR LOVES US. THE GREAT

CONDUCTOR WANTS US TO GET ALONG. YES, WE ARE ALL DIFFERENT. Different customs, different foods, different mannerisms, different languages, but not so different that we cannot get along with each other ... IF WE WILL DISAGREE WITHOUT BEING DISAGREE-ABLE. THE GREAT CONDUCTOR has often been referred to as OUR FATHER. Being OUR FATHER, he has made it possible to live together as one great peaceful family. He has made it possible, by giving US THE POWER TO CHOOSE. WILL WE USE IT SENSIBLY OR WILL WE USE IT FOOLISHLY? WE HAVE THE POWER... THIS GREATEST POWER... THE POWER TO CHOOSE.

Choosing Happiness

Almost everyone could find himself 100 to 500 percent happier, if he could recognize and realize that he possesses THIS GREATEST POWER . . . THE POWER TO CHOOSE . . . So many people have a little happiness and then try to hang on to it. Some people as soon as they find themselves a little happy, wonder what is wrong and especially begin to wonder if it will last. There was a play on Broadway in which the heroine walks out on the stage (she had just returned from her honeymoon) and states she is so happy "she could die." Just imagine . . . here is a person who was searching for happiness . . . now that she has it "she could die." What a terrible MISUSE of the GREATEST POWER . . . THE POWER TO CHOOSE. Is it any wonder that we see so little happiness? Those who have it are so afraid that they cannot hold on to it, that they lose it almost as fast as they find it.

Sometime ago a young man told us this story. He said, "I was going with a young lady. We became very fond of each other. We decided to become engaged. So happy were we in our engagement that we decided to culminate our happiness in marriage. We were married. We fixed up a very attractive little apartment. In fact, it was the envy of all our friends. My wife was working. I was working. We had a car. We had a little money in the bank. We were really and truly living a heaven on earth. But, from time to time, I would talk with some of my friends, and they seemed to feel that it wouldn't last. They told me that it couldn't last. They would say, 'Look at the Joneses, how happy they were the first few months of their married life. Look at them now, how much trouble and worry they have. Look at the Smiths. They were happy, too, the first few months of their married life. Look how unhappy they are now.' I heard this so many times that I thought that my wife and I were living an unnatural life instead of a natural one, that any day this heaven-on-earth marriage balloon would burst. I would go home, after talking to one of these people who said it was too good to last, and say the same thing to my wife. 'Dear, this is too good to last. It is too heavenly. It just can't go on.' Before long, things began to happen. My wife lost her job. I lost my job. We had to give up our car. We had to give up our beautiful little apartment that we had fixed up. We had to go back and live with mother, and on top of it all, my wife became a mother herself. What's the good of living," he cried out, "if every time you get things straightened out, something comes along to spoil it." He wanted to commit suicide. He felt that if THIS IS LIFE, then you might as well end it now.

We finally showed the young man that had he used his GREATEST POWER... THE POWER TO CHOOSE... HE COULD HAVE AVOIDED ALL OF THIS DIFFICULTY. We showed him that he did not have to CHOOSE

TO BELIEVE his friends who told him that married happiness does not and cannot last. We told him about a wonderful statement that a woman wrote in her book that would have saved him all this difficulty. Florence Scovell Shinn, author of the "Game of Life and How to Play It" and also, "Your Word Is Your Wand" states in the latter book that *NOTHING IS TOO GOOD TO LAST*. We explained to him that there isn't anything that will come along to spoil your life, if you use your POWER TO CHOOSE CORRECTLY. If you use your POWER TO CHOOSE that NOTHING IS TOO GOOD TO LAST, it is surprising but true, that things will run along smoothly and beautifully for you, even beyond your fondest dreams. *HERE IS THE SECRET OF KEEPING THINGS RUNNING SMOOTHLY*. But, you must constantly remind yourself that when everything is going without trouble that THAT IS THE WAY IT IS SUPPOSED TO BE. The stars don't bump into the moon; the moon does not crash into the sun; the sun does not crash into the earth. Certainly, if the stars and the moon and the earth, traveling at a tremendous pace don't conflict with one another, why can't our lives run along smoothly without the conflicting forces that so many people encounter. Our lives can run along without friction, if we could only realize the full import of the POWER TO CHOOSE. THE POWER TO CHOOSE THAT NOTHING IS TOO GOOD TO LAST will make a change in your life far greater than one could even dream of. As one man said, "Our heaven on earth is right here, but the trouble with most of us is that we don't take advantage of it."

Everywhere you go you hear of people who are getting along beautifully, and then seem to have trouble holding on to this smooth living. A man is getting along exceptionally well in his work. He is happily married. He has money in the bank. He drives a big car. He is sitting on "top of the world." But can he stand it? No! He doesn't see anyone else living so smoothly. He thinks he is better than the next fellow. He becomes over-confident. Over-confidence always leads to carelessness. This carelessness leads him into trouble of one form or another. NOW HE IS DISCOURAGED. Didn't he have everything he wanted? Wasn't he happy? Didn't he go to church and live according to the rules? So he started to look for something to blame. He comes to the conclusion that there was something outside himself that caused his trouble. He didn't do anything to cause it. Certainly not. But let's analyze his case, and what do we find. He was getting along fine. He wasn't short in anything. He made one little mistake. He allowed himself to become overconfident. Instead of thanking God for his good fortune and choosing to keep it that way, he chose to become careless and . . . not realizing, deliberately choosing to do something to GET BACK INTO TROUBLE AGAIN. This overconfidence has done as much to spoil and frequently to ruin as many lives as any other reason we might know of. Very little is ever said about overconfidence. We are not aware of it. It overtakes us because we have failed to recognize this GREATEST POWER . . . THE POWER TO CHOOSE . . . with the result that we are not careful at a time when we should be. Nature does not want us underconfident . . . but she does not want us to be overconfident. Millions of people have had a taste of overconfidence . . . without recognizing it. If they don't recognize it, they may be kicked down by it, and may never get up again. Then when it happens, it takes the spirit out of their lives. They are defeated and beaten. They cannot analyze what happened, with the result that another life joins the great ranks of discouraged people.

George gets a raise in salary. He comes home as happy as can be. He says to his wife, "Let's go out and celebrate." They call up another couple and go to some night club to celebrate. They start to drink. Before long George is making love to the other man's wife. His wife is now making love to the husband of the other couple. Now George doesn't like it. They start to argue. They come home in a rage. The argument continues into the early hours of the morning. After it is all over, George wishes he had never gotten the raise. Then, he sits down and begins to complain. He complains that his happiness did not last long, that his good luck was short-lived. But why? Because something outside himself brought it about? Because God did not want him to be happy? Why? You know why . . . now. George's good fortune made him overconfident. His overconfidence led to carelessness . . . carelessness almost always leads to trouble.

Most people cannot stand life when it runs along "TOO SMOOTHLY." They crave excitement. They crave it because they choose it. This choice brings them into a troubled state and then they say "THIS IS LIFE." Life did not produce the trouble. We bring it about ourselves with our BAD CHOICE OF THOUGHT.

From time to time we hear people say, "If I can put this deal across, then I don't care what happens." "If I marry George, then I don't care what happens." "After we get the mortgage paid, then I don't care what happens." WHAT A TERRIBLE CHOICE OF THOUGHT! How stupid! Can you see why there is so much trouble in the world, and why so few people are really happy? Imagine choosing the thought... "I don't care what happens." It is almost like going into a restaurant and saying, "I don't care what you serve me as long as it is food." They may serve you food that is so badly burned that you can't even eat it. They may serve you meat that you can't even cut. They may serve a vegetable that is so badly rotted that you can't even look at it. BE CAREFUL. It is just as easy to be careful, as it is to be careless. YOU DO CARE WHAT HAPPENS AND YOU KNOW IT. Keep thinking good thoughts. Keep thoughts that will help you, not harm you. It is important, because through this GREATEST POWER... THE POWER TO CHOOSE... LIFE BECOMES WHAT YOU THINK AND CHOOSE IT TO BE.

Our parents, our grandparents, our great-grandparents and people for generations back have so completely filled our minds with the thought that we must have trouble; that this, that, and the other is too good to last; that we of this modern day and age have come to inherit these thoughts which *keep the world in mental bondage.*

THE POWER TO CHOOSE gave the young man in our story a NEW FREEDOM. He slept better. He felt better. He realized that there was nothing outside himself trying to hurt him or destroy his happiness. He began to live. HE FOUND A NEW LEASE ON LIFE. He began to realize that there *WASN'T SOMETHING* THAT ALWAYS HAPPENS TO SPOIL HIS LIFE. *THAT SOMETHING* was his own failure TO CHOOSE CORRECTLY. Once he realized this simple, yet POWERFUL FORCE, his whole life changed. He knew that IT WAS HIS OWN THOUGHTS... HIS

OWN CHOOSING that caused his trouble and not some unseen force or power outside himself. (Read this last statement again and again.)

All over the world people CHOOSE TO BELIEVE that if it isn't one thing, it's another. People everywhere are bewildered by the thought . . . if it isn't one thing, it's another. A man is working steadily . . . everything is moving along without friction . . . EVERYTHING EXCEPT HIS OWN THINKING. He starts his mind into action. He says, "Yes, I am working now, but how long will it last?" Before long, he is out of work. The grocery bill begins to mount; the back rent becomes a worry; work is not in sight; his child takes sick; then he takes sick. A big doctor bill faces him, together with all the other expenses of the household. The man has to go to the hospital. The hospital bill makes life even more uncomfortable. Finally, the man goes back to work. He begins to pay up his debts. He is just about straightened out and paid up on all his bills when something else appears . . . and so . . . with a few experiences of this kind he becomes a CONFIRMED BELIEVER in the thought . . . THAT IF IT ISN'T ONE THING, IT'S ANOTHER.

During all this trouble period, he found himself carried away with his trouble and his trouble thoughts. He never did think clearly, mainly because he was never taught to think clearly, and he just never did learn to think clearly on his own. He had his "ACRES OF DIAMONDS," but he never found them. He remained poor in his thoughts, and poor thoughts bring poor results. Had he discovered his GREATEST POWER . . . THE POWER TO CHOOSE . . . he would then have realized that most of his trouble was due to his own poor thinking. THEN IF HE HAD DISCOVERED THAT NOTHING IS TOO GOOD TO LAST, he could have avoided his difficulties and instead of expecting trouble, he would have expected his smooth-running life to continue.

It isn't easy to live an even-going life, when we notice that everyone around us is filled with trouble, difficulties and disappointments. However, when we begin to realize that those who are filled with troubles and difficulties are using their GREATEST POWER . . . THE POWER TO CHOOSE . . . AND USING IT INCORRECTLY, then we begin to understand why things happen the way they do. Is it any wonder that so many people "knock on wood" when things are going along nicely. The fear THAT IT IS TOO GOOD TO LAST is obvious and apparent. We must constantly remind ourselves . . . THAT NOTHING IS TOO GOOD TO LAST . . . and before long we will begin to believe it. When enough of us begin to believe it and practice it . . . we will . . . just as Columbus discovered a new world in 1492 . . . DISCOVER A NEW WORLD OF REAL LIVING.

One of the greatest of religious leaders, head of one of the large Eastern religions, said, "How can I be happy, when the rest of the world is unhappy?" A very good question, and being a very wise man he presented a very interesting problem. However, if we see no man happy then we come to the conclusion that life is not meant to be happy. When we are happy for a short time, we must of necessity come to the conclusion that it is not meant to last. But, why not? If this great religious leader had said instead, "Look at me . . . look how happy I am . . . you can be the same as I . . . if you will follow my teachings."

Then his millions of followers would have felt that it is natural to be happy, and at least one of the great religions of the world would have had millions of happy people. Again, we see that one man can change an entire group of people, running into the millions. Like many of our new inventions, no one thought of them before. Likewise, before Florence Shinn came out with the statement NOTHING IS TOO GOOD TO LAST . . . people thought that happiness could not last . . . because so few people had been able to demonstrate it. This great religious leader has THE POWER TO CHOOSE. He chose to believe that he could not be happy because the rest of the world was not. What was to stop him from choosing to set an example of happiness for his followers? Nothing, but his OWN CHOICE.

The same conditions that prevail with an individual can also prevail with a whole country. So many people remember when everything in the nation was going along smoothly. Almost everybody was working, there was very little unemployment. People were buying new cars; stocks were high; property was high; everybody seemed to be making money. Most people seemed to be riding on the crest of the waves. For a short period of time it seemed as though the world was having one of the greatest periods of prosperity that it had ever seen. But many people from the richest to the poorest, from the weakest to the strongest, from the lowest to the highest walks of life, began to feel that IT WAS TOO GOOD TO LAST. Little by little this thought began to fill the minds of the people everywhere. Things began to change. People became cautious. Stocks began to topple. Banks began to close. Everywhere there was nothing but darkness and despair. A land that yesterday was prosperous, was now thrown into the depths of depression, all because from the richest to the poorest, people felt that IT WAS TOO GOOD TO LAST.

What would have happened if these same millions of people who said it was too good to last would have used their GREATEST POWER and had CHOSEN TO BELIEVE THAT NOTHING IS TOO GOOD TO LAST? THEY WOULD HAVE FOUND A WAY TO KEEP THINGS RUNNING ALONG SMOOTHLY. As one man said, "This is truly a great country." When the country seemed to be at a standstill and was not going forward, the automobile came along and kept everybody busy and progressive. When we seemed to catch up with ourselves with the automobile and it seemed that everything would be at a standstill, the airplane began to pick up the slack in our production. Then when the airplane seemed to fill its need, the radio began to take up the slack . . . after radio came television. THIS ONE MAN CHOSE TO BELIEVE THAT NOTHING IS TOO GOOD TO LAST. *SOMETHING GOOD CAN HAPPEN* . . . just as easily as something bad. WE MUST USE THIS POWER TO CHOOSE CORRECTLY OR IT WILL WORK THE VERY OPPOSITE OF THE WAY WE WOULD LIKE LIFE TO BE.

There are still millions upon millions of people in this world who have nothing. There are still millions upon millions of people on this earth who do not have a single change of clothing. Millions are not properly housed. The world as a whole is still unlearned and uneducated. According to the reports, two-thirds of the world still eat without knives and forks. Even in this country, there are still millions of people without bathtubs, without decent living quarters, without hope of ever seeing a better way of life.

> LET US CHOOSE TO BELIEVE
> *THAT SOMETHING GOOD CAN HAPPEN.*
> WHY MUST WE ALWAYS USE
> THE OLD MODEL... THAT
> SOMETHING BAD WILL HAPPEN?

We begin to realize now that through the GREATEST POWER... THE POWER TO CHOOSE... that man has come a long way since the first man walked the face of the earth. The world, as a result of modern inventions is reaching a point that it is gradually mastering the forces of nature, in as far as the mechanical perfections that go to make life more enjoyable are endless. With this mastering of nature, we begin to realize now that we have a bigger job... MASTERING OURSELVES. We have gone through the stone age, the wood age, the iron age, just going through the mechanical age... we are now entering the MENTAL AGE. Man has been using... those who have used it... THE POWER TO CHOOSE and not realizing it. Now that we realize it... we make the great discovery that most of our troubles, our difficulties, and our miseries are *MAN MADE.*

Man has been making himself a mechanical life of ease and pleasure; while at the same time he has been making his mental life more and more complicated. It need not be; not any more. NOW THAT HE HAS DISCOVERED THIS GREATEST POWER... THE POWER TO CHOOSE... HE CAN CHOOSE TO LIVE... LIKE A MAN.

No longer can man blame something outside of himself. Man must blame himself. Man does what he does because... HE CHOOSES THUS TO DO. Maybe we won't admit it, but it is true. For years man worked the whole day through, sometimes putting in 12 to 14 hours a day, with little or no time for leisure. As a result of modern inventions, man has more time for himself. Man, therefore, is at the present time, beginning to fathom the art of real living. He must learn how to live because he has so much leisure time on his hands. As long as he has so much time on his hands, he must be able to use it sensibly. If he doesn't, he will bring destruction upon himself. Man has found that tasks that were difficult years ago, are now simplified by machinery. Man will now find time to learn how to live. In learning how to live, he will recognize that the most important task is TO LEARN HOW TO LIVE WITH HIMSELF. He will learn to live with himself when he begins to use THE GREATEST POWER THAT HE POSSESSES... THE POWER TO CHOOSE.

This GREATEST POWER... THE POWER TO CHOOSE... will make life for him what he always wanted it to be; not to depend upon something outside of himself, but to depend on that great POWER WITHIN HIMSELF, THIS GOD-GIVEN POWER WHICH MAKES HIM A MAN. He will realize that life does not depend on money, machines, cars, homes, furs, and so-called wealth... but upon his MIND POWER given to him by the UNIVERSAL MIND POWER of which he is a part, and through which all that he desires can come to pass.

Man must realize that the most important thing in life is LIFE. Therefore, he owes his first duty to this LIFE which he possesses. If he takes care of his LIFE, it will be what he wants it to be. If he neglects his own LIFE . . . it will be what he does not want it to be. After the UNIVERSAL POWER gives man LIFE . . . then it is up to MAN TO CHOOSE TO DO WITH IT AS HE SEES FIT.

May we remind you of a poem we came across some time ago:

"I shall pass through this world but once
Any good, therefore, that I can do,
Or any kindness that I can show
To any human being,
Let me do it now. Let me
Not defer it or neglect it,
For I shall not pass this way again."

Therefore, the fact remains that inasmuch as we are going through life JUST ONCE, we should choose to make life a confident one, instead of a timid one . . . that we should choose to make a calm life rather than one of restlessness . . . that we should choose to have poise rather than confusion . . . that we should choose to make the most of life for ourselves and everyone else around us . . . rather than spoil our own lives and those about us. We have the POWER TO CHOOSE . . . LET US USE IT TO THE BEST OF OUR ABILITY. As we use our own minds to CHOOSE THE BEST so we will find that the UNIVERSAL MIND will come to our aid and assistance to help us choose the BEST. Together we cannot fail. WE MUST SUCCEED!

Just an Afterthought

Now that you have read *"YOUR GREATEST POWER,"* do you feel better? Sure you do. Then read it over and over again.

Anytime you find yourself a little disgusted, disturbed, or upset, read it. You'll feel better.

Keep a copy at your bedside. Read a little before you go to sleep. You will feel better and stronger the next morning.

Why not send a copy to someone who needs it? It will be appreciated, to be sure.

Hidden Treasure

It exists in self-help books such as *Your Greatest Power*. Here's how to find it.

By W. Clement Stone

Let's try an experiment: When you see a word, phrase or sentence that is underscored in this article, just copy the number beside it and write down the thoughts, if any, that flash in your mind. Try it! Something wonderful may happen to you if you subsequently relate the idea, suggestion or principle to yourself. I'll explain why the experiment later.

Everyone loves an adventure story! Countless readers have been intrigued with tales of: pioneers and cowboys who opened the American West . . . Flash Gordon and Buck Rogers keeping Planet Earth safe from evil forces of outer space . . . brave explorers going into deep jungles filled with danger to find ruins of past civilizations . . . swashbuckling seamen fighting off the attacks of pirates . . . and stories of: TREASURE . . . hidden treasure—lost gold mines and—sunken treasure ships. These are among the stories that have caused so many of us to daydream. Perhaps each of us, at least once, has fantasized finding a map that would lead us to our particular fanciful TREASURE. The word itself conjures up visions of chests laden with gold, silver, jewels beyond price.

Stories of great adventure appeared in the news media recently that may trigger such a dream and stimulate our imaginations to help us materialize maps whereby we shall find hidden treasures. But this applies only to those of us who have learned HOW TO develop the habit of taking ACTION when we recognize a usable principle and relate it to ourselves from what we read, hear, see, think or experience.

Treasure Beneath the Sea

While reading the *Chicago Tribune* of Sunday, January 21, 1979, a headline caught my eye: "Drama, Treasure Beneath the Sea." Written by Carol Oppenheim, a *Tribune* writer and certified scuba diver who went into the sea with the treasure hunters, the article related the story of the discovery of the Spanish galleon *Concepcion*. As I had learned at an early age HOW TO Recognize, Relate, Assimilate, and Apply principles, it flashed into my mind that the concepts in Carol's account would be an excellent basis for this article. The following is a summary of Carol's article:

> The *Concepcion* sailed from Mexico in 1641, heavily loaded with silver coins, gold ingots, Chinese porcelain and countless tons of other booty claimed by the Spanish crown. Not listed on the manifest were contraband smuggled aboard by the officers and crew, which may have accounted for 20 to 50 percent of the cargo.

A few weeks out of Vera Cruz, the *Concepcion* ran into an eight-day storm. With her masts gone, she limped toward Puerto Rico to make repairs. Eighty miles off Hispaniola, now the Dominican Republic, the ship rammed into the coral reefs and foundered.

In 1687, William Phips found the wreck and, employing native divers who could stay underwater only three minutes at a time, recovered 32 tons of silver.

Burt Webber, 36, who grew up in central Pennsylvania, developed a "fascination with water" when he was 6 years old. When interviewed, he said, "We had a mountain stream running into a mill, and I would swim in it, fantasizing about being on the bottom instead of the top . . . I began reading books on shipwrecks, and <u>I knew I wanted to dive.</u>"[1] At 16, <u>Webber sold his coin collection to buy a scuba tank.</u>[2]

Webber <u>"wanted to join the Navy but could not pass the physical because of his asthma. Instead, he enrolled in the Divers Training Academy in Miami."</u>[3] In 1961, he "was hired by the Museum of Sunken Treasure in the Florida Keys." <u>He took part in many treasure hunts,</u>[4] some of which <u>"met expenses."</u>[5]

Five years ago, <u>Webber decided to "shoot for a big one."</u>[6] He and Jack Haskins, 44, another treasure hunter based in Florida, were competitors until <u>they decided to join forces</u>[7] a decade ago. Haskins became Webber's <u>researcher,</u>[8] making annual trips to Spain to study naval archives. In 1974, <u>Haskins came across documents</u>[9] detailing the aborted voyage of the *Concepcion*. <u>He deduced that Phips hadn't picked the wreck clean</u>[10] . . . what remained would be very lucrative, easy to find and easy to salvage since the shoals bottomed at an average depth of 65 feet.

Armed with this information . . . <u>a consortium of 30 investors</u>[11] raised $450,000 and set up a corporation now known as Sequest International <u>to negotiate a contract with the Dominican Republic</u>[12] providing for a 50-50 split of the treasure.

Equipped with a <u>magnetometer</u>[13] to record anomalies in the coral, Webber and Haskins, accompanied by a crew of divers, American map and coin <u>experts</u>[14] and a Dominican naval officer, searched the reef for five months in 1977. They found 13 wrecks . . . none the *Concepcion*. <u>"I bet we went right over her,"</u>[15] Haskins said later, "but our mag' wasn't sensitive enough to catch it."

A year later, the treasure hunters learned <u>that the log of Henry Phips's ship had been found. It contained the precise compass points for the location of the lost galleon.</u>[16] In mid-November, carrying a newly developed portable magnetometer, the group set out again aboard the *Samala*. On the sixth day of the renewed search, <u>the divers found an iron strap and a 17th century Spanish olive jar. Three days later—November 30—they found the first silver coin.</u>[17]

"Then we just kept pulling up coins—130 that first day . . . " plus cups, plates, candlesticks, candle snuffers and more olive jars. They found so much they decided that numismatist Henry Taylor would have to move his operations to shore. Taylor chipped away the shards of coral and bathed the coins in muriatic acid. What he saw were rough-shaped circles containing about one ounce of silver, bearing the cross and shield of the king of Spain and the dates 1630 through 1640—proof, he and other experts said, the coins were from the *Concepcion*.

"... The crew twice has discovered a complete chest of coins fused by the coral into a solid 180-pound mass."

Webber refused to discuss the potential value of the booty. Published reports place it at $40 million, but there is speculation it might be as much as five times greater. The salvage operation is expected to continue for months, interrupted only by trips to Santo Domingo to unload the treasure and take on food and water. Haskins believes the section of reef now being worked was not the location of the *Concepcion*'s main hold . . . and may not even have been touched by Phips's divers.

Important Points in Discovering Hidden Treasures

I have had many investment opportunities submitted to me... among them, to become one of Burt Webber's investors in the search for the *Concepcion*. However, because I had treasure maps of my own, I decided against joining the consortium. On my maps, "X" marks the spot (the goal) where there are riches... and many of them are treasures money can't buy. I am now sharing with you several of the important points necessary in reading or interpreting any map that leads to the discovery of hidden treasures.

Do you want to find a hidden treasure? Now you can. But, like Burt Webber and Jack Haskins, you must carefully study, understand and comprehend why it is imperative to follow directions to achieve your objectives. It may be tough to get started, but it will become easier and easier as you get experience in developing the necessary habits of thought and action as you travel toward your destination.

So Obvious It Isn't Seen

Long ago, I developed the habit of underscoring words, phrases and entire sentences while reading a newspaper, magazine, book or other printed material for the purpose of recognizing key ideas that symbolize principles such as those employed by Burt Webber and Jack Haskins that made their dreams become a reality . . . principles so obvious that they may not be seen unless you establish the habit of Recognizing, Relating, Assimilating and then APPLYING those which can bring you to where "X" marks the spot on the map.

The interpretation of the underscoring above can be a guideline in helping you to develop an accurate map to find any treasure you may choose to seek. But you must first know specifically what you want and develop an intense desire to get it. That is what Burt and Jack did. That is the one thing that separates the achievers from the dreamers.

As you read on, I shall describe the principles I recognized. This may help you to design your treasure map. Let's compare notes: If you followed the instructions in the introduction to this article, you will want to refer back to the numbers and compare your notes with mine as to what each idea you selected symbolized or represented.

17 Principles

1. A desire that motivated Burt to set a definite goal: to dive.
2. Paying the price and... Budgeting time and money.
3. Learning from defeat... "With every adversity, there is a seed of an equivalent or greater benefit for those who have PMA (a Positive Mental Attitude)."
4. Gaining experience in seeking a treasure.
5. Again, learning from defeat... The value of perseverance.
6. Aiming high... Definiteness of purpose.
7. The Master Mind Alliance.
8. Accurate thinking... Teamwork.
9. Controlled attention. With a definite goal, one is apt to recognize that which will help him achieve it, particularly if he develops a burning desire.
10. Thinking... Planning and... Study time.
11. Use of Other People's Money (OPM).
12. Good legal advice to get the cooperation of the government and prevent confiscation of the treasure.
13. Use of modern equipment.
14. The employment of experts.
15. PMA... Learning from defeat... Accurate thinking (to get better equipment).
16. "Success is achieved by those who try and maintained by those who keep trying with PMA."
17. "What the mind of man can conceive and believe, the mind of man can achieve for those who have PMA."

The list includes many of the principles to be found in Napoleon Hill's *Law of Success*, *Think and Grow Rich* and *Success*

Through a Positive Mental Attitude, coauthored by Dr. Hill and me. In addition, you may wish to reexamine the story "Drama, Treasure Beneath the Sea" to determine whether other principles, not mentioned, are applicable such as: Going the extra mile ... Self-discipline ... Applied faith ... Pleasing personality ... Personal initiative ... Enthusiasm ... Creative vision ... Maintaining sound physical and mental health ... Using cosmic habit force (universal law).

Do You Want to Find a Hidden Treasure? Here's How!

Do you want to find a hidden treasure. I have my treasure maps. Now you can have yours. Just use your mind power as Burt Webber, Jack Haskins and everyone else has who found treasures—tangible or intangible—including the true riches of life. They Recognized, Related, Assimilated and APPLIED the PMA principles revealed to you in this article.

The map is now in your hands. *Will you dream of achievements ... or achieve your dreams?*

Reprinted from the April 1979 issue of *Success Unlimited* magazine. Copyright 1979 by Success Unlimited, Inc.

How to Become a Mental Millionaire

Preface

by Judith Williamson

The Napoleon Hill Foundation has been the beneficiary of numerous good things from W. Clement Stone's estate in the past decade. One of the invaluable items gifted to us is a series of "lessons" that J. Martin Kohe created in 1952 when conducting his "How to Become a Mental Millionaire" course.

Upon reading these lessons, the thought struck me that Kohe intended this series to correspond with his book *Your Greatest Power*. This book is short, to the point, but theoretical in nature. In order to compensate for the lack of "how to" application that was not included in the brief text, Psychologist Kohe developed 20 strategies, or lessons, to correspond to the "right to choose" theme of his book. Once you have read *Your Greatest Power*, right then is the time to begin Kohe's lessons for creating any desired transformation in your life.

As an educator, I have studied Bloom's Taxonomy of Educational Objectives. If you too are familiar with this hierarchy of learning, you already know that it reads from the bottom up like rungs on a ladder or stair steps. According to Bloom, the six stages of learning are: Knowledge, Comprehension, Application, Analysis, Synthesis, and Evaluation. In order to advance in your learning, you must process through the six stages successfully for full integration of the lesson being taught. You might consider Walter P. Chrysler's story involving his love affair with the automobile to review how this works. In order to create the Chrysler Corporation, Mr. Chrysler processed through the six stages of learning one by one first as a backyard mechanic and then progressing to a corporate CEO.

You too must integrate the lesson on more than just the knowledge level if you are to make a difference in your life.

W. Clement Stone and Dr. Hill both reiterated "action is the key." Action equals application, and that is precisely what Kohe's lessons bring to us. Knowledge first, understanding second, and application third. This process guarantees success in any endeavor as long as you are consistent and persistent in your approach.

Success = Thought + Action. Given this little formula, is it any wonder that Kohe was not finished with his lesson on your power to choose when he finished *Your Greatest Power*? As any good teacher would do, he repeated the lesson using twenty different applications to make certain that you get the point—and, more importantly, that you get the effect—SUCCESS—in your life.

It is with great pleasure that I bring these lessons to you from the Napoleon Hill archives for your immediate use. Do not let these applications remain untried. Remember, action is the key. Unlock the key to your full potential and become the Mental Millionaire that you are fully capable of becoming. Begin the adventure and reap the reward. Unlimited success to you!

>JUDITH WILLIAMSON
>Napoleon Hill World Learning Center
>at Purdue University Calumet

Introduction

by Judith Williamson

Martin J. Kohe's *How to Become a Mental Millionaire* is a phenomenal book that, if you are lucky enough, comes along in your lifetime. Perhaps you have read *Your Greatest Power* by Kohe. If so, you can view this book as a companion book, a "Bearings Book," that will enable you to put into action what Kohe so eloquently discloses as your greatest power—your power to choose. The twenty lessons in *How to Become a Mental Millionaire* instruct you step-by-step in putting theory into practice through simple terminology and equally simple action steps.

In motivational literature many books fall just short of taking you through those final steps to greatness. Kohe's book is different. Being a psychologist by profession, Kohe understands the human psyche and mankind's reluctance to get started toward whatever goal or objective that is set. The maxim, "Do It Now" often seems to be best applied to someone else.

Everyone knows that before we walk we crawl, and before we crawl we scoot, and before that there are even more preliminary stages prior to advanced walking. But, just look at us today. Most of us walk with little or no trouble at all! Success is no different. Each accomplishment is a series of steps that build one upon the other until what appears to be an overnight phenomenal success actually takes several years or even decades of power walking to achieve. By reflecting on the process and then taking the sequence of prescribed steps, success becomes something that is achievable for everyone. Now, let's take a closer look.

Do not confuse success with only financial riches. Success means different things to different people; however, according to Napoleon Hill's research into the lives of 500 successful men from business and industry, success can be gauged by looking at twelve different manifestations or signs of success in a person's life. Hill calls these the "Twelve Riches of Life" and they are listed below:

1. A Positive Mental Attitude
2. Sound Physical Health
3. Harmony in Human Relationships
4. Freedom from Fear
5. The Hope of Achievement
6. The Capacity for Faith
7. Willingness to Share One's Blessings
8. A Labor of Love
9. An Open Mind on All Subjects
10. Self-Discipline
11. The Capacity to Understand People
12. Financial Security

How do you assess these riches in your own life? Using a scale of 1-10 with 1 being the lowest and 10 being the highest, rate yourself on each of the riches. Next, add up the scores and divide by twelve. The number you end up with can be labeled your average Success Quotient. This will be your overall assessment of the state of riches in your life. Are you a 7, 8, 9, or even higher? What are you going to do about improving your score?

A more visual and interesting way of looking at this data is in the form of a circle. Draw a circle and divide it into 12 equal parts resembling the spokes on a bicycle's wheel. At the outer rim of the circle, label the twelve riches. Divide each line into increments of 10 with 1 being at the circle's center and 10 being the circle's outer rim. Next, plot your score on the line by placing a dot on the score you indicated. When all 12 scores are plotted, connect the dots. What does your wheel of success look like now? Will the configuration you created roll, or will it bump along clumsily?

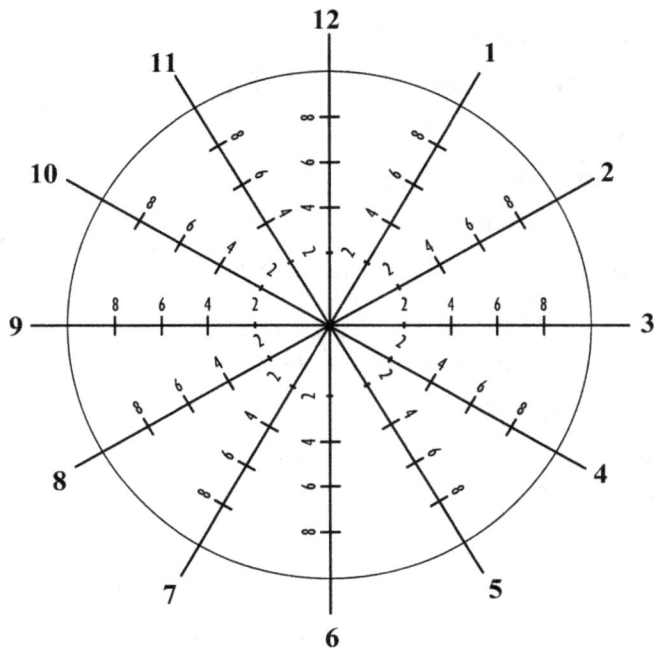

As you can infer from the exercise, your life's riches must be in balance, or you will be out-of-sync and encumbered as you attempt to reach current and future goals. Would it not make more sense to synchronize the 12 riches in your life first and then move more efficiently toward your ultimate goal, your life's purpose?

You've heard the saying, "As within, so without." Reflect on this statement as you journey toward success. Choose to work on yourself first, and within a corresponding length of time what you think about you will become. Napoleon Hill states that "What the mind can conceive and believe, the mind can achieve." You too can become what you dream about, but first let's learn the process by uncovering some common and some not so common techniques that Martin J. Kohe shares with us in his very practical and inspiring work, *How to Become a Mental Millionaire*.

My promise to you is that if you follow Kohe's curriculum in detail, you will be a person changed for the better when you finish this book. If you only read the book for the information herein, you will become a better reader but not necessarily a more successful person. In order to become a full fledged "mental millionaire," you must examine where you are now so that you can follow Kohe's map in the next 20 chapters to reach your targeted destination. Maps are meant to be followed, not merely read. A map implies action. Commit, here and now, to take yourself on a journey of a lifetime that will unlock the treasure chest of your dreams. You, and only you, can complete your journey. Will you stay the course or will you remain an armchair traveler? Only you can decide. Take my advice, and "Stay the Course." You will know the difference.

>
> JUDITH WILLIAMSON
> Napoleon Hill World Learning Center
> at Purdue University Calumet

Lesson 1

Power of Mental Pictures

Dear Reader:
In this our first lesson, Psychologist Martin Kohe gives us a very powerful exercise for expanding our inner vision and then manifesting that very vision into our reality. After demonstrating our imaging power in creating mental pictures, Kohe guides us in producing mental pictures or images in our mind's eye that will assist us in fulfilling our dream. This process of seeing what we would like to manifest, prior to it appearing in our life, is in reality engaging our subconscious mind to work with us in the creation process. Napoleon Hill states that the subconscious mind works very much the same way as film in a camera. He states that the subconscious mind "is capable of receiving any image that is transferred to it by the conscious mind under the influence of a strong emotion . . . . Getting good pictures with this camera is like getting them with any other—the focus must be sharp, there must be good exposure, and the timing must be right."

It is not necessary to understand how thoughts become things more quickly through our mental imaging any more than we need to understand the intricacies of electricity. What we do need to know is how to throw the switch and turn on the light. It is important to note that the subconscious mind cannot distinguish between fact and fiction. Therefore, by imaging in our mind's eye preferred future outcomes in the here and now, we are actually creating our future one mental picture frame at a time. When we spend time in the theatre of our mind, we star in our own very best performance. That, dear reader, is time well spent.

—Judith Williamson

A tooth grows from the inside. So, we must
change our inner thoughts . . . as we change
our inner thoughts about our financial positions,
the outward change is bound to come about.

–YOUR GREATEST POWER

If you have read my book, *Your Greatest Power*, you realize that you possess the power to make life according to your own choosing. You are to be congratulated that you chose to go ahead with this course on "How to Become a Mental Millionaire." Because, honestly, what more could you ask? If you are a mental millionaire, you are bound to make money, if that is what you want. However, most money millionaires rarely become mental millionaires. They depend too much upon money to get them what they want out of life. The result is that you see very few happy money millionaires. They can be, if they so choose, but they have become so accustomed to getting what they want with money that they fail to realize that there is another way. So, prepare yourself as you go through these lessons. You will learn every trick in the game of life. Nothing will be left out.

The first step in becoming a mental millionaire, in learning to take every trick in the game of life, is to watch your mental pictures. I say "think of an automobile and immediately your mind sees a picture of an automobile." I say, "think of an airplane and immediately your mind sees a picture of an airplane." I say, "think of a beautiful garden and immediately your mind sees a picture of a beautiful garden." I say, "think of yourself as a successful person and immediately your mind sees a picture of yourself being successful."

How simple this all sounds, but it is true, isn't it? You see now why almost everybody likes the movies. You see now why almost everybody enjoys television—the reason being that the mind works in pictures. Your whole life depends upon the kind of pictures you choose. Contrary to general belief, it doesn't take long to change conditions—they change as fast as you change the picture, and you can change the picture in an instant.

To illustrate, here is the famous story of Columbus and the egg:

As you know, it was Columbus' theory that the world was round. Everyone else said the world was flat. Columbus said, "Give me ships and men and I shall prove that I am right." Finally, he was able to start out on his voyage, and he did discover America, he did prove to the then civilized world that the world was round. Upon returning to Spain, a banquet was given in his honor. Everywhere around the banquet hall he heard people saying that there was nothing to it—how could he miss America, all he had to do was to keep on sailing. This bothered Columbus—to think that before he had proven his idea that the world was round, everybody was against him. In fact, he had been perceived as a crazy man and had been threatened with jail time. So, when they were all seated at the banquet table, Columbus began: "While we are waiting for the food to be served, I have an egg here and I would like to see someone make the egg stand on end." The first man to his right tried it—the second, the third, and so on. No one could make the egg stand on end. In a chorus, they all exclaimed: "It can't be done." Columbus responded, "Now watch." He took the egg, tapped it lightly, and then the egg stood on end. Everyone shouted, "Oh, that's easy!" Columbus retorted, "Yes, it's easy when someone shows you how!"

Don't continue to go through life thinking that life is hard. You have the "power to choose," to think that life can be a grand and glorious experience. We have spent a lifetime looking for a way to simplify this business of living. It is a whole lot simpler than most people are willing to admit. Yet, we have so complicated life that we think—"This is the way it should be." Don't allow yourself to "continue to choose" making life a difficult experience. We have seen people living beautiful simple lives. But we think that this is the exception—it doesn't have to be the exception—unless we choose to believe it.

Please bear in mind that although Columbus discovered America, it was here all the time! This means that the things we want out of life—whether it be health, happiness, wealth—are here right now for us to choose them, to claim them as our own if we so choose. One important thing I would like to impress upon your mind right in this very first lesson is this: nature did not put a slot in your head like a piggy bank. So, if you add a thousand dollars to your possessions, you do not put this thousand dollars into this slot so that it goes into your "head account." The only thing that changes is your thought or your picture. Now you have a picture in your mind of having a thousand dollars more than you had the day before. Actually, the only thing that we have to watch is our mental pictures, that is the only thing that will actually change. Start working on your pictures now and a change in your life will begin.

I hope you are feeling well; but if you are not, the first smart thing to do is to put a picture in your mind of feeling fine, feeling strong, feeling good, everything you eat agreeing with you, sleeping well and restful, getting along fine.

During the war Winston Churchill was unusually calm for a person who had so many responsibilities, hardships, and difficulties to contend with. He was asked how he was able to keep so calm and poised in such trying times. He answered, "I think of only one thing at a time."

Here is one of the most powerful thoughts you will ever come across: You can think of only one thing at a time. You can keep only one picture in your mind at a time.

Therefore, if you want to be well, keep the picture of being well in your mind. At first, it may seem as though you are kidding yourself. Maybe so, but it works. For example: a man working in a factory was always boasting about how well he was. He was never sick. He had never missed a day because of colds and the like. He, however, went about kidding those who were not well. One day, five of his coworkers decided to see how smart he was. This man—I will call him Joe—walked into work "feeling fit as a fiddle." Shortly afterwards, one of the "five in the plot" walked up to him and said:

"Joe, what is wrong with you? Don't you feel well? You look sick."

Joe told this fellow to quit kidding him. The second fellow walked up a little later and said:

"Joe, what happened to you? Don't you feel well? Didn't you sleep well last night? You look terrible."

Joe replied, "That's strange. That's what Jack (the first fellow) told me."

The third fellow came along a little later and exclaimed, "Joe, what on earth is the matter with you? You frighten me. You are as white as a sheet. What happened to you?"

"I was all right when I came in today. But, that's what Jack told me. That's what George (the second fellow) told me."

To make a long story short, by the time the fifth fellow was through with Joe, Joe—who had walked into the shop a well man—went home a sick man.

You have experienced just such an incident time and time again, throughout your lifetime. Someone meets you on the street and tells you you are looking fine, you perk right up! Someone else comes along and asks what is the matter with you. Immediately, you begin to wonder what is wrong. Now, keep repeating these remarks and before long, the picture becomes a part of your thinking.

So, regardless of how you feel, keep putting a picture in your mind of being well. If necessary, tell it to yourself a thousand times a day. Put a picture before you of someone who looks a perfect specimen of good health, look at it as often as you can, especially before going to sleep at night. (I will explain more about this in a later lesson.) Every time you look into a mirror, tell yourself you look fine. Walk around with this picture in your mind. *You can think of only one thing at a time.* Make it good.

Do you want friends? Then put a picture in your mind of having a lot of friends. Visualize these people coming to your home and you going to theirs. See yourself out with helpful and friendly people. Put the picture in your mind of being popular with all kinds of nice and encouraging friends. See yourself friendly. See yourself with the kind of personality you would like to have. Keep a model picture in front of you. See yourself as this model person. Before long, you will see that this principle will work faster and easier than anything you have ever tried. It goes to the core of getting what you want.

Do you want money? Then put a picture in your mind of "being in the money." See yourself with a lot of money. See yourself buying the finest and best of everything. See yourself dressed in the "best." To affirm this fact, I'll tell you a story of a man who had very little money. This man went to a place where they sold "stage money" and bought a "big roll." Around the bogus roll of money he put several real dollar bills. Every time he put his hand in his pocket, he felt this big roll of money—giving him a picture of "being in the money." It wasn't long before he really was in the "real money."

Don't you see that when you put a picture in your mind of something you want—just that very minute—the law of attraction starts to work. You put a picture in your mind of eating—immediately your mind starts to think of different foods. You then begin to go somewhere food is to be had. Before you know it, you are sitting down and eating! This action is a result of your "picture of eating."

The trouble with most of us is that we are so busy with everything else that we fail to realize just how our mind works. If you want money, you must first put a picture in your mind of having money, the next step is to decide how much you want, the third step is to decide when you want it. To simply say you want money is not enough. It does not stimulate the ego enough. How much do you want? Set the amount. Then set a date when you want to have this amount. If you say you want a thousand dollars in ten years, what stimulant is this? But if you say you want ten thousand in ten years, then we find ourselves stimulated to go ahead and accomplish this result. The ego must be constantly stimulated. We do it with mental pictures. Once you decide how much and when, then keep putting this picture in your mind, remind yourself night and day, as often as you can—but, don't talk about it. Every time you talk about it, you lose some of the stimulant. Furthermore, many of your friends may not be too encouraging, they may even be critical or even spiteful. Make out a card with the amount you want and put it in a place where you will be constantly reminded. You must constantly hold to the picture. Daily reminders will hold the picture.

Do you want success? Then put a picture in your mind of being successful—act like a success, walk like a success, talk like a success. What is success? (I will cover that in another lesson.) In the meantime, does success mean having a lot of money? Then see yourself living in a beautiful home, driving a big car, wearing the finest of clothes, and with lots of money to spend. Think of someone who is successful, and keep thinking of yourself as this person. See yourself in a successful business. If you are in a profession, then see yourself in a beautiful office, with many people calling to see you, seeking your services. If you are employed, then see yourself growing in the company for which you work, see yourself occupying one of the executive offices, see yourself progressing year after year. *See the picture* and then get busy making the picture come true.

Do you want to live life beautifully? Then put a picture in your mind of living this kind of life. Don't try to keep up with the Joneses now. It isn't important. Now, the important factor is to choose everything that will make life beautiful. Remember that when you meet someone on the street, this person doesn't say, "How much money did you make today?" Usually, the remark is, "How are you?" However, if you have mental pictures of living a beautiful life, you won't be asked how you are, but someone may instead say, "My, but you are looking fine." If you want to live a beautiful life, you will naturally watch your actions, your thoughts, your expressions so that you will be a constant pleasure to have around. People will begin to take to you, like you, and will want you around. Others will envy you because you have something that no money can buy—poise, pleasantness, friendliness, beauty in living. May I remind you of the famous statement: "Look at the lily, look how beautifully it grows, yet King Solomon in all his glory cannot compare."

Thus, we can readily see the power of mental pictures. We also realize that we choose these pictures. It is up to us and no one else—not some power outside of ourselves—but to us. Everything starts with a picture. Someone once said: "The very fact that you can picture it, shows that it is possible." Certainly, Graham Bell had a picture of the telephone before it became a reality; Edison had a picture of the electric bulb before it became a reality. So it is with us—we make the pictures in our own minds of which I will help you make them realities. These lessons will show you how to get what you want; and not only to get what you want, but will also show you the right thing for you to have. That is important too. So, make a list of the pictures you want to see realized:

Picture Possibilities
- Good health
- Friends
- Money
- Success
- Living beautifully

Each morning and each night before going to sleep, picture what you want from life. During the day remind yourself that you can think of only "one thing at a time"—choose it well.

> *Your mind belongs to you exclusively.*
> *Take possession of it, direct it to specific usage,*
> *and make life pay off on your terms.*
>
> —Napoleon Hill

Lesson 2

Power of Self-Confidence

Dear Reader:

Having confidence in your own personal ability to achieve your definite major purpose in life is of such absolute importance that Kohe places it as the second lesson in this course. If you cower in a corner sucking your emotional thumb, you will never experience success. This is a certainty, and so critical to your understanding that the author gives several illustrative examples that cause you to reflect on the concept of self-confidence. When you tell yourself that you are not good enough, that you are inferior, that you lack the brain power, that you are unequal and that you are unworthy, you underscore those very same traits within yourself. As you do so, you also dig yourself into an even deeper hole of despair and inaction. Perhaps you have heard that one of the techniques in reversing depression is to do something, any thing. Action neutralizes depression and oftentimes reverses it. Ralph Waldo Emerson states that if you want something badly enough, you should "Do the thing, and you will have the power." Acquiring self-confidence is about doing versus thinking. You may not get it exactly right the first few hundred times, but soon you will have more hits than misses.

At this point, you may be asking exactly what is it that you should be doing? Well, in this lesson you learn how to feed your mind positive mental images, to act in the way in which you prefer to be treated, to relax and to renew your mind in order to alleviate daily stress, to practice affirmations, and to control your thoughts at will regarding self-confidence. This lesson is priceless since once you acquire the above strategies in developing and maintaining your self-confidence, you will never look down upon yourself again. It is only when your outlook is positive that you can envision yourself as a success. That, dear reader, is the only way to see the shining star that you really are.

—Judith Williamson

It is easy enough to blame conditions; it is easy enough to blame relatives; it is easy enough to blame the government; it is easy enough to blame anybody and everybody and everything, if one chooses to do so. But, any person who truly recognizes this greatest power . . . the power to choose . . . begins to make progress, not only in his business life, but also in his social, family and personal life. He begins to realize that he is the one that is doing the choosing and that friends, although they mean well, cannot do his choosing for him, nor can his relatives. Consequently, he develops real self-confidence based upon his own ability, upon his own actions, and upon his own initiative.

–YOUR GREATEST POWER

One of the greatest psychologists of our time once said, "With self-confidence you can do anything. Without it, you can do nothing." So great and so important is self-confidence that I want you to have this lesson early in the course.

Today, success can be made a mathematical certainty. In the previous lesson you learned that if you want success in any direction, you must first put a picture in your mind of the thing—accomplishment, desire, ambition—that you want realized. Once you have the picture, you need a motivation force. This motivating force is self-confidence. Go out and get it. To this end, I would like to bring to your possession the following three poems which have tremendous driving power. Any of these will give you confidence. Using one or all of them will give you that specific drive necessary to make your dreams come true. I suggest that you learn them, put a copy where you can see them, and constantly remind yourself of their message. Here is a famous one by Edgar A. Guest:

It Couldn't Be Done

Somebody said that it couldn't be done,
   But he with a chuckle replied
That "maybe it couldn't," but he would be one
   Who wouldn't say so till he'd tried.
So he buckled right in with the trace of a grin
   On his face. If he worried he hid it.
He started to sing as he tackled the thing
   That couldn't be done, and he did it.

Somebody scoffed: "Oh, you'll never do that;
   At least no one ever had done it";

But he took off his coat and he took off his hat,
   And the first thing we knew he'd begun it.

With a lift of his chin and a bit of a grin,
   Without any doubting or quiddit,
He started to sing as he tackled the thing
   That couldn't be done, and he did it.

There are thousands to tell you it cannot be done,
   There are thousands to prophesy failure;
There are thousands to point out to you, one by one,
   The dangers that wait to assail you.

But just buckle in with a bit of a grin,
   Just take off your coat and go to it;
Just start to sing as you tackle the thing
   That "cannot be done," and you'll do it.

This poem has helped thousands of people and it will surely help you. In other words, if you choose to tackle the things that cannot be done, you will do it.

The following is another mighty powerful poem. I think you'll agree that it is almost impossible to fail if you follow the suggested thoughts:

Success

If you want a thing bad enough
To go out and fight for it,
Work day and night for it,
Give up your time and your peace and your sleep for it.

If only desire of it
Makes you quite mad enough
Never to tire of it,
Makes you hold all other things tawdry and cheap for it.
If life seems all empty and useless without it
And all that you scheme and you dream is about it,
If gladly you'll sweat for it,
Fret for it,
Plan for it,
Lose all your terror of God or man for it,
If you'll simply go after that thing that you want,
With all your capacity,
Strength and sagacity,
Faith, hope and confidence, stern pertinacity,
If neither cold poverty, famished and gaunt,
Nor sickness not pain
Of body or brain
Can turn you away from the thing that you want,
If dogged and grim you besiege and beset it,
    You'll get it!

—Berton Braley

You can surely realize that if you choose, as the poem points out, to allow nothing—absolutely nothing—to stand in your way of getting what you want, you will get it. As I promised you, you have the power to choose. I will guide you to getting not only the things out of life you want, but also living a life of which you will be proud, and so will those around you.

The following is another selection that has been of great help to me and to my students. These same students have said that as a result of this selection, they were able to overcome the feeling of failure. They have committed it to memory, and I think that you should too. Once you begin to think positively, an immediate change will come over you, and progress will begin almost immediately. If we have been thinking negatively, then by all means we must have substitutes handy to offset these negative thoughts. Throughout our lives we are choosing. Our negative thoughts want our attention. Because most people are negative, they too are quick to help us think negatively. Therefore, we must reverse the thought. When you hear a negative statement, immediately reverse it. Substitute a positive thought. These poems will help you more than you realize at the moment.

Thinking

If you think you are beaten—you are,
  If you think you dare not—you don't,
If you'd like to win, but you think you can't
  It's almost a cinch that you won't.
If you think that you'll lose—you're lost
  For out in the world we find
Success begins with a fellow's will,
  It's all in the state of mind.
If you think that you're outclassed—you are,
  You've got to think high to rise,
You've got to be sure of yourself before
  You can ever win a prize.
Life's battle doesn't always go
  To the swifter or faster man,
But soon or late the man who wins
  Is the man who thinks he can.

—WALTER D. WINTLE

Again, you noticed in this splendid selection that you are constantly being called on to choose—choosing to win or fail, thinking you can or can't, succeeding or not. The power to choose is yours. The more positive thoughts you choose, the more positive you will be. The more positive you are, the more confidence you will have. With self-confidence, you can do anything.

Many times a person fails to make progress because he feels that somewhere along the line he was not given the brain power to succeed, that his brain is inferior to those who seem to be more successful than he. I had the same trouble years ago. I too felt that because I did not get good grades in school, because I did not make much progress immediately after leaving school, I was working with an inferior brain. I would like to tell you a story regarding the brain.

There was once a Frenchman, a Mr. Tallyrand, Napoleon's right-hand man. This man was a mental giant and was one of the smartest men in France. He was getting on in years, and yet he retained his brilliancy. A group of French scientists and doctors went to him and asked him a favor. They wanted his brain—after he had passed away, of course—so that they could examine it, experiment with it, and find out why he was such a brilliant person. They explained that if he consented, and if they found out what they were looking for, they could change the mentality of the world. Mr. Tallyrand didn't completely comprehend why it was his brain that was so important, but if they felt that way about it, he would help them by letting them have it. He gave them a written promise to this fact. Sometime later, this mental giant passed away and as planned, these scientists and doctors took the brain out of his head, brought it into the laboratory, and began their experiments. After their day's work was over, they placed the brain on a slab in the laboratory.

It so happened that in the same laboratory there was a student doctor who was also studying and experimenting with brains. He was working with a brain which had belonged to a laborer. When he finished his day's work, seeing another brain on the slab, he assumed that this was where he should also place the laborer's brain. When the senior doctors came in the next morning to continue with their experiments, they saw that there were two brains on the slab and could not tell which was theirs.

We can clearly conclude from this story that it is not a question of brain power but simply a question of "choosing." The brilliant man chose to develop his brain by studying, reading, and learning. The laborer, choosing to believe that he could do nothing with his brain, resolved to remain a laborer and did nothing to develop his brain power.

Can you see how important it is to properly make your choice? If you choose to be a failure, that is exactly what you will be. If you choose to be successful with whatever you undertake, no one in the world can stop you. You must realize, therefore, that success can be, in reality, a mathematical certainty.

Now, I want to tell you two very helpful stories that will bring confidence to you. There is a fable that is told about two cats. One was an alley cat, the other a Persian cat. The alley cat—as the name implies—lived in the alley and was very fortunate when he could find something to eat. He was kicked around and thrown about all the time; on occasion, cans were tied at the end of his tail by mischievous boys. One day, the alley cat came to learn about another type of cat—a Persian cat—who was permitted in the richest of homes, given the best of foods, allowed to lie on the most expensive of sofas, and was petted, pampered, and waited on.

The alley cat could not understand why the Persian cat was so highly favored. The alley cat said to himself, "One of these days, I am going to ask the Persian cat why it is that he has the best of everything and I can only eke out an existence." A few weeks later, the alley cat did get his chance.

"Will you do me a favor?" the alley cat said to the Persian cat.

"What is it?" the Persian cat replied.

"Why is it that you are able to come into the best of homes, fed the purest of foods, pampered, petted, and waited on while I am being kicked around with hardly anything to eat?"

The Persian cat replied, "Sure, I will tell you." He raised his head, drew himself to his full length, and said: "The reason is because *I am some cat.*"

The alley cat got the idea. He walked away from the Persian cat and drew himself to his full length and said, "*I will become some cat, too!*"

It was not long before the alley cat too was given finer foods and allowed to lie on the richest and most extravagant of sofas. He too was petted, pampered, and waited on. According to the story, even the fur on his back changed!

My dear friend . . . if you have been an alley cat, do not blame yourself. Somewhere along the line, you have been told to "be yourself." You will continue in your present state of affairs and conditions. But, if you make up your mind to be your "better self"—and I take it you did or you wouldn't have enrolled for this course—I say to you that it is only a matter of time until you too will be the "Persian cat."

So many students have reported to me that they never thought the time would come when their friends and associates would approach them for advice. But, as they continued to be their "better selves," their friends did come, they did look up to them, and they did desire to serve them and wait on them.

Carry yourself erect. Hold yourself up high as though you are *some cat*. You will feel better, you will act better, and you will have more confidence in yourself. Be your "better self" at all times, especially at those times when something worthwhile is at stake—a promotion, a better job, an election to office, or whatever it may be. Whatever you do, do not hesitate to be your "better self."

Some of your friends may call you egotistical. The average person fears, more than anything else, the thought of being called egotistical. This fear makes people crawl into their shell and become timid, shy, and backward. Let me explain the true psychology regarding egotism.

Let's suppose that there's a promotion in store for you in your company and you feel that you deserve this promotion. You go to your employer and in a loud, careless method of expression, say to him, "I can handle this job. I can take care of this branch as well as anybody here. I know that I am just the man that you are looking for to handle this job." Naturally, if you state your case in a loud coarse manner, your employer will say to himself, "Well, this fellow surely has a lot of ego. He is the egotistical type. I don't dare trust him with our branch office." On the other hand, if you go to your employer and in a confident, calm, clear voice say to him, "Mr. Employer, you are looking for a man to handle our branch office. You know that I have been a hard and faithful worker. You know what I can do; and I feel sure that if you will give me an opportunity, I will prove to be an able and qualified branch manager." If you do this in a *straightforward, confident manner*, your employer would not think that you were egotistical but the right person for the job.

Egotism is simply a matter of expression. If you express yourself in an egotistical manner, people would naturally say you are egotistical. If you express yourself in a direct, confident manner, they would not say that about you. If you strut down the street or about your place of business in a manner that gives one the impression that you are the king or queen of this great USA, then your fellow workers have the right to call you egotistical. However, if you walk around with your head up and shoulders back in a confident manner, no one will say that you are egotistical. The only difference between a confident person and an egotistical person is the manner of *expression*.

Sometimes, regardless of how hard you try not to be, someone will call you egotistical. I remember when I was in school someone in my class was always able to express himself without any difficulty. He could stand up in front of the class and tell us how something ought to be done. Quite frequently, a group of us would get off to one side and "discuss" this fellow called Bill. We had always referred to him as being egotistical—I too was among this group, simply because I could not do what he was doing. Today, I can look back and clearly see the reason why I called Bill egotistical—it was in defense of my own timid, backward personality.

I know, today, there are many people who think that I am egotistical. I know why they think as they do—they simply cannot express themselves as I do. No matter how hard you try not to be egotistical, there will always be someone who will call you such and will try to prevent you from becoming what you want to be.

Only recently, I read an article in which the following question was asked: "Is it possible for a leader to be modest?" The answer was in the negative. It is almost impossible for a leader to be modest. A leader must set his case before others; a leader must express his "better self"; a leader will defend his convictions because of his aggressiveness and forcefulness.

My dear friend . . . if you desire to develop leadership, forget your modesty. Modesty is a virtue, but it interferes too greatly in expressing that great "better self" of yours.

For many years, I was under the impression that the expression "the meek shall inherit the earth" meant that the timid, shy, backward people are the ones who will inherit the earth. I soon began to realize that this statement was almost impossible. How could anyone who is backward, timid and shy, inherit the earth. What would he inherit? What would he accomplish? What would he do in this world?—just sit back and be a "do nothing?"

What this expression means is this: a person with confidence will inherit the earth. It takes a person who truthfully and honestly expresses his "better self" to inherit the earth. It does not mean that the meek, the timid and shy, the backward, and the unheard of, shall inherit the earth. Read these last few sentences over many times. I have frequently found, through my contact with students, that it is such simple thoughts as these that prevent the progress they so justly deserve.

This brings to mind another true story. This particular man's experience cost him five thousand dollars. If you use the moral of this story in the right way, it should be worth to you five thousand dollars over a period of years. It is about a man who was a manufacturer of a fair-sized company. I will point out to you how easily a "bad case of nerves" and a feeling of "being ill at ease" can be eliminated.

This manufacturer found that when business would not go exactly the way he wanted it to go, he would become very irritable and nervous. He would constantly growl at his employees. He managed to make it very uncomfortable for his salesmen. It wasn't long before he had developed such a bad case of nerves that he was unable to go to his business at all. In an attempt to rebuild his physical condition, he hopped from one doctor to another. Not one of these doctors was able to help him at all. He was unable to sleep at night and as a result of this, became unbearable to his family. In fact, his "case of nerves" got so bad that it seemed as though he was going mad. The inability of the doctors to help him gave him a feeling of gloom and despair.

One day a friend asked what his problem was. After hearing the situation, the friend exclaimed: "Why don't you go and see Dr. Brown, out in Nevada? He can help you."

"No, I don't think there is any doctor in the country who can do me any good," responded the manufacturer.

The friend persisted, "I know he can help you. You cannot go around the way you are now. Go out to see him and I know he can take care of you and put you back on your feet."

Finally, the manufacturer gave in, "All right, I will go out to see him."

Arriving at Dr. Brown's office, the manufacturer said, "Dr. Brown, I have come a long way. You can see that I am a very nervous man. If you cannot help me, I want you to say so. I do not want you to tell me that you can help me and then find myself disappointed."

Dr. Brown replied, "I will guarantee to cure you."

The manufacturer was somewhat astonished at this answer and asked him to repeat what he had just said. "All right," the manufacturer went on to say, "How much will it cost?"

"How much money do you still have in cash?" Dr. Brown asked.

"Twenty-five thousand dollars."

"This cure will cost you five thousand dollars," replied Dr. Brown.

"Five thousand dollars! That is a lot of money, and you guarantee this cure?"

"Absolutely," responded Dr. Brown in a confident manner.

"Well, there is no sense in my carrying on the way I have," and the manufacturer proceeded to write out a check.

Accepting the check, Dr. Brown stated: "Now, I am not going to give you any medicine; I am not going to ask you to indulge in any exercise; I am not going to advise any rest cures; I am going to ask you to promise that no matter what I tell you to do, you will do."

"Well, I have already paid you so I suppose I shall have to carry out your suggestions."

Dr. Brown persisted, "Now, I want you to promise that you will."

Finally, the manufacturer promised to follow the doctor's instructions.

Dr. Brown proceeded, "The next time you find yourself irritable and nervous, the next time you find yourself ready to scold someone, the next time you feel as though you would like to 'fly off the handle,' the next time anything arises which you would ordinarily be upset about, I want you to say to yourself as strongly and loudly as you can, *'I don't give a darn!'* "

In disbelief the manufacturer looked at Dr. Brown, "Are those your instructions?"

"Yes, that is all, and you promised to carry them out!"

The very next day the manufacturer received a telegram from his place of business stating that he should return at once or else the business would be gone. He sat down and responded with a telegram that read, "I don't give a darn!"

Anything that would subsequently come up to upset him, the manufacturer would emphatically retort with an "I don't give a darn!"

Another case in point came up one day when he was to meet some friends at a designated time and place. The train he was supposed to take to get there was delayed two hours. Ordinarily, he would have been frantic, but not this time. Once again, he shrugged it off with an "I don't give a darn!"

Within thirty-days, the manufacturer became a perfectly "calm" man. Nothing seemed to bother or upset him and so he returned back to his place of business. The salesmen all commented on what a changed man he was, how much more tolerant and reasonable. More business started to pour in and the employees became more productive. It wasn't long before the business was back on its feet. His family and friends wanted to know of his cure, but he refused to tell.

The results that will come from this story will surprise you. I have had such absolutely amazing results which are very difficult to believe. For instance, one young lady admitted that whenever she would miss catching the bus in the morning, she'd be so irritable that it would impede her from doing a good day's work. Upon hearing the manufacturer's story, she put this principle to the test. She, too, started to say to herself "I don't give a darn" whenever she'd miss her bus. The same applied whenever any of her co-workers would criticize her. She admitted that for the first time in her life she was not bothered by criticism.

I will tell you another story of a woman who had been troubled with high blood pressure. She had spent a fortune in the hope of curing it. Lo and behold, within a week's time of using the "I don't give a darn" attitude, her blood pressure went down 80 points.

Doctors, who have taken my training, have reported that applying this principle in their practice has brought about many unusual results. Salesmen, who have hesitated to call on their customers, have discovered that using this principle has transformed them.

Most of us are "too serious" anyway. We are constantly being told that life is difficult, life is a battle; and as soon as we look at it as being different, we are very often criticized. We are told that we don't really know what life means.

As we go along in these lessons, we will learn what life really means. In the meantime, when someone tries to make you "too serious," say to yourself, "I don't give a darn." You will not only save yourself many difficult hours, but many doctor bills. You will reach a point when very few things will bother you. You will be strong because you will understand how to handle yourself and how to protect yourself from these people who insist that life is a "battle."

I do not know whether you have done what I am now going to talk to you about, but I have found that most people have. Years ago, I would stand before the mirror and utter: "You dumbbell. You fool. You haven't any brains. You will never get anywhere. You will never be a success." I did that so many times that I became afraid of everybody and everything. If you, too, have done this—stop it. Enough of this!

Instead of talking to yourself in a negative way, talk to yourself this way: "Jack, John or Mary (whatever your name may be) I have confidence in you. You are going to do the things you have always wanted to do. You are going to be a success. You cannot fail now. From now on you are going to be your 'better self'." Talk to yourself this way for about two minutes every morning before going to work and about two minutes before going to sleep at night. If you do, I promise you, you will have more confidence in yourself than you ever have dreamed possible. Be not afraid of talking to yourself in this manner.

The trouble is that some of us have so degraded ourselves by our negative mental thinking that we have placed ourselves into the "alley cat" mentality. Instead, turn about—face and become the "Persian cat."

Many of my students have objected to "talking" to themselves. They suspect that the next thing I'll demand from them is that they cut out paper dolls, and thus find themselves on their way to the insane asylum. Talking to yourself, my friends, is the same as anything else we may do. Take an automobile, for example; put it into the hands of a careful driver, and it becomes a means of convenience and pleasure; put it into the hands of a fool, and it becomes a means of destruction and a possible instrument of death.

I believe you are sensible people or you would not have taken this course. Use it to talk yourself up and it will become a means of convenience and pleasure. Use it to talk yourself down and may God help you!

Some of the greatest people in the world have used this method to help themselves. It is hard to believe, but the records prove it. Take President Theodore Roosevelt, for instance. He had a picture of Abraham Lincoln in his office. Whenever he was in doubt about doing something, he would stand before Lincoln's picture and say, "Abe, what would you do if you were in my place?"

Many an outstanding minister has publicly confessed to standing before a statue of Jesus and asking, "Jesus, what should I do in this case?" It has been reported that Jack Dempsey, a well-known fighter, would stand before a mirror for some twenty minutes and talk to himself, telling himself that he would win the fight, that he would not be afraid, that he would succeed just as he had done before. It is important, very important—few people realize—to make this behavior a part of one's life in order to make life what one wants it to be.

We are constantly being criticized. We are criticized at work, at the club, at home, and even at church. Sometime this criticism is so great that it takes all the spirit out of us. It would truly be a wonderful thing if we had someone to booster our egos. But, where are you going to find these people? For every wife who encourages her husband, there are probably 500 who don't or won't. For every employer who encourages his employees, there are probably 50 who don't or won't. For every friend who encourages us and tells us how good we are, there are probably 10 who don't or won't.

So, where are we going to get this needed confidence to help us obtain what we want? We get it from our own choosing, from our own encouraging, from our own self up-building. These "mirror talks" are important. Start this habit now and do it for as long as you live. You will never be sorry. Remember the following seven pointers and your confidence will grow daily, yearly, and constantly throughout your life:

1. Tackle the thing that cannot be done, and you'll do it.
2. If dogged and grim, you besiege and beset it, you'll get it.
3. The man who wins is the man who thinks he can.
4. You have the brains to do what you want.
5. Be your "better self."
6. "I don't give a darn!"
7. Choose to talk yourself . . . up.

Do not take yourself or anyone else "too seriously."

If you know your own mind, you know enough to keep it always positive.

—Napoleon Hill

Lesson 3

The Secret of Dealing with People

Dear Reader:
Our ability to get along with people will either make or break our opportunities for success. Even if you possess profound knowledge and skill, unless you can interact positively with people, your success profile will be extremely impaired. W. Clement Stone knew this and that is why he debated with Napoleon Hill as to which of the 17 Principles of Success was of the utmost importance. Stone declared that it was having a Positive Mental Attitude while Hill debated that it was having Definiteness of Purpose. In the end, both are correct because these two principles go hand in hand in the success journey. Success, on the highest levels, will not be achieved unless one uses a combination of these two mutually beneficial principles. Andrew Carnegie related the Charles Schwab story to Napoleon Hill during one of the early interviews. Mr. Carnegie informed Hill that Schwab earned a salary of $75,000 per year, but because of his ability to get along and to work collaboratively with all sorts of people, many times he was awarded a

yearly bonus of $1 million. Being given a bonus that exceeds your salary because you utilize a positive mental attitude is well worth your investment time. Kohe provides several powerful strategies, that although not unique or profound, enable the average person to upgrade his skills one hundredfold. These tips can propel you to higher and higher positions both on the job and in everyday life if you use them.

Avoiding criticism that addresses personality rather than behavior, sandwiching criticism between praise, knowing how to use the stress eraser of "I don't give a darn," and other simple techniques for dealing with people may not earn you an Oscar or a fat bonus, but these techniques will earn you a good night's sleep. That, dear reader, is information worth its weight in gold.

—JUDITH WILLIAMSON

> Stop to think about it . . . you can choose to be friendly, or you can choose to be unfriendly. You can choose to be helpful, or you can choose to refuse to help. You can choose to be cooperative, or you can choose to be stubborn. You can choose to get excited, or you can choose to be calm. You can choose to lose your temper, or you can choose to overlook the matter which would ordinarily cause you to be upset. You can choose to be lovable, or you can choose to be bitter.
> –YOUR GREATEST POWER

One of the biggest problem that we have in life is in dealing with people. I have worked with over 10,000 people during a quarter of a century, and I have come to the conclusion that although there are many, many ways and tricks in dealing with people, the most workable and most practical methods for everyday usage will be found in the following five ways. Rather than give you a whole volume on dealing with people, I shall keep it down to five ways which you will use almost everyday of your life. Some of these methods you no doubt have already been using.

Fine—now, use them even more—and most of your problems in dealing with people will be eliminated.

1. DEAL WITH PEOPLE'S HABITS RATHER THAN WITH THE PEOPLE THEMSELVES

The first way—and most important—is to deal with people's habits rather than to deal with people themselves. In dealing with people, I find it difficult to know where to start. However, in dealing with a person's habits, I come right to the point and save much difficulty. For example, I hear people saying, "I hate his guts." The person speaking did not say, "I hate him . . . no . . . but, I hate his guts"—meaning, of course, that the individual is all right, but he dislikes his characteristic of being "so forward." The point is, you realize that you can tolerate the person but dislike his "forwardness." Once you begin to separate the habit from the person, you realize that you can get along so much more easily. You admit that the person is not "perfect," but you remain friends with that person although you are not for that person 100%.

Don't we do that with our best friends? Even our best friends have certain habits that we do not like. But, we overlook them, don't we? We keep their friendship and we like them for all their "good" habits. This is so true in the business of life.

Let us suppose that you have a young man working for you. He is reliable, dependable, loyal, and a good worker. However, he has the bad habit of coming in late for work. If you are not careful, you will begin to concentrate on this habit until you cannot stand him around. You fire him. Afterwards, you realize that you have lost a good worker. If you had come right out and criticized him, perhaps he would have held it against you. But, if you had called him in and told him that he was a good worker, loyal and reliable, who had a problem of getting to work on time, he wouldn't have been as hurt because you criticized his actions and not his personality. His bad habit of coming to work late was what you disliked, not him personally. If you took this approach, in eight out of ten cases, this situation would be cleared up. You can, in most cases, correct a bad habit; but it would be too difficult to attempt to correct the individual.

Let us realize another important fact. Just as a cat lives "nine" lives, so we live "four" lives—social, business, family, personal. Each of these lives are lived almost separately from the other, yet all in the same life and in the same personality. For example: when you dress for the social life, you put on "your best"; when in business, you dress for business comfort; when home, you dress "any old way." True? The same can be said for when we eat: when you are out socially, you eat with your very best table manners; when in business, you are not quite so careful; when home, you eat in a way that's most comfortable for you. True?

We don't dress the same and we don't eat the same in our different lives. This classification helps us better understand the habits of people in their "four" different lives. We find that the people with whom we do business are not necessarily the ones we want in our families. Likewise, there are people in our families with whom we would not like to do business. Knowing that a person lives four different lives, enables us to adjust more quickly to that person. We recognize that his habits will, of necessity, be different in each life. We will be more patient, less critical, quicker to understand, and more easily able to adjust to that individual.

Wherever possible, deal with people's habits rather than with them personally. Separating the habit from the person will become an interesting and fascinating game. You will not take the other fellow "too seriously" and this is a wonderful habit for all of us to cultivate. As you develop the habit of separating, you will find that there will be very few people that you won't like. In fact, there will hardly ever be one you would immensely dislike. This is because you will discover that it isn't the individual you dislike but the habit that the individual has unfortunately acquired.

In the first lesson you learned that if there is someone with whom you would like to get along, you would have to put a picture in your mind of getting along. This is the best way and the quickest way to proceed. If you deal with their habits, you will make the picture so much easier since you don't have to face it and since you would realize that it isn't the entire person whom you dislike.

In dealing with people, it doesn't take long to realize that the average person does not like to be "bossed." Yet, most of us walk around, unaware, that "bossing" is going on all around us. Some people never overcome this bad habit. This brings us to the second step I would like to bring to your attention.

2. SUGGEST AND REQUEST

This simply means that instead of telling people what to do, ask them, request them to do it. To illustrate: about twenty years ago a woman came to see me. She was about to get a divorce. She could not get along with her husband and had finally decided to divorce him. Someone had suggested to her to come to see me. It didn't take long for me to see what her trouble was. For example, she would say to her husband, "Give me the paper." He would answer, "Get it yourself." She would say to him, "Let's go to a picture show." He would answer, "I don't want to." This went back and forth for twenty long years. Is it any wonder that she wanted to get a divorce!

This woman subsequently learned to use the "suggest and request" technique. She would begin by saying, "Will you let me have the paper?" and he would respond with "Why sure, here it is." She would ask him, "Would you like to visit the Browns?" and he would respond, "All right, call them up and if they are home, we will go." She would ask him, "Would you like to go to the movies?" and he would respond, "Very well, if there is anything worth seeing, I'll go."

She then reported to me the results this technique produced. "I could hardly believe my ears. He does almost everything I ask him to do!"

For twenty years, this woman could not make her husband do what she wanted him to do. "Why," you ask yourself. Simple—when she would tell him to give her the paper, he would say to himself, "I'll show her who's the boss around here." When she wanted him to go somewhere, he would say to himself, "I'll show her who's boss."

"Suggest and request" is a habit that if you haven't yet learned how to use, start using it right now! Make it a lifelong habit! It will pay amazing dividends in your social, business, and family life. The most successful employers are constantly "suggesting and requesting" to their employees. As a result, they do not incur any labor problems. People are happy to work for them. They would be heard saying, "I have a wonderful boss. He never tells me what to do; he asks me." You will find that it is very easy to suggest and to request. Once it becomes a habit, you will find a new thrill in getting people to do what you want.

Now, we come to the biggest stumbling block in dealing with people—criticism.

3. PRAISE FIRST AND THEN CRITICIZE

Criticism is a great problem. Everyone doesn't have to face a gun or go to battle, but everyone has to face criticism. Some people never learn; others learn the hard way. Some people suffer all their lives as a result of criticism; others are so critical that they make themselves and everyone around them disgusted and bitter. We must divide this problem into two classes: when the criticism is given to you and how to use criticism to respond.

When someone criticizes you, don't conclude that the criticism is given to hurt you. Actually, this criticism is given to help you, to build you up, to make you stronger. I suggest you look for the lesson in "criticism." If you do this, I guarantee you,

you will be glad that someone took the time to "criticize" you. To better understand this, let me tell you a remarkable story.

There was once a little Italian newsboy who was selling newspapers in the city of Chicago. One day he walked up to an elderly lady and asked, "Lady, will you buy a paper from me?" The lady turned around and responded, "I would not buy a paper from you, you dirty little wop!" She could not have insulted the boy any worse no matter what she said. This response was an awful slap in the face for the little fellow. He did not sell any more papers that day. He went home and cried himself to sleep. However, the next morning when he woke up, he said to himself, "Maybe that lady was right; maybe I haven't kept myself as clean as I should."

That day, the little Italian boy returned to work all cleaned up. He not only made up his mind to keep his body clean but to stop using the slang and to stop swearing. To his amazement and surprise, he noticed that he was selling more papers! It wasn't long before he made a little money and opened up a newsstand. This little stand was as clean as anyone could expect. He made money and before long opened up a regular business. The store was immaculate. It grew and prospered until it became one of the big department stores in the city of Chicago.

When a person becomes successful, newspaper reporters and magazine writers interview them, asking them what factor or factors contributed to their success. When these reporters approached the Italian merchant and asked him what had influenced him most in his life, he would relate the story I have just told you. He went on to further add, "That lady made me realize the value of cleanliness."

From this story, we deduce that criticism was responsible for the Italian merchant's success. It was bitter, to be sure, given in very bad taste—but that was what really did the trick! Too many people would be hurt by the use of such language and hurt to such an extent that they would never overcome it.

You must always remember that criticism does not come into your life to hurt you. Look for the lesson in the criticism and you will see that every criticism is to help you up the ladder of better living, better successful living. I have experienced many bitter encounters with criticism, but in each and every case the criticism brought me more success and improved my methods of doing the tasks at hand.

It is a pity that there is so much criticism in the world. Everybody seems to be criticizing everybody else until life becomes unbearable at times. Life has become a task and a battle for most people because they are constantly facing criticism. It seems that all they have in their lives is criticism. Some people become so discouraged that they never get a taste of real living. But, why are we so critical? Why are people so quick to find fault? Why is there so little praise and so much criticism? Here is the answer:

There is a Gulf Stream, a hot stream of water that runs along the Atlantic Coast past Florida and then goes up around England. If it were not for this Gulf Stream, it would be too cold for people to live in England. However, nobody pays any attention to this Gulf Stream, it just goes its own way. This underlying current is taken for granted. So too in life. There is an underlying current, one wherein everybody is seeking perfection. People wrongly assume that perfection can be attained through criticism rather than praise. Remember the old saying, "More flies are caught with honey rather than vinegar," and you will understand how praise is used to sandwich criticism for the best possible outcome of all concerned.

4. WATCH OUT IN LOOKING FOR PERFECTION

Husbands are criticizing wives—they want their wives to be "perfect." Wives are criticizing husbands—they want their husbands to be "perfect." Parents are criticizing children—they want their children to be "perfect." Children are criticizing parents—they want their parents to be "perfect." Employers are criticizing employees—they want their employees to be "perfect." Employees are criticizing employers—they want their employers to be "perfect." Voters are criticizing politicians—they want their politicians to be "perfect." Politicians are criticizing voters—they want their voters to be "perfect." Ministers are criticizing their congregation—they want their congregation to be "perfect." The congregation is criticizing their ministers—they want their ministers to be "perfect."

Everybody is criticizing everybody! Is it any wonder that life becomes so difficult at times? Is it any wonder that people have adopted the idea that life is a battle and a struggle? Is it any wonder that from time to time someone gets the idea of taking his own life? Sometimes the criticism piles up so high that the individual finds it almost impossible to withstand.

Seeking perfection has its good points, but why expect the other fellow to be perfect? If your wife is reasonably perfect, you are a lucky husband. If your husband is reasonably perfect, you are a lucky wife, and so on down the line. It is good to seek perfection in machinery—the perfect automobile, the perfect washing machine, the perfect radio. With human beings, however, it takes time, a lot of time, and a lot of patience to become perfect. Let us not be so demanding, let us be reasonably perfect, and we will get along well. Work for perfection, if you want, but in so doing don't make everybody's life around you miserable.

Now, you will understand that the next time someone criticizes you, they simply want you to be perfect. Criticism will no longer bother you for you will know why it is given to you. You will be more tolerant and more patient towards others. You will realize that when you criticize someone else, you are doing so because you want the other person to be "perfect."

Because of this underlying current to seeking perfection, many of us forget and subconsciously find ourselves turning to criticism without thinking. For example: this is Easter Sunday. The lady of the house has been hopping around for three weeks to get an Easter outfit. She finally succeeds. She has her suit, hat, pocketbook, gloves—everything to match! She is so proud of herself. She comes downstairs all dressed up and says to her husband, "Well, dear, how do you like it?" Eight out of ten husbands would ordinarily take a look and would answer, "For goodness sake, where did you get that hat?" Of course—BOOM! The war is on! She, naturally, becomes angry and starts to pout, maybe even holler something like, "You make me tired. I chased all over town trying to find a suitable outfit and all you can say is 'the hat . . . .' Oh, go jump in the river!" Easter Sunday is spoiled; everybody is angry with everybody else; the happy marriage has been given another blow.

Oh, if only we would learn to praise first and criticize afterwards . . .

Could not the husband have said, "Why dear, that is a beautiful suit, I like it, it makes you look as sweet as can be" and the wife would reply, "Gee, I'm glad you like it, dear. I looked around for three weeks before I found what I wanted." He would then continue, "But dear, that hat, it doesn't match your suit," to which she would answer, "You are right, dear, that's what I told the saleslady. I told her it doesn't match. All right, I'll take it down and change it tomorrow."

Well, has anyone been hurt? Of course not. Easter Sunday isn't spoiled, the marriage goes on smoothly, and everyone is in agreement. Oh, how easy we could make our married lives . . . if we would only choose to praise first and criticize afterwards!

From my dealing with thousands of people, I have found that the husband does not mind working all day long, paying the bills, sending youngsters through school. If only he would receive a pat on the back once in a while! The same applies to the wife who, likewise, does not mind working in the kitchen, taking care of the children, keeping the house in order. If only she would receive a pat on the back once in a while!

The world is starved! —starved for a little praise, a little appreciation.

Sometime ago I went to visit some friends. We were all going out later that evening. The husband had just bought himself a new suit. When he came downstairs, he happily asked, "Well dear, how do you like it?" She took one look at the suit and shouted, "Look at those sleeves, look how short they are!" The poor husband went into a rage; he started to holler—actually, you couldn't blame him. Looking at me, he exclaimed, "Look at that woman, all she could say is the sleeves are short, everybody else liked the suit, but no, she can only see the short sleeves!" He just couldn't contain himself.

Later that evening when we were out together, all you could hear him talk about was the short sleeves. Could she not have used the simple technique of "praise first and then criticize!" She could have let the short sleeves go for the time being. Instead, she could have said, "Dear, that is a beautiful suit, I like you in grey, it makes you look ten years younger." She could have made him so happy . . . then, she could have said, "But dear, the sleeves are too short." No one would have been hurt, the evening would not have been spoiled, and the marriage would not have lost any of its beauty.

How true this is with children! The child brings home a report card and what happens? Nine out of ten parents would start complaining and raise the devil because the report card was not better. Only recently I heard a story of a young high school girl who came home with a report card having "only two A's." The mother went into a rage. She began to yell as loudly as she could, "Two A's, you should have had four A's." The young girl was almost sick.

How often have we had that happen to us? Parents have a very bad habit of "seeking perfection" in children, many times criticizing so severely as to render the child disheartened. Could not the parent have praised the good part of the report card and later find fault with the other part? This would undoubtedly save the child's agony and possible serious dislike for the mother.

Be careful. Unfortunately, this situation happens too often. It is just as easy to help someone as it is to hurt them. So, why not take the obvious and apparent road in the art of praising? Praise is the secret to dealing with people—if you stop to think about it.

- If there is someone you like, that person praises you.
- If there is someone you don't like, that person criticizes you.

Never forget these statements. Always remember the importance of praise when dealing with people.

For many years I could not figure out why George was going out with Mary. He would see her for six consecutive nights a week and would complain that he could not see her on the seventh. Then after about a year or two of being married, George didn't even want to go home! Why?

Before getting married, George was always telling Mary how wonderful she was and Mary was always telling George how wonderful he was, how much she loved him—praise, praise, praise. After getting married, praise stops and criticism takes over. They each in turn criticize the other. They want each other perfect! Before marriage, they "saw" each other perfect; now, all they saw were faults. Therefore, the couple thus conclude that marriage is not what it is supposed to be.

Too many people start out by praising others. Before long, what happens? For instance, if you keep praising a child—if you are not careful—before long you will have a spoiled child on your hands. If a husband keeps praising his "little woman"—unless she is an unusual person or unless she has studied the art of dealing with people—she becomes a spoiled wife. The same holds true regarding the wife, the employer with his employee, and so on. So, what do we do? We stop praising and start criticizing. Once in this habit, we usually find ourselves stuck at this position for the very simple fact that praise didn't get us where we expected.

We know that criticism is not the answer. Then, what is the answer? The lady of the house knows that she cannot bake a cake or bread with flour alone, she must mix milk or water with it. The man of the house cannot do a cement job around the house using cement powder alone, he must mix water with it if he wants the powder to stick. So, "we must mix praise with criticism" if we want it to stick.

Take your child who plays the piano, for instance. You say to him, "You played beautifully today." The next day the child refused to play the piano. He reminds you that the day before you told him that he played beautifully. Therefore, practice was not necessary. Now, you start to criticize and the trouble begins. Most people would throw their hands up in the air and say, "I just don't know what to do!"

Follow the pattern I will suggest to you and your difficulty will be over. True, the child played the piano well. Say to him, "You played beautifully today and I feel sure you will do even better tomorrow." No "spoiled" child is produced here, instead you have given the child something towards which to work.

I will give you another example. You tell your wife, "Gee, this is a delicious meal!" The next day she may fall back in her cooking. You can't understand it. Did you not praise her on her cooking the day before? If this happens, then mix it; mix it like this: "Honey, dinner tonight was so delicious. You know I am expecting many more like this." She is thrilled with the praise. In the meantime you have given her something towards which to work.

You praise your husband. He took you out and showed you a great time. You praise and praise him. Then you find you cannot do anything with him. If you notice this, say to him, "Honey, we had a wonderful evening tonight. I thank you so much. I know you'll see to it that we have many more extra special evenings like this." Mix the praise with the criticism.

You may have someone working for you. You praise him continually. You may have a spoiled worker on your hands. Then, mix the praise with the criticism. In fact, it may not even be criticism but something towards which to work. You might say to the worker, "That was a fine sale you made this week." You keep praising and before long you cannot do anything with him. You wonder why. Now, you know why. So, the next time he makes a good sale, say to him, "You made a fine sale this week. I know you can make many more."

Mixing praise with criticism—making statements of better work, better performance—will prevent the harm that may come from mere praising. We must be constantly on the alert in expressing ourselves. We must be positive, not negative. By choosing to use praise and criticism to the best of our ability, by choosing to praise first and then criticize, we will have chosen to make the most of our dealing with people. Choosing to think before we speak, choosing to express ourselves positively, will bring us untold dividends.

Just as we train ourselves to express ourselves positively, we realize that by "seeing" the good in the other person, we "bring out" the good that is inherent in that person. This brings us to the fifth way of dealing with people. It is a thought that brings untold success. You may have used it many times yourself without realizing its great possibilities. We have seen the most stubborn and difficult person "melt" under the following treatment.

5. FIND OUT WHAT IS THE OTHER FELLOW'S HOBBY

One of my resident school students came in one day complaining that his new manager did not like him. I told him to find out what his manager's hobby was.

The manager happened to be a "camera nut (aficionado)." I suggested to my student that he buy him a book on photography and a certain specific small gadget to put on his camera in order to enable him to take better pictures. Within two week's time of receiving this gift, the manager was as nice as he could be. It is the old psychology: "An apple for the teacher." The results work wonders in school as well as in business.

Another of my resident school students told me this story. He learned that in the next department from where he was working, there was a job opening for an assistant foreman paying $50 more a month than his present salary. No one was applying for the job because the foreman was very mean. Due to his training and believing that he could get along with him, my student applied for the job and got it. Immediately, he was sorry. The foreman was even meaner than expected. Being disgusted at this outcome, my student tried to find out what was the foreman's hobby. However, he was unable to engage the foreman in a conversation.

This job change, plus the difficulty with his foreman, began to take a toll on my student's health. Luckily, one day he went to a Sportsman's Show—a show where all kinds of sporting goods such as hunting and fishing were displayed. While admiring a bowl of fish, the foreman happened to appear in front of him. "I didn't know you were interested in fishing.

Why didn't you say so? Where do you go fishing? How have you been making out?" he exclaimed.

From that moment on, my student no longer had problems with his boss. They began to have a beautiful relationship. Unbelievable? Maybe, but we have never seen it fail.

Another case in point: A young man came to me sometime ago complaining that he was working with a girl whom he just couldn't stand. He had asked for a transfer and the company refused. Jobs were scarce at the time so he continued to stay with his job and with the unreasonable girl. He asked me what he should do. I suggested he find out what her hobby was. He did and they became very good friends. They even walked to the bus stop together after working hours.

What a difference it makes knowing the other fellow's hobby! It is a wonder worker to be sure. People who have no interest in you will suddenly become fond of you when they learn that you share the same hobby. Likewise, you too, will discover that the people you would ordinarily not like will suddenly be liked, upon learning of your shared interests. The hobby is a common meeting ground—like a lodge brother—it is an attraction for the other.

The same can be said for traveling. You know how much more interested you are in those people who happen to come from the same state as you. In traveling abroad, Americans tend to seek other Americans for company and conversation.

We will cover this thought in another lesson. It is a thought worth repeating.

In looking for a mate, marry the person you like rather than the person you love. The chances for a successful marriage are great if you share the same interests—if you like to skate and he likes to skate, if you like to swim and he likes to swim, if you like to travel and he likes to travel, if you like the opera and he likes the opera, if you like to dance and he likes to dance, and so on. If you don't share similar interests, it will really be difficult to make the marriage work. It can be done, of course, but where the likes are the same, it is almost a certainty.

In conclusion, use these five great principles in dealing with people. These techniques will solve most of your problems. By making good mental pictures of the people you want to get along with, you will be creating that very outcome in your day-to-day existence.

> *A positive mental attitude
> is an irresistible force that knows
> no such thing as an immovable body.*
> —Napoleon Hill

Lesson 4

How to Get Ahead Financially

Dear Reader:

Too often a person may solicit advice on a thousand and one things without regard for the accuracy of the information. Personal health issues such as diet, exercise and the newest fashion trend all account for many of the fads that cycle through society today. However, when it comes to finances, people often get very accurate and time-tested advice, but fail to use it. The distant future can make financial preparation and planning seem irrelevant to individuals that live in the here and now. This is a mistake, but a mistake that you can still correct if you follow Kohe's five-step formula.

Give yourself a chance to warm up to the concepts, and then begin to follow the directives one at a time. Begin with making certain that you are paying yourself first from your earnings. A suggested amount to deposit into savings is 10% of your weekly salary. This amount is to be "untouchable" so that it can accrue earnings when deposited in a savings account or invested in a money market over a period of years. By paying yourself first, you are retaining a sizeable portion of your salary for use later in life. If you fail to do this, you are relying on luck, chance, good fortune, lottery winnings, inheritances, or other unlikely sources of revenue that seldom materialize in life.

It has been said that "Goals are dreams with feet," and when it comes to savings, dreams without observable and measurable results are useless. By not paying yourself first, you leave your future livelihood to chance. This is not the methodology of becoming a Mental Millionaire. Mental Millionaires comprehend the success formulas and put them into practice. Understanding what is needed is the first step, but nothing happens until action is taken on what you know to be good for you. That, dear reader, is the very foundation of financial planning that will place you on the road to becoming a Mental Millionaire.

—JUDITH WILLIAMSON

Our financial condition is a thought first, and then a reality. If we want to change our financial picture, we must first change our thought. If we choose to change our inner thoughts . . . our outer conditions must change.
–YOUR GREATEST POWER

Everyone in America—for that matter, everyone in the world—wants to have financial independence. We know that not everyone is interested in money. However, as long as it takes money to buy the necessities of life, we must have it. It is perfectly all right to say you are not interested in money, but be careful or you will find that money is not interested in you either. It is a pity how many wonderful people there are who would like to do so much for mankind but have no money with which to do it. Money is essential in making this world a better place in which to live.

Money is like anything else. It can be used to do good things or it can be used to do bad things. If you choose to make bad use of money, don't blame the money. If you choose to make good use of money . . . hurrah, it is good money! Do not say that money means nothing. It does. Anyone with a little common sense knows that! Choose to use it well and you will have no reason to feel bad towards money.

Too many people say that "money is the root of all evil." Actually, it is the "love of money" that is the root of all evil. To put it bluntly, if a person wants money bad enough, he does not care what he does or how he does it in order to get it. This is when money becomes "evil money." Money itself is not evil. It is the use of money, whether you choose it for good purpose or bad purpose, that is the problem, not the money per se.

Here is a suggestion I made sometime ago which would eliminate once and for all the idea that money is evil. Money means "service." If the electric company or gas company gives good service to their customers, they will make money. If, on the other hand, they render bad service, they won't make money. If a doctor gives his patients good service, he makes money, for they will return to see him. If you give your employer good service, he will pay you; if not, he won't.

It's very clear to see that when we render good service, we will make lots of money and when we don't, we make no money. It's up to us to choose in which direction we want to go. It is true that you can give great service and not be paid for it. However, these cases are few and far between. When the world becomes spiritually minded, then and only then would the money stop being so important. So, for those of us who wish to bring about this beautiful spiritual world, let us render great service with or without money. When money loses its importance, the genuine service of man will endure.

I would like to clear up a very important point which may be confusing to some of my students. Many of you might say, "If I were not so 'darned' honest, I could get somewhere." Allen, in his book, *As A Man Thinketh*, says that a person does not succeed because he is dishonest, nor does a person fail because he is dishonest. The dishonest person succeeds because he is a hard worker, a schemer, a planner, a person with an insatiable desire to get ahead and make money. The honest person fails to succeed because he is not willing to work hard, is not a schemer, a planner, or possesses a strong desire to get ahead and make money. To assure myself that you understand Allen's statements—that you firmly grind them in your minds—I want you to read this paragraph over again—again and again, if necessary.

For many years I labored under the idea that if one wanted to become financially independent, one had to first "be smart" and second "be a big money maker." I have, however, found that they are both untrue and unnecessary. I know, and so do you, that many people who have become wealthy and financially independent were not "smart," and not "big money makers." Then, you would ask, "How did they accomplish financial independence?" Well, I will now outline the various steps necessary to bring financial growth and financial independence.

STEP 1: PAY YOURSELF FIRST

It doesn't make any difference how much money you make. What makes the difference is how much you pay yourself. Suppose one man makes $100 a week (we will call him Brown) and another fellow (we will call him Smith) is making $50 a week. Brown doesn't pay himself anything—he lives up to the very last cent. Smith, on the other hand, pays himself at least $5 a week. Which of the two will be better off at the end of a year, 10 years, etc.? What a difference between the two men! In other words, Brown was actually working for nothing while Smith was making at least $5 each week—Smith was making more money than Brown!

Then what happens to Brown? He is making $100 a week. You know that that is not enough, everything keeps rising, and before long he goes to get a loan from a bank to tide him over. He asks to borrow $250, but walks out of the bank with only $225. What happened to the other $25? . . . bank's expenses, my friends. Borrowing money costs more money. Brown thus pays towards the loan week after week. At the end of the year he finds it necessary to renew this loan. This cycle keeps going on and on with Brown becoming more and more disgusted with his financial position since he is getting nowhere.

Now, let's suppose that Brown realizes his difficulty and decides that he is going to pay himself first. He would begin by paying himself at least $10 each payday. At the end of the year he'd have saved $520. Now, he no longer needs the loan. In five years he will have accumulated $2,600. He is surely on the road to financial freedom.

Before proceeding to the next step, let me continue along this line of reasoning. It does not make any difference as to how much money you make. You probably have had the following experience. You make $50 a week, you live on $50; you make $100 a week, you live on $100; and so on. Every time you increase your earnings, if you are not careful, you increase your scale of living. It is good to increase your way of living and to move on to the luxuries of life, but we must always—and I cannot emphasize this enough—always pay yourself first, or else you will be headed towards disaster.

Many of the boxers who made as much as $1 million a year have wound up with no money at the end of their fighting careers. Many of the big money-making ballplayers have also found themselves penniless at the end of their careers. The best example of this was our beloved Babe Ruth. In spite of all the money he made throughout his career, he found himself penniless. What a pity!

In fact, if one were to take a survey, one would find that the percentage of big-money makers who have become financially independent is much smaller than one would ever think. Charles Schwab, Andrew Carnegie's right-hand man, was making over a million dollars a year. Yet, Mrs. Schwab could barely make ends meet. This is due to the fact that Mrs. Schwab lived lavishly by putting on parties that cost thousands upon thousands of dollars, entertained royalty, and spent indiscriminately. When Mr. Schwab's income stopped, he found himself in financial trouble.

Obviously, you see that it doesn't take long to realize that it isn't how much money you make that really counts but how much you pay yourself. Set aside money each payday, pay yourself, do not save for a rainy day. Saving money for the future, that is old psychology—rather save money for going into possible business for yourself, buying a home, traveling, further education, interesting experiences in later years. Saving money for a rainy day means that you are expecting trouble, expecting sickness, expecting inability to work, expecting accidents to happen. Instead, save money for a future filled with great experiences, a life to which you look forward.

Pay yourself at least 10% of your earnings. If you can pay yourself more, that's fine too, but the rule is for at least 10%. You can spend the remaining 90% if so desired for you are still providing for your future needs. This is called "healthy" living.

If you are saving 10% towards insurance premiums, that's very good. The insurance people suggest that you put aside another 2% to ensure that you don't borrow against your policy when you need money in a hurry. If you are saving 10% towards the mortgage in your home, that's also considered "healthy" saving. Sometime ago a friend of mine advised me that if I ever bought a home to pay off the mortgage as soon as I could. He further added, "You can make enough for groceries, and you don't ever have to worry about 'bad times'." What a wonderful suggestion. If every homeowner were to do that, there would never be any so-called "bad times."

As I told you in the book *Your Greatest Power*, "bad times" are only for those people who do not understand the "power of choice." If you choose to pay yourself first, and to pay off the mortgage, it is almost impossible to incur "bad times."

Another good feature of paying yourself first—at least 10%—is that you *always* have cash on hand to buy what you want. You do know that when you pay in cash you save money. You are able to always take advantage of a "bargain." You are able to go wherever you want and buy whatever you want. You will not be obligated to pay off debt to anyone. That's when you will experience your first taste of financial independence! This brings us to the next step.

STEP 2: FIND PROFITABLE EMPLOYMENT FOR YOUR MONEY

This is easier said than done, but I will help you. When you have your money working for you, it is the same as having someone working for you. So, let's see what you can do towards finding profitable employment for your money.

A very interesting woman told me the following story: Realizing that her husband would never be a big-money maker, she began to save every cent she could. Before too long, she went out and bought a house with the money she had accumulated. It was a two-family house. This allowed her to rent the other half and still have money coming in. She lived upstairs and rented the downstairs. She continued to save and stint until she went out and bought another two-family house. With two rents coming in, it wasn't long before she had saved enough money to again go out and buy another two-family house. She went on to do that several more times.

"Now my husband is fifty-five years old and he can quit working any time he wants," she proudly stated.

Simple enough? Remarkable enough? Smart? I say she was sensible rather than smart. She realized her husband would never make big money and instead of becoming discouraged, she looked for a way to help him out. She found the way. You too can see the possibilities even if there isn't any big money coming into the family. You can start small, pay yourself at least 10%, and then find profitable employment for this money.

Another woman, seeing that her husband would never be a big-money maker, took it upon herself to do something about it. You see, he was a carpenter and whatever he made during the summer months, they would eat up in the winter months. This went on for several years before she became disgusted. She then told her husband that the following spring he was going to work for her. She took the money she had saved during the summer and went out and bought a lot. She told her husband to build her a house on the lot. He did. They were so poor that they had to move into the house before it was even finished and sold it even before the furniture was all set up. Making a nice profit on the house, she went out and bought another lot for another house to be built. The story repeated itself for a period of twenty years. You can imagine how wealthy they became.

Smart? Again, I say sensible. This woman too followed the rules: one, pay yourself first; two, find profitable employment for this money. These two rules are bound to lead to financial freedom, especially if one follows intuition—given to you in Lesson 17.

Many years ago a young man came over from Scotland and found a job in the lumber regions of this great country. He was making all of four dollars a week. Within a few years he had saved $400. He then moved to the west coast where he bought an old ship. He fixed it up and began to haul freight. The venture was such a success that he went out and bought another ship, fixed it up, and now he had two ships hauling freight. He continued to do this until he became a millionaire.

For a very long time, you have known that if you wanted to go to China or Japan you would have to take a Dollar Steamship. Yes, the man who started with four dollars a week was Mr. Robert Dollar who later became the millionaire boatman. Opportunity is always knocking at your door—if you prepare for it.

One of my resident school students was a truck salesman. He told me how in the past fifteen years he had been selling trucks. He would see a certain man come in and buy a truck, with hardly enough money for a down payment. Before long, this man would come in and buy another truck, then another and another. My student went on to say that he had seen several times how men would start with one truck, and before long build themselves a fleet of trucks, and with it, of course, financial freedom.

Sometime ago, I heard a college president make a very interesting statement. It is a little slangy—I hope you will excuse the language—but I feel it has a great thought: "A big shot is a little shot that keeps on shooting." Let us never forget this, especially if you want to become financially independent. The lady with the two-family houses started with one house; the builder's wife started with one house; Mr. Robert Dollar started his steamship business with one boat; the truck fleet owner started with one truck. Let's not lose sight of this. We see these wealthy people and we wonder how they did it. We think it is impossible, out of our reach. I say, analyze them—as I've done in this lesson—and you will see that the greatest percentage of great fortunes have started with one house, one ship, one truck, one store, one step forward. In this country, no one need ever be discouraged for opportunity is everywhere.

STEP 3: BE VERY CAREFUL ABOUT YOUR FIRST EXPERIENCES AND ASK QUESTIONS

So many people who decide to become financially independent start out all right and then become confused in their very first experience. This results in their taking a loss, sometimes never recuperating from it, and remaining in "hot water" all of their lives. My mother used to say, "Don't learn to shave on your own beard, learn to shave on the other fellow's beard." Meaning—find out from the other fellow what to do and ask questions.

Andrew Carnegie once said, "Other men's brains have made me rich."

Why must we learn everything the hard way in the university of "Hard Knocks?" Henry Ford always said, "I can learn anything I want from the men who know." So, let us ask questions, let us find out what to do. We are told that advice is "cheap." This is very true, especially if we go to the people who "know."

A doctor spends about ten years to become a doctor, a lawyer spends about six years to become a lawyer, a dentist spends about seven years to become a dentist—and yet, we expect to do certain new things well, without asking questions.

Let us suppose that you wanted to open a hardware store. The sensible thing to do is to go around and ask as many hardware men as you can for their advice and suggestions. Most of these men will tell you in an hour what it took them twenty years to learn. If you were to open the hardware store on your own and you don't ask questions, your experience in learning the business might cost you dearly. Instead, if you were to ask questions of these men, you would know what to do, how to do it, and how to avoid the many pitfalls that might come your way.

To illustrate further . . . I know of a man who had an idea, an idea that has been put into effect thousands of times throughout our country. This man was going to buy a business, his wife would run it by day and he by night. Once the business began to show a profit, he would quit his job and be a businessman in every sense of the word. This was a very good idea, with one exception. Let me explain.

One day this man saw an ad in the paper. He went to see the store that was for sale, liked it, liked the price also, and said to the owner, "I'll buy it!" Never having had any previous experience, the man proceeded to close the deal. He went to the bank, the bank's notary public made out the papers, the money was given to the seller, and the buyer took over the business. The very next day, all the creditors came to him demanding payment for their unpaid bills. The new owner explained to them that it was the previous owner who owed them money, not him.

The creditors pointed out to him that he should have been represented by a lawyer. The lawyer would have seen to it that all unpaid bills were paid before handing any money over to the seller. But, it was too late now. The bills were greater than the value of the store. So the man lost his business, lost his money, and almost lost his credit. What a terrible experience! The law was very clear, and he could not get around it.

Be very careful with your first experiences. Never buy a business without a lawyer. The lawyer knows what to do to protect you and your interests. He sees that you get everything that is your due. Finally, he makes certain that the previous owner's bills are paid in full before you take ownership. This leaves you in the clear financially.

Watch your first experiences!

Suppose you are buying a home for the first time. I say, get a lawyer, protect your interests. The bank will make out all the papers, of course, but they will not protect your interests, as they should. To illustrate: a man bought a four-family house. He made the deal without a lawyer. After buying the house, he found that he had four garages behind his building and no driveway. The driveway belonged to the owner next door. The man had no recourse but to get a lawyer so arrangements could be made for him to use the driveway and thus access the garages.

It cost this man as much for a lawyer after he bought the building as it would have before buying the building. All these aggravations could have been avoided. You could have taken this approach—of not being represented by a lawyer—only after having had the experience of several real estate purchases. Only then would you know what to expect. For the first few times, have a lawyer ready to help you.

Likewise, if you are selling your home for the first time, have a lawyer represent you. Let me also illustrate: a man sold his home without being represented by a lawyer. The day after all the papers went through, the new owner came to his door wanting the house. Puzzled, the seller went on to say, "I have no place to go." The buyer responded, "I'm sorry, this house belongs to me now and I want it." The seller is now forced to get a lawyer. The lawyer goes to court and obtains a thirty-day stay so his client could find a place.

It cost this man as much for a lawyer after selling the house as it would have before selling the house. The lawyer would have seen to it that provisions were made to allow him thirty days in which he could find a new place to live. The bank had not made this provision, and no one else had allowed for it.

If you are building for the first time, be sure you have an architect. He will protect you and save you untold agony later. Let me tell you what happened to one of my resident students who had bought a lot and had decided to build. My student made all the arrangements with the builder and the builder started the job. The following Sunday—the day one would usually go—he went to see how the building was coming along. Lo and behold, the foundation was being erected on the wrong lot! What an expense that ensued! If he would have obtained an architect, the spot for the building would have been staked out and no unnecessary expense would have been incurred.

Watch your first experiences!

Ask questions. Ask people who know. People are so willing to help, so gracious to be of service, and so flattered to think that they would be approached for advice. The difference between success and failure is in having the knowledge of what to do and what not to do. The saddest words in life are, "If I had only known!" We are so anxious to get ahead that we fail to make sure that we are on the right track. Intelligent people—the ones from whom you expect more—sometime go ahead with a project without first getting all the details, lose large sums of money, then blame everyone around them. The truth of the matter is that they "chose" to do this without first asking questions. Again, we have a case of "bad choosing." This brings us to the fourth step.

STEP 4: DO NOT INVEST IN A BUSINESS WITH WHICH YOU ARE NOT FAMILIAR

Sometime ago a very wealthy man told me this story. He had been approached by his brother-in-law with an idea for a business that would be a sure money maker. He was asked to invest $50,000 in this enterprise for which he had no previous background or experience, and he did so. Two years later the business failed and he lost his $50,000 investment. After this happened, he stated, "I learned a very important lesson; that is, not to invest in a business in which I am not familiar."

Another story about a man who owned a small railroad came to my attention. This man sold his railroad for $1 million. He was later approached by some men who were interested in busses and was asked to go into the bus business. Knowing nothing about the bus business, he reluctantly agreed to join them. Needless to say, several years later he lost every cent of the one million he had invested. Why did he lose? The answer is simply: because he was not familiar with the bus business. He knew nothing about it.

Some people say that it is the smart person who gets ahead financially. This man was smart enough to have one million but not smart enough to pay himself first. He should have said to these men, "Just a minute, before I give you my million I will first take 10% for myself, and then I will invest $900,000 with you." With the 10% he could have then taken out an insurance policy whereby he would have been paid $100 a week for as long as he lived. As it was, he was broke and had to finish the last years of his life in an "Old Folk's Home." He had been smart enough to accumulate one million but not smart enough to pay himself the 10%.

Here's another story that bears out what we have been discussing in this lesson. A man worked himself up to be worth a quarter of a million dollars. A relative in the insurance business said to him, "Imagine that you have two hundred thousand instead of a quarter of a million dollars. Give me fifty thousand and I will give you a policy that will pay you fifty dollars a week for as long as you live." The man responded, "Don't be silly. I can open a business with $5,000 and make myself $50 a week. Why should I give you $50,000?"

The depression came along and this man lost all his money. His wife, who had not worked for 20 years, had to go back to work, so did his son and daughter. The four of them together could barely make $50 a week. Smart enough to make a quarter of a million dollars, but not smart enough to pay himself 10%. How many hundreds of people have had such similar experiences?

Of course, we know that we should not invest in a business in which we are not familiar. Neither are we familiar with the future. Therefore, it is wise to invest in our future. These comparatively new types of insurance policies —investing now for future payments—take a load off the average person's mind and lets the insurance companies handle it for us. Not only that, but instead of putting "all of our eggs in one basket," we protect our way of life and keep away from the strain that comes with the constant worry about the future. These policies need not be paid in a lump sum. They can be paid in installments, and allowed to accumulate to a sum that will then repay us so much a week or a month for as long as we live.

STEP 5: DO NOT FORCE YOUR MONEY TO MAKE FANTASTIC RETURNS

It seems that almost everybody is looking for "easy money." The result is that the crooked elements in life are always working out plans for just such "easy marks." How many times has the Brooklyn Bridge been sold? How many times do you read in the papers of people who were sold smuggled diamonds, worth hundreds of thousands of dollars, for just a few thousand? Then these people find out that the diamonds are worthless! How many schemes and plans have been "cooked up" for centuries by dishonest people to take advantage of the "get-rich-quick" minded individuals? The schemes seem endless; the "suckers" are countless, not only among the poor and uneducated, but among the very wealthy as well. How many millions upon millions of dollars have been invested in worthless stocks, and so much of it has been sold by mail! Imagine, people actually buying this kind of stock by mail! What imaginations they must have!

If you have a few extra thousand dollars or a few hundred dollars, don't buy stocks by mail. How do you know the company even exists? How do you know what the company represents? If this company was as good as claimed, they would not need you. They could go into the banks and get all the money needed. Why, then, do they come to us? Because, the banks will not give them any money. The banks would investigate and reveal that the company was not a legitimate business.

Do you want to invest your extra money? Then, buy legitimate stocks. Do you like General Motors? Then, buy yourself some General Motors stock. Do you like General Electric

Company? Then, buy yourself some General Electric stock. Go to a legitimate broker in your town or city—you will find their names in the phone book, tell them how much money you have, and they will advise you on what to buy. They will also guide you into building a "nice nest egg" in the stock market. Each day you can pick up the paper—the stock edition—and see just where your stock is. If you should need money, either your stock broker or your bank will lend you money on your stock. Your stocks may go down, but the chances are, you will not lose everything. Your broker will tell you whether to hold on or sell the stock. In other words, you can sell it when you want. The stock sold by mail, or by dishonest stock salesmen, cannot be sold nor borrowed against it.

So, where are you? You may not make as much money in the "listed" stock market, but neither is there risk. If you force your money to make "fantastic" returns, you are headed for trouble. Be careful. As the Better Business Bureaus throughout the country emphasize, "investigate before you invest." Why be in a hurry to lose your money? Why complain when you lose? It is your fault—for "bad choosing"—that would bring about any damage.

I know of a man who once said, "I'm tired of taking other people's advice, I am going to use my own judgment." Not a bad idea. It is very good to depend on your own ability and your own judgment. As you go along in this course, you will more and more depend on your own judgment. However, we can always ask the other fellow, especially if he is experienced and we are not, for his opinion and *then* use our own judgment.

Well, this man went out and without asking anybody bought some lots. He lost the lots and several thousand dollars. He had been advised against it but he was not going to "listen to anybody else." (In Lesson 17—Intuition—you will learn how to make healthy and happy decisions.)

Continuing in this line of "not asking questions," a man who owned a drugstore refused to put his savings in a bank. He would save his money in the basement of his store—in cigar boxes! A fire broke out in the store and the $10,000 he had saved went up in smoke. The man committed suicide. How foolish can we be—trying to be our own banks, our own insurance companies, our own stock brokers, our own investors?

Ask questions, find out from those who have had experience. Why be in a hurry to invest without first investigating? Get the other fellow's experience and then if you still desire to do so, make your own final decisions. If things don't work out, you have no one to blame but yourself. Blame your own "bad choosing" and you will learn to live a healthy and successful financial life.

Again, I remind you of the five steps to financial freedom:
1. Pay yourself first
2. Find profitable employment for your money
3. Be very careful about your first experiences and ask questions
4. Do not invest in a business with which you are not familiar
5. Do not force your money to make fantastic returns

*A closed mind stumbles
over the blessings of life
without recognizing them.*
—Napoleon Hill

Lesson 5

Psychology of Trouble

Dear Reader:
Although this is a short lesson, do not overlook its significance. In dealing with the Psychology of Trouble, Kohe looks trouble directly in its face and names it for what it really is—a lesson to be learned. These lessons may not be personal lessons but rather societal lessons or even cultural lessons. Trouble created in our world is always the result of wrong thinking. As we grow in understanding, and allow right thinking through the selection and maintenance of good thoughts to prevail, our troubles will diminish.

Trouble is not sent to us from Infinite Intelligence as a punishment for bad behavior, but rather is directly related to the effects that bad behavior brings about in our lives based on our power to choose. On a personal level, trouble results when an individual makes a choice that is based on wrong thinking. On a societal level, trouble results when groups of individuals make a collective choice based on wrong thinking. Choice is the catalyst that brings good or bad happenings into our reality. As Shakespeare states, "There is nothing either good or bad, but thinking makes it so."

When we learn to focus on good thoughts, right thinking will result and the effect will be wholesome, not troublesome. Mental Millionaires understand this concept fully and store up treasures for themselves in their minds. No moth or thief can touch these treasures. Safely, they are locked away in the mind's treasure chest and accessible at a moment's notice. The wings of thought are swift and carry us to our treasure instantaneously. Mental Millionaires know that these unseen treasures contribute to the good life. That, dear reader, requires us to "Accentuate the Positive, Eliminate the Negative and don't mess with Mr. Inbetween" as the song states.

—JUDITH WILLIAMSON

The world will start getting better
the very minute we choose to make it better.
–YOUR GREATEST POWER

Wouldn't it be a grand and glorious feeling if there were no trouble in the world? It would be "heaven on earth." Isn't that so? Well, in these lessons you will learn how to avoid trouble and how to handle trouble. Once you begin to understand trouble and the purpose of trouble, you will see a complete change come over your life.

In the "Secret of Dealing with Trouble" (refer to the Appendix), you have learned that troubles are really lessons to be learned. Be sure to read this lesson. Just as soon as I stop talking about trouble and start talking about lessons, you will lose the fear of trouble. Lessons are always stepping-stones. Every time you learn something, you feel stronger. That is the reason you are taking this course—to be stronger.

In the "Psychology of Trouble" you will learn that trouble does not come into your life to tear you down and make you weaker, but to build you up and make you stronger. If you are disappointed in obtaining that something upon which you had your heart and soul set, it is only because you have unconsciously set a force in motion that will bring you something bigger and better. Then, why are you afraid? You are afraid because you have been led to believe that trouble comes to you as a punishment, that everybody has trouble; so, naturally, you must have trouble. Now you see how silly your choices have been. If one person chooses to go swimming in the ice-cold lake, does that mean that all of you have to follow suit? Because one person has trouble, does that mean that everybody has to have trouble?

For years this may have been true. Now that we know God loves us, we know that there is nothing outside of ourselves that is sending us trouble. It is our own "bad choosing." I say, everybody has his troubles and let it go at that. That is the same as saying that every automobile tire gets punctures, so your tires will get punctures. We now have tires that are puncture-proof and blow-out proof; we can no longer say we must have punctures. Now we say, "buy puncture-proof tires and be free from punctures." I contend the same thing in this lesson regarding trouble.

The Greatest Psychologist who ever lived said, "He whosoever doeth good . . . what wrong can come to him?"

Today we say, "He whosoever doeth good ideas choose, . . . what wrong can come to him?"

So, I come back again to my original thought that trouble comes from choosing bad ideas. Good living, smooth living, beautiful living, all come from choosing good ideas. Our job, therefore, is to learn to choose good ideas, keep choosing good ideas, and life will be what we choose to make it.

From now on when you see someone in trouble, don't do what I used to do—wonder when this same trouble would strike me next. Instead, say to yourself, as I do now: "Too bad that person does not know what I know. If he did, he never would have made that mistake."

A doctor makes more money than the shoemaker, a dentist makes more money than the window washer, a lawyer makes a better living than the garbage collector—Why? Because they went to school and studied, they prepared themselves for a better living. Each individual must prepare himself for a better way of life. One does not help a sick fellow by crawling in bed with him and saying, "Move over, I'll get in bed and be sick with you too." Oh, no! So, too, in life you don't crawl into the other fellow's bed of trouble, you try to help him, try to lift him up. By making yourself strong, you automatically help him to carry on. By improving yourself, you improve the world. When enough of us make it our business to improve the world, it will really be improved.

Look around you and what do you see? We used to use gas mantles, but now we have electricity. Why?—gas mantles were too much trouble. Now we have self-starters on our automobiles. Why?—people broke their arms trying to start their cars. We have air-conditioning. Why?—man says it is too hot in the summer time. Wherever we go, we see these improvements.

You may remember when Mother used to spend a whole day down in the basement washing clothes. She would come up all worn out. Today, the lady of the house pushes a button and the washer does the work. All of these improvements have come about because of "trouble." Yet, one says that "trouble" is our enemy when in actuality it is our "friend." Just as a friend wants to help make your life more enjoyable, so "trouble" wants to make your life better and more enjoyable.

So, why be afraid? Clearly, trouble does not come to your life to hurt you, but to help you. Please bear in mind that most troubles are "man made." Don't create any trouble for yourself; those that do come into your life are coming in to improve your life, so relax. Trouble is your friend, not your enemy. If you are good, choose good ideas and your life will be good, too.

Lesson 6

How to Control Your Nerves

Dear Reader:
Here in this lesson is a technique that Kohe teaches regarding right and left nostril breathing. The purpose of this practice is to steady your nerves, achieve an overall sense of calmness, eradicate worry, and eliminate negative thinking. This meditation technique called by Kohe the "Human Barometer" is a stress-reducing skill that Yoga students from India master during their apprenticeship. Not being popular in our culture, this lesson on nostril breathing may seem silly, simpleminded, and useless upon first encounter. However, if you agree to try the procedure for several days, and then consider the results, you may find that your paradigm was the one that needed to change.

Too often our imaginations are suppressed and our creativity suffers because we do not approach subjects with optimism. Life teaches us how things work, and these ruts in thinking become imbedded in our brains. New approaches are not congruous with past experiences. This causes cognitive dissonance and forces us to consider whether the old way or the new way is best. Change is *created through dissonance. Things that support our current beliefs do not change our behaviors. Things that do not support our beliefs cause us to change and grow.*

In becoming Mental Millionaires, one must be open to new approaches to old issues. Suspending your disbelief, even temporarily, opens up new concepts that just might hold the key to your personal greatness. One little technique, one piece of advice, one missing ingredient, or one change in thinking might be just the "little extra" needed to give you that boost as you work to become a Mental Millionaire. That, dear reader, is the acorn that matures into the giant oak. Cultivate it wisely.

—Judith Williamson

We can control our thoughts . . . and by controlling our thoughts . . . by using this greatest power . . . the power to choose . . . we are indirectly able to control conditions.

–YOUR GREATEST POWER

One of the most difficult problems that one has to face in "choosing correctly" is in controlling the nerves. Be sure to read the "Human Barometer" (found in the Appendix). The nerves are constantly demanding attention. This attention is drawn to our minds in so many different ways that it is easy to understand why humans have gone for so many centuries believing that there is some power outside themselves which is controlling them. Certainly, the average person says, "I didn't think of that terrible thing; why did it come into my mind?" He can find no answer. The answer is that there is something outside of himself that is causing it. Now, however, we have the answer.

As you will read in the "Human Barometer," the Yoga students of India are much more advanced than the American Psychologists. Yoga students are much more interested in answering the question "What is life and how does it work?" than they are in making money. Unfortunately, the American Psychologist who is not successful financially is not considered to be very good. This is explainable since under our present societal conditions, making money is more important than making a life. However, because the Yoga has been able to devote himself to his body and his mind, and to meditate and study so much more, he is far more advanced. He has, therefore, given us what I consider to be one of the greatest bits of information that gives us the absolute proof—each one of us can do his own choosing.

In the "Human Barometer" you will have everything explained to you regarding the left and right nostrils. You will be told how they work and of the various reactions a person has or may have from time to time. You must be constantly on guard regarding these reactions. If you are, you will very quickly begin to realize that you are doing the choosing, although other influences may seem otherwise.

I must warn you, too, that it is very easy to forget about the effects of the left nostril or the right nostril especially when everything is running along smoothly for a period of several months. Then when a negative reaction occurs, you will wonder what has happened. The first thing the average person reaches for is an aspirin, which is perfectly all right. However, if you are going to rely on aspirins, when are you really going to become a "master of your thoughts?"—one time it is an aspirin, the next time it is a cocktail, the next time it is a vacation, the next time it is something else, and always it is "the next time." So, for most people life is just one "darn" thing after another.

On the other hand, if you keep constant watch over the left and right nostril breathing, you will learn to control yourself, you will save yourself hundreds of bad hours and hundreds of thousands of bad thoughts from running through your mind; and more than anything else, you will really begin to feel the "power of choice." Once you gain this self-mastery, you will then begin to choose to believe that life can be beautiful. You will save yourself and your family many doctor bills, many a moment of anxiety, the fear of thousands of things—as pointed out in the "Human Barometer." Your entire family will benefit far beyond your imagination!

Another word of warning: do not discuss this lesson with people who have had little or no study of the "power of the mind." They may laugh at you, ridicule the entire idea, and before long you will have lost the most important lesson in your life.

There is an old saying, "The fool laughs at that which he does not understand." Too many people do this very thing. They laughed at Ford when he rode his first horseless carriage down the street, they laughed at Columbus when he said the world was round, they laughed at Edison when he said he was going to turn night into day. Thus, you can readily understand why these great dreamers and doers were ridiculed. People react this way when they do not understand how these dreams are meaningful. They are sure to laugh at something like the "Human Barometer" simply because it sounds too good to be true.

In my resident school classes I constantly have the same problem, so I know that experience bears out my point. The lesson on the "Human Barometer" is such a wonderful lesson that the Yoga calls it the "Million Dollar Breath." You wouldn't sell it for any large sum of money once you got it to work and learned to depend upon it!

Remember, it is impossible to have any serious negative or destructive idea going through your mind unless the left nostril is empty. You won't be bothered by little negative thoughts, such as someone telling you that you are a fool. So what? Someone else may say to you that you do not know what you are talking about. So what? Whenever you have a very serious negative thought running through your mind, you have a problem. But, now you have the answer—the Yoga breath. Consequently, you can handle the smaller negative thoughts without too much trouble. Now, you can handle the very serious negative thoughts. Your power to choose looms up greater than ever before. Then and only then can you say "Life is what you choose to make it."

From time to time my resident school students have made some very important discoveries of their own. Sometimes when you have a very negative thought bothering you and you would like to get rid of it, try the left nostril. Not getting the desired results, you try the right nostril. Sometimes, too, if you ever had an operation on your nose, or if you had your adenoids removed, there may have been a change made in the flow of your nostrils. Frequently, the left nostril may be blocked for one reason or another so you work through the right. You want results. Experiment until you have mastered this great simple principle.

I have often been asked if one can eliminate all these negative thoughts through ordinary deep breathing. In most cases, the answer is "yes." However, most people are not deep breathers and, as a result, very few will master their nerves through constant steady deep breathing. In very serious situations, ordinary deep breathing will not solve the problem.

Remember: Read Appendix 1 and avoid very negative thoughts by watching your left nostril.

> *Change your mental attitude and the world around you will change accordingly.*
> —Napoleon Hill

Lesson 7

Power of the Imagination

Dear Reader:

Napoleon Hill states: "Creative vision is definitely and closely related to that state of mind known as faith, and it is significant that those who have demonstrated the greatest amount of creative vision are known to have been men with a great capacity for faith. This is both logical and understandable when we recognize that faith is the means of approach to Infinite Intelligence, the source of all knowledge and all facts, both great and small."

Kohe believes the above statement and also emphasizes that imagination and creative thought go hand in hand. When thoughts are creative, something happens. Our lives are impacted because action has occurred. Thoughts by themselves are not creative. Nothing happens with a thought until it becomes a creative thought. When it is creative, it is born into our world. Thoughts that are birthed into existence then create our reality. Since what we think about we become, it is only evident that the part of our thought process that is creative can determine our world.

The Twelve Riches of Life exist in our mind. If we view ourselves as a financial millionaire, we act the part and cause our body language to exude millionaire status. We are not literally carrying around our million dollars on our person; however, our person invariably displays this richness. Peace of mind is another million dollar asset not purchasable at any price. This state of mind which exists first mentally for us is simultaneously demonstrated on the physical plane. The experiences are identical for the remaining ten riches.

The point is that our million dollar attributes are all mental—even financial assets. If you think you are a millionaire, you are. Likewise, if you possess great wealth but think like a pauper, you are that too. That, dear reader, is the truth stranger than fiction. First, you change your mental picture, and then your mental picture changes you!

—JUDITH WILLIAMSON

Let us choose to believe that something good can happen.
Why must we always use the old model . . .
that something bad will happen?

–YOUR GREATEST POWER

What a tremendous power is the power of the imagination! It has made some men giants, while at the same time it has made other men pygmies. It has given some people the greatest of happiness, while at the same time it has made others sad. It has given some people peace of mind, while at the same time it has made others most disturbed. Everywhere you go, everywhere you look, no matter what you may be doing, the "power of the imagination" is playing an important role. Why?

Coué, the famous Frenchman who was able to gain such remarkable cures with his system of conscious auto-suggestion, wrote a most unusual book called *How to Gain Self-Mastery through Conscious Auto Suggestion*. In this book he states: "All of our actions come from the imagination." Never forget this statement. Carry it around with you wherever you go. It will change your life. It will make your life what you "choose" it to be, give you all the things that are worthwhile in life, lift you up when you are down, give you courage when you need it. It will make your life so much more worthwhile; and best of all, things which ordinarily bothered you, won't.

When Coué said that all of our actions came from our imagination, he didn't mean—and neither do I—the ordinary "garden variety" type of imagination, he meant "creative thought." In other words: "All of our actions come from our creative thought." It is a truly wonderful fact that nature so constructed us that thought alone will not necessarily create anything.

"A thought does not mean anything until it becomes creative." If this were not so, most people would not live very long. So many people have made the statement to the effect that they wished they were dead—but nothing happened. Many go around wishing and thinking some awful things about themselves—and thank goodness, nothing happened. Many people have said that they are losing their minds or that they will lose their minds—nothing happens. The reason nothing happened is simply because the thought did not become creative. If a person persists in this form of thinking and it does become creative, then there is a chance that the thought will come to pass.

For example: Suppose there is someone that you do not like, and you say to yourself, "I would like to punch him in the nose," but you don't. Yet, you keep thinking about it and keep saying it to yourself every time you see this person. Then one day, without thinking, you walk up to this person and you hit him. You can't understand why you did that—*but now you do.* The thought became creative and you acted upon it. Keeping the thought constant in your mind, continuing to keep it alive, makes it creative—and finally, it becomes a reality!

As you know, thoughts become things. The thought constantly worked on becomes a thing—then it is creative. So, let us always remember that a thought does not mean anything until it becomes creative.

Before long, we realize that everyone of us is a "creator." Therefore, we can create good for ourselves or we can create poverty, we can create a beautiful life or we can create a miserable life, we can create what we want or we can create what we don't want. It is up to us. As I told you in my book *Your Greatest Power*, you choose. You create according to your choice. It is up to each individual to choose and to create as he sees right and fit. This course—these lessons—in which you are now engaged, will give you all the best to choose from. You will learn how to use every trick in the game of life, nothing is left out.

Unfortunately, our imaginations must be constantly guarded and watched. Just as when you drive your automobile, you must be constantly alert to what is going on around you. The imagination is like the automobile. It is constantly in motion and it is always active during the time when we are not asleep. Therefore, we must watch it, we must be careful that we do not let our imaginations run away with us, and we must control them constantly.

We start to do this by first realizing that we do "our own choosing." That is possible because "God loves you." There is no one outside yourself who can hurt you. God doesn't hurt you. The only one who can hurt you is yourself through your own bad choosing. So, with the greatest power that you possess—the power of choice, and now with the power to create—you are able to make life what you want it to be. What a thrill that should be to you—if you realize it!

Let me tell you a true, almost unbelievable, story that took place during the French Revolution. A man, who happened to be a school teacher, was accused of speaking against the French government. Actually, he did not, but he was so charged and thus brought before the court where he was found guilty and sentenced to jail for a period of twenty years. The reputation of this specific prison was that no man had ever come out alive from there. However, this man vowed that he would come out alive.

Once in prison, this vow was soon forgotten upon seeing how filthy this place was—the floor was plain dirt, the bed was only a sheet of metal with a little straw over it, the food was far from the best, the only light was that which was coming through the bar-covered window, rats were running all over the place. What a sight to behold! Frightened by all this, the Frenchman began to lose control of himself. He wondered how any living person could endure such a life. He didn't eat, he didn't sleep, he was a complete mental wreck. Then, he remembered his vow—the promise to himself that he would come out alive.

The Frenchman began to take charge of his mind. He imagined that the ground was not so bad—after all, farmers live on the soil, the bed was not so bad—he would become accustomed to sleeping on it, and the rats—well, the rats showed him that there was still life around. He asked the jail keepers to bring him whatever books they could; and they did. At night when the stars were out, he studied them, oblivious of the bars in the window.

The story goes on to tell that this man lived his twenty years in jail and that when he finally came out, he did not look one day older than the day he went in. Hard to believe? Yes, what a wonderful use of the imagination! What wonderful creative thought!

One is inclined to believe this story to be true for one sees it all around. Some people have everything that one could ask for to make them happy and yet, they are unhappy. Others, who have almost nothing except the bare necessities of life, are always smiling and living so happily that one would think they didn't have a worry in the world.

This leads me to another story about a king who was very sick. There was no cure for the king. One of the wise men said that if the king would wear the shirt of a happy man, he would be well again. So, messengers were sent all over the country trying to find a happy man. Finally, they came to a field where a man was working and singing and showing all the signs of being extremely happy. Going up to the man, the messengers said, "We see you are a very happy man."

"Yes," replied the worker, "very happy."

"That's fine," said the messenger, "our king is very sick and the only thing that will cure him is that he should wear the shirt of a happy man. Please give us your shirt."

The workman opened his coat, looked at the messengers and said, "I'm sorry, but I don't have a shirt."

This, of course, is only a story, but how true it is in real life. People who appear to have every reason to be happy are not, and people who outwardly appear to have nothing to be happy about, really are. What is the reason? You know what it is—it all depends on how you imagine yourself.

Another story which shows the power of the imagination, or creative thinking, is told about a man who never had very much. He had worked for the same boss for many years and during the last ten, he had not gotten a raise. His wife always made him feel small and his daughter had little respect for him. Indeed, he was a mental bankrupt!

One day while at work, he got a telegram. It read:

John Brown, we are happy to inform you that your uncle George Brown passed away and left you $50,000 in his will. Will call on you in a few days to complete the details.
Signed . . . Gallagher and Gallagher, Attorneys.

Well! As soon as he received this telegram, he became a changed man! He stormed into his boss's office and with a raised voice exclaimed how in ten years he had never received a raise and if he did not get one right away—and a substantial one at that—he would quit. The boss responded by telling him not to get so excited, that he would take care of him.

At home that evening, his voice rang out while exclaiming to his wife that tonight was Tuesday and he did not want the regular Tuesday night hash—he wanted steaks! He made her go to the butcher to get some. He then told his daughter, in a good loud voice, to go upstairs and bring him his slippers. What a completely changed man!

The next day, the boss gave him a very fine raise in salary, his daughter gains new respect for her father, his wife begins to realize that her husband is a *man* after all. All proceeds fine until a week later when another telegram arrives for John Brown informing him that he was not the John Brown who was to receive the $50,000 but the John Brown from a neighboring town!

Actually, this man never really had the money in hand, but the "thought" that he did have it was there, it was real, it was creative, and he lived as though he did have the $50,000 in hand. What a tremendous power is the power of the imagination!

All of our actions come from our imagination. The man in prison acted in such a way that it did not bother him too much—he lived through it beautifully. The man without a shirt was a happy man—even though he did not possess the wealth of a king, who on the other hand was miserable. The man who had $50,000 only in his creative thought—lived as though he really did have it.

Oh, if only we could get this power of the imagination working as it should . . .

. . . Life would be truly wonderful!

. . . Life could be a truly happy experience!

. . . Life would truly be simplified!

Why have we made life so complicated? Why have we made it so difficult? Why have we made life so full of unhappy experiences? I have attempted to answer these questions in my book *Your Greatest Power*. Simply stated: one has chosen badly. By choosing correctly, one saves most of the difficulty in life, life is simplified, and one is able to control one's imaginations.

The truly Great Psychologist said, "Unless we become as little children, we shall not enter the Kingdom of Heaven." Many times it takes a childlike faith to stop the complications of life. It takes a childlike faith to realize that "life can be beautiful." Don't let anyone spoil it for you. If you find someone trying to spoil it for you, don't argue with him, leave him alone for he is not ready to think the way you do. He will learn it eventually, but trying to convince him is simply a waste at the present time.

Now, we begin to be aware that there are "magic words" around us and here are two great ones: just imagine. Now, just imagine that you feel fine. What ensues? Almost like a flash, you create the thought that you feel wonderful. Imagine that you feel bad, and in a flash, before you realize it, you don't feel so good. Imagine that you are somebody, and in a flash, you stick out your chest and begin to walk as though you are the most wonderful person in the world. Imagine that you are lucky, and in a flash, good luck comes to you from many different directions.

The reverse also holds true. Imagine that you are unlucky and immediately you begin to attract unlucky situations, wondering what has happened to you. Imagine that no one likes you, and that is exactly what takes place. On the other hand, imagine that everybody likes you, and all of a sudden you find yourself popular and being sought after.

All this occurs simply by using the magic words: just imagine. Your thoughts are now creative, and before you know it, you see the thought in action. Be sure that you are using "just imagine" for your good.

From what you have gathered in this lesson and from the stories I have related, you can now draw one of the great lessons in life: *All real life is within . . . not without.* Why keep yourself in a mental dungeon?

Money is important—certainly I told you that in an earlier lesson. A home is important for good living, clothes are necessary for modern-day living, stocks and bonds are all nice to have, automobiles and jewelry all go to make the outer life complete, and love for your family and friends are all part of the making of life.

All of these things, in the final analysis, are thoughts. Therefore, *what is truly important are our thoughts.* So, in the meantime . . .

   . . . If you want peace of mind (your thoughts must be peaceful)—just imagine life is peaceful.

   . . . If you want money (your thoughts must be for making money)—just imagine that you are making money.

   . . . If you want success (your thoughts must be for success)—just imagine that you are successful. . . . If you want happiness (your thoughts must be happy thoughts)—just imagine that you are happy.

   . . . If you want beautiful living (your thoughts must be beautiful thoughts)—just imagine that life is beautiful.

Do not let what goes on outside of your life affect your "inner" thoughts. It is in your inner thoughts that you really find life. The richest kind of life is a life filled with rich thoughts. Let us realize that we live with our thoughts more than we live with the things of life. If we can realize this, we can master every difficulty and find that life can be beautiful.

> *A man is no greater than
> the thoughts that
> dominate his mind.*
> —Napoleon Hill

Lesson 8

New Psychology of Success

Dear Reader:
This lesson on success is innovative because it tells us that our old definitions of success no longer work, and probably never did. Kohe emphasizes that tales told about heroes and heroines during school years do not measure up to current expectations about what we admire in life. This is a shocking aspect of how history places individuals in a positive light, when perhaps they should have remained in obscurity. Individuals like Napoleon, Charles Schwab, Eastman and others were outstanding "successes" in an area of their lives, but dismal failures in other areas. When their biographies are researched, no one would want to model the catastrophic outcomes of their lives. Yet, they still are placed on pedestals as worthy examples of success. Kohe affirms that we have the success model all wrong.

Herein is the lesson to be learned. Success comes to individuals through different accomplishments that have occurred in their lives. Success can be financial, social, familial, or personal. Optimally, it is all four. Kohe calls a person with success elements in all four of these areas a "four square success." Extreme success in only one or two of these areas leads to an imbalance in lifestyle. A life focused on only one type of riches will be out of sync with the culture in which the person lives. Benjamin Franklin states: "Moderation in all things." Perhaps this is another way of saying balance is an enviable state of affairs. Not too much and not too little.

Kohe admonishes us to think outside the box. He asks us to examine what a true success looks like, talks like, behaves like, and feels like. Having more does not bring success into a person's life, rather it is having the quality of the trait rather than the quantity that brings ultimate satisfaction. Perhaps you already head the list on being a four square success! That, dear reader, is something for you to think about as you read the next Fortune 500 list.

—JUDITH WILLIAMSON

We have gone through the stone age, the wood age, the iron age, just going through the mechanical age . . . we are now entering the mental age. Man has been using . . . those who have used it . . . the power to choose and not realizing it. Now that we realize it . . . we make the great discovery that most of our troubles, our difficulties, and our miseries are man made.

–YOUR GREATEST POWER

Everybody wants to be successful. In school I was taught all about successful men and women. By the time I left school, I had made up my mind that one thing I would do for myself in this lifetime was to become *successful*. Unless I did become successful, I will have failed—failed my teachers, my parents, and most of all myself. I was taught about Napoleon—was he not a poor boy who became a great military genius? I was taught about hundreds of poor boys who became great men—if they could, so could I!

When we go out into the business world, we are constantly reminded that successful people have money. So, to be successful, we too must have money. Money becomes a very important part of our searching for success. With all this in mind, we set out on our goal. We scheme, we plan, we struggle to make money—is that not important to be a success? When we do not receive the feeling of importance through money, we try to find it in politics—city councilman, state representative, mayor of the city, governor of the state. I conclude that "opportunities for success" are all around me.

I start out optimistically—it won't be hard to become successful. But . . . it isn't long before I find that there are not too many chances to become a governor, a mayor of the city, or even a city councilman. With a family, trying to make ends meet, and sending the children through school, money is not too free. The years start to fly by, success begins to wing away, I am not making the progress I expected, here I am with life half over and I have not succeeded. I become a little disappointed—I have not come up to my expectations. Certainly, I will not become a Napoleon. I settle back and begin to feel that I have failed. I trudge along, going to work, paying the bills, hoping now that maybe my children will do what I failed to do. My hopes rise—yes, that's it, my children will be the successful ones. I will help them, I will get behind them, I will give them an education, I will bask in their success, I will transfer my hopes to my children—maybe that's the answer!

But, is this really the answer? I have built a "Psychology of Success" that has actually created a "Psychology of Failure." All over the country our mental institutions are filled with mental patients, most of whom are failures. These people have failed to make life what they expected it to be. They become discouraged and lose themselves entirely—thus, you become a "mental case." According to the present standard of success, they are failures. On and on we go making people feel that they are failures in life—due to our present "Psychology of Success." So, what can we do about it?

Let me change the "Psychology of Success" so that everybody, with a few exceptions, can be successful. Psychologists have recognized this very serious problem and all over the country today, there is a decided effort to change the old "Psychology of Success" to the "New Psychology of Success."

The "New Psychology of Success" goes away from the idea of becoming a Napoleon. If you truly analyze Napoleon, what would you find? Instead of being a great military leader, he was one of the worst butchers that the world had known up to his time. Hundreds of thousands of men lost their lives to make Napoleon a "great leader." So badly did he manage his war ambitions that thousands of men lost their arms, their legs, their eyes. Worst of all, he so drained the manpower of France that France, due to the shortage of men, has never been the same since. So, now we will no longer teach our children to become Napoleons. Thank goodness for that!

Just as the cat lives nine lives, so we live four lives—a business life, a social life, a family life, a personal life. (I discussed this a little in Lesson 3.) This now gives us four chances to be successful:

1. *Business*—make lots of money, build a fine business
2. *Social*—have lots of friends, a home filled with company and parties, go out a great deal with other people, visit them, belong to various clubs and organizations, take a part in them, be a good member or even an officer
3. *Family*—be a good husband or wife, be a good mother or father, raise a family, do all that is possible for our fathers and mothers
4. *Personal*—this is really the most important one

Ever since man has walked the face of the earth, and has had to decide on a "Psychology of Success" of some kind, he said, "He who conquers himself is greater than he who conquers a city. What gaineth he, if he gain the whole world and loseth his own soul." Socrates, one of the world's early great philosophers, had a school for young men who wished to be able to think well and for themselves. Over the doorway of his school he had an inscription which read, "Know Thyself."

Four chances for success . . . isn't that better than the old psychology? No need for people to become discouraged for not accomplishing a great deal in the commercial world. Suppose one did not make a lot of money or build a big business or not become a mayor or governor? One has other ways of being successful. One can be a social success, a family success, or a personal success.

Let us look at some of the successes of life:

Andrew Mellon, who was at one time Secretary of the Treasury of the United States, was worth $123,000,000. Was he a business success?—Certainly. Mr. Mellon was a divorced man. Was he a family success?—No. Then, let me simply say he was a business success and let it go at that.

Eastman, of the famous Eastman Kodak Company was worth $55,000,000 at the time of his death. Was he a business success?—Certainly, and served a great purpose to the American way of life. Mr. Eastman committed suicide. Was he a personal success?—No. Then, let me say he was a great business success and that he brought happiness to millions of people. I will not say he was a success in every sense of the word. He certainly was not a four-square success.

Thomas Edison, the great inventor, was a millionaire. Was he a business success?—Yes. Edison had a very nice family. Was he a family success?—Yes. Edison got along beautifully with Edison. Was he a personal success?—Yes. On the social side, Edison simply did not care for it. Was he a social success?—No. Let me expand on this. A huge banquet was held in one of the large hotels in New York City to honor Edison. Everybody of any importance was there but the honoree. The chairman of the arrangements committee went to the telephone and called Edison, who lived just across the river in New Jersey, to inquire if he would be there. Edison replied, "Do I have to?" . . . Here we clearly see that Edison was a business success, a family success, a personal success, a social failure—he just did not care for the social life!

There are very few outstanding men and women in this world who are four-square successes. It is difficult to find them and even to name them. In case you want one or two illustrations, I will mention Henry Ford. Having made two billion dollars, Mr. Ford was surely a business success. He was well known in the Detroit social circles, so he was a social success.

He had a very fine family, so he was a family success. After having made his money, he began to get along nicely with Henry Ford, so he was a personal success. Here we have one four-square success!

Bing Crosby has been pointed out as being a four-square success. So, these people are around, to be sure. But, for most of us, if we are a success in one category or another, that should suffice to make our success psychology helpful instead of harmful.

Sometime ago a man came into my life who walked around with his head drooping, his eyes dull, the expression on his face showing defeat. In talking to him, I learned that he had never made a lot of money, he could hardly make ends meet, he was lucky if he could save a little money to take a summer vacation. He was, indeed, depressed. Upon talking further, I discovered that he was a married man who had been married for twenty-five years, he had never left the house in the morning without kissing his wife goodbye, he had four sons—three of them in the service and the fourth was too young to follow suit, and he gave his boys a good education. This man was definitely a family success!

For the mere fact that he had not made a lot of money—been the kind of success that people talk about—this man went about like a "beaten" man. Yet, he was truly a grand success. If every man would be a "family success," would we have any trouble in this world? Theodore Roosevelt, one of our United States presidents, has told us that whenever he heard a reformer, the first thing he would ask him was, "How are *you* getting along in *your* home?"

Let us always remember that we all have four chances at success. If we succeed in any one of the four, we will have done all right. If we succeed in two, fine; three, even better. If we can be a four-square success, so much more good fortune to us. Let us no longer be governed by the old Napoleon idea of success. Let us teach our children many of the heartaches that so many millions of people have endured due to a bad "psychology of success."

So many men walk around with the idea that success will come with retirement, when they are ready to hang up their working clothes and take it easy. Then they will be able to bask in the sunshine of their success.

I will tell you a story about a man who started out in life with the idea that he was going to retire at an early age—that would really be a successful way of living! Thus he went into business, became so busy making money that he never found time for his family. He extracted all the work he possibly could out of his employees, paying them as little as he possibly could. He took advantage of his customers at every turn and opportunity. He carried on like this for forty years and he did make enough money so that he could retire. At the point of retirement, he discovered that this was not what he wanted after all. Forty years of the worst kind of living! Could he not have been decent to his employees, taken a little time out for his family, given his customers a reasonable and fair opportunity in his business transactions?

Sometimes we think the millionaire is free to live as he wishes. A story is told of a millionaire who wanted to open a gasoline station. Upon relating his intention to his family and business associates, he was met with: "If you do, we will disown you." "If you open a gasoline station, we will have to call a psychiatrist to see what is wrong with you." So, he had to forego his whole idea. Finally, the years went by and he retired. What was the first thing this man did? You guessed it—he opened up a gas station!

Retirement is a wonderful thing, but why wait? How do you know when you are going to have enough money to retire? One man told me, "I have enough money to last me for ten years; if I live any longer than that, I don't know what I am going to do." Isn't that a fine way to retire? He no sooner decides to quit working that he starts to worry. Some men will quit working when they reach a certain age. How do you know what is the right age? What happens to many people who retire? Usually, they don't live very long. Did you know that insurance companies will not insure a retired worker or a businessman?

If your work is going along nicely, and you don't mind going to the shop or office, why do you want to retire? If your business is going along beautifully, and you don't mind going to the business, why do you want to retire? What, then, is it that you want to retire from anyway? If you want to retire from worry, you can do that now—why wait a minute longer? That is what this lesson is intended to teach you. Its purpose is to help you become a "mental millionaire" so you don't continue to worry, and so that you will live as you go. When you say you are waiting to retire, you are actually saying that "you are going to start to live when you retire." Now, think it over, are you going to waste the best years of your life before you start to live?

Remember to live as you go along—not for some future moment in time. Mentally live the very best you know how to live right now. Don't sacrifice a moment of your precious time. Be a mental millionaire—that's what these lessons are teaching you. If you are a mental millionaire, you will make money if you so want, but you will not place money success ahead of "real living." You will not have to wait.

You will enjoy life as you go. We have seen that even the millionaire could not do what he wanted, even though he was a millionaire. Money will not give you the freedom you want. Freedom comes from good thoughts, from living as you go and doing things that you want to do. If you want to take music lessons at fifty, then go right ahead. If you want to take dancing lessons at sixty, they go right ahead. If you want to learn to paint at seventy, then go right ahead. People may laugh at you, your relatives may object, your associates at work may think you are a little "off"—go right ahead anyway. When you are able to paint, dance, play a musical instrument, they will say, "Oh, I didn't think you had it in you!" Show them, or better still, don't tell them but surprise them with your new—found ability. Not so long ago there was an article in the paper telling about a man who was starting in medical school at seventy—at eighty he would be able to practice medicine. What a different world we are living in today!

Now, you realize that if you are seeking to find success in retirement, do not wait until a certain age, or until you have accumulated a certain amount of money, but rather find it in living as you go. This brings me to the very thing the "New Psychology of Success" is advocating: *The most successful person in the world is the happy person.*

This "New Psychology of Success" has come about because man has found that money does not give happiness, peace of mind, quiet the nerves, avoid heartaches that come through "bad choosing." The magnificent and joyous part of this psychology is that everybody can be happy, everybody can be successful. The happy person does not hurt anyone nor is he envious of anyone. The happy person certainly would not have to gain what he wants through wars and destruction. Oh, what a different world this will be when the "New Psychology of Success" begins to dominate the life of man! It will truly be a great world! Something to live for? Then, why wait?

You don't have to wait. Parents and teachers, work to make children happy instead of making them successful according to the old psychology. Your children will be happy. Don't do anything to destroy their happiness. They will grow up into happy boys and girls, then into happy men and women, then on into the years when they have decided to no longer work and to do some of the things they wanted to do.

Too good to be true? May I remind you that nothing is too good to be true. Mental institutions will no longer be overcrowded, the mad rush to "keep up with the Joneses" will stop, diseases will diminish, the old Psychology of Success will no longer drive man to an early grave. *Man will live.* Man will still accomplish and go on to bigger and better things in life. The scientist will continue to make life easier for millions. Everyone will continue to make the world a better place in which to live, but they will do it without all the misery and war and destruction of human life and spirit.

In the next lesson you will learn the secret of happiness. It is easy to apply and very easy to understand. Once understood, you will find that you can become a happy person. It is really so simple. It depends simply upon your choosing to do one simple little thing—so, read on . . .

Lesson 9

Secret of Happiness, The Power of Joy

Dear Reader:

Lesson 9 is not only a primer on Positive Mental Attitude but a review course as well for those of us who are Positive Mental Attitude enthusiasts. Kohe pulls out all of the stops here as he details example after example of just how our thoughts continue to shape our world and thereby shape our earthly destiny. Enough, you might be thinking! I get the concept already, but do you really? Have you let some negativity take up residence in a small corner of your mind? Have you agreed to another's negative viewpoint because their argument had worn you down? Are you negative because you find it easier to choose the lower road rather than the higher ground? Stop it! You are only hurting yourself in the long run.

Hill reminds us that habits are first cobwebs then cables. Habits begin with thought. Positive habits develop due to right thinking and negative habits develop due to wrong thinking. Use self-discipline right now to control any negativity that might seep into your consciousness. Weed it from your mind garden for good!

Once you are in a positive frame of mind, continue to expand this awareness. Be a good-finder. Focus on the positive rather than the negative. Look for something to praise rather than something to complain about. When times become trying, enumerate all the blessings you encountered during the day. At bedtime, instead of counting sheep, recall with gratitude all that was positive in your day. Soon, you will see the riches that were previously hidden arrive on your doorstep in abundance. You may even ask yourself why they took so long to find you. The important thing to note is now that you know how to bring them home to roost, you keep doing what works. That, dear reader, is the way you create a true millionaire's lifestyle. No amount of money can buy the joy and happiness you will accumulate when you focus on the habit of right thinking. So, think positively.

—Judith Williamson

We have the power to choose . . . let us use it
to the best of our ability. As we use our own minds
to choose the best so we will find that the universal
mind will come to our aid and assistance to help us
choose the best. Together we cannot fail.
–YOUR GREATEST POWER

Actually, it is very easy to be happy. It is so easy that it takes a lifetime for most people to grasp it. We know now that you can keep only one thought in your mind at a time; therefore, think of something happy and you are happy; think of something sad and you are sad. That's it! Simple enough? Think about it. Each day make up your mind to think of something happy—each day, each hour, each minute. Choose to think a happy thought—"God loves you," for example. There is nothing outside yourself to hurt you. Then, choose to make yourself happy with your own thoughts.

STOP. Read the preceding paragraph over at least three times before proceeding.

During the war, I was walking into my resident school and as I did, I was whistling a song. A resident school student said, "You mean to tell me you can whistle at this time?" My answer was that I knew that many of our boys had lost their lives that very day, I knew that many of them had lost their arms, legs, eyes, and were wounded in other ways, I knew that hundreds of thousands of people were in hospitals all over the world, I knew that millions of people were sick, I knew that millions of people did not know where their next meal was coming from, I knew thousands of people were in mental institutions, and I knew that there were hundreds of thousands of cripples all over the world. When one thought of all those things, who then would have a desire to live? However, when I think of that party I was to attend, that vacation I was to take, that new car I was to buy, that dance where I was to go, that wonderful good friend I was to see, that delicious steak or meal I was to have—then I want to whistle. The student said, "I see what you mean."

There it is again. When you choose happy thoughts, you are naturally happy. If you choose sad thoughts, then you find yourself sad. It is up to the individual to decide which thought he will choose. He has this power; that is why it is the greatest power that man possesses. God is the greatest power there is, but man does not possess God. Man was given the power to choose by God, which makes it the greatest power that man possesses. Let us not make the mistake that we have pointed out in my book, *Your Greatest Power*, of not using our power to choose.

A great religious leader once asked, "How can I be happy when the rest of the world is unhappy?" In his day, although he was a great religious leader, he did not know about the conscious and subconscious minds. Consequently, he did not know that you can keep only one thought in your mind at a time. Therefore, do not wait until the rest of the world is happy—you start it . . . you be happy, others will see you . . . they will follow . . . it is time we changed this world from the sad one it has been to a happy one . . . that it can be . . . when enough of us choose correctly.

A person may say a thousand nice things about you and you may never pay attention to any one of them. But, let him say one nasty thing, and see how angry you become. If he is our best friend, we immediately forget all the nice things he said; and if we are not careful, we wish immediately to break up the friendship. Husbands and wives living together may say ever so many nice things to each other—fine. But let either the husband or the wife say something nasty to the other, the one who is affected by the statement immediately becomes angry, and in some cases becomes so angry that they are ready to start divorce proceedings. How many divorces have started from one nasty statement?

So it is in seeking *happiness*. The truth is that we have more nice experiences than we have bad ones. The truth is that we have more good in life than we have bad. But, we forget the good—and concentrate on the bad—and make ourselves unhappy. We see so few happy people that we think, we too, must be that way. When you see someone unhappy, that person is choosing unhappy thoughts. You know that now. So, why should you be unhappy because he is unhappy? He does his own choosing and you do yours—which will it be? Are we going to build a happy world for our children or allow them to inherit the same kind of world that was given to us?

Reflect on the following statements:

Ella Wheeler Wilcox said: *Always think success . . . no matter what happens.*

Disraeli said: *All my successes have been built on my failures.*

Lincoln said: *A person is just about as happy as he makes up his mind to be.*

I say: *You cannot fight life . . . you have to understand it.*

I understand now why so few people are happy. They do not realize that they, and no one else, do their choosing. They choose. Therefore, they can choose to be happy or they can choose to be sad. I used to think that God decided that—He has. When you know that God loves you—that He doesn't hurt anyone, that it is we who hurt ourselves—when we understand that, then we stop fighting life, we stop fighting God. Use this Greatest Power and let us make ourselves happy through our own thoughts.

One of the greatest discoveries that has ever been made in the field of mind study is that *there are only two natural fears:* (1) the fear of falling, (2) the fear of a loud sound. All the other fears that have come into your life have come into your life somewhere in your past life. In other words, *all other than the above two fears are man made.*

For years doctors and psychologists have tried to find out what you have just read. How did they find out? About twenty-five years ago the doctors and psychologists examined about five hundred babies. They tried to scare these babies in every conceivable fashion. They tried putting mice in their cribs, snakes, fire—nothing scared them—but when they broke an empty bag filled with air, the loud sound made each baby cry. When they held the baby in such a way that the child thought it was going to fall, then the baby began to scream.

What a truly great discovery? Now I have something to go on. I know now that all other than these two fears are man made. Again, I come to the conclusion that we "do our own choosing." Now I know that man has been choosing his thoughts badly and has used them to make himself sad instead of happy. Now we can look back over our lives and see how foolish we have been. We can look back over our lives and find out what we did that may have made us sad. We can look back over our lives and trace those experiences that have given us a lot of trouble and have kept us in bondage. Instead of letting these things bother us unconsciously (as they frequently may), we are able to understand them now and throw them out of our harmful thinking.

For example: A woman living on a farm would have apples stored in the basement during the summer for winter use. When winter came, she would send her ten-year-old son down into the basement for apples. She told him to bring up the speckled apples first, because they had to use those first. So the young lad went downstairs, went from bushel basket to bushel basket and picked out the speckled apples, brought them upstairs, and mother was happy because her son did what she had told him. The following Saturday, she sent him downstairs and told him again to be sure to bring up the speckled apples. So again, he went to the basement, went from basket to basket and picked out the speckled apples and brought them up to his mother. His mother was proud; her son had done exactly as she had told him. This went on week after week, all winter long they had speckled apples. Silly? Foolish? But how many of us have not been using the speckled apples instead of the good ones?

When my mother was living, we were always using the broken and cracked dishes. We asked Mother why we did not use the good dishes, for we had two good sets in the dish pantry. Mother would say, "We have to save them." We saved them; very seldom used them; time moved on; Mother passed away. Then, we called in the "junk man" and sold him these dishes. You can imagine what we got for these dishes! Yes, someday we will use them. Why didn't we use the good ones? Why?

One of my resident school students told me that when his mother-in-law died, they found drawer after drawer full of unused towels and linens. Yet, all the time that she lived, they used all the torn towels and thin ones. Some of them were so thin that your hand would come through the towel. Another told me that before she heard the speckled apple story, they ate all of their meals in the kitchen. After hearing the story, they ate many of their meals in the dining room. One man who loved his wife bought her a beautiful fur coat. She wore it five times in five years. He asked her why she did not wear it more often, and she said she was saving it.

So many men buy a suit of clothes with two pairs of pants. What happens? He saves one pair, never uses them, finally finds a need for them, then finds that they are now too small, or that the coat has faded, or that the moths have gotten into them. The result is that the second pair of pants, instead of being really useful, has been of little or no use.

A housewife buys some nice new furniture for her home. What is the first thing that she does? She puts covers on them. Why?—To save them. Save them for what? How many suites of furniture do you buy in a lifetime? So, we go through life with second best, afraid to use what we have. Saving furniture is a small item compared to what some people do. In the days gone by, the parlor (the front room) was closed all week long. On Sunday, Grandma would open the parlor—then it could be used and that's all! Some people go even further than that. They buy themselves beautiful homes, furnish them elegantly, then they fix the basement and live in the basement. They save the rest of the house. Why? Simply because they never have trained themselves to live now. Someday they are going to live. Someday they are going to enjoy themselves. Someday they are going to live the way they always wanted.

Too many of us "put off" using what we have, put off living to "Someday." This day may never come because the habit of living this way has so completely involved us that we can't change later in life, it has become too late.

A millionaire was addressing his group of salesmen. He knew that his men were somewhat envious of him. So, he proceeded to prove to them that this envy was unnecessary. He went on to say, "Yes, fellows, I have more clothes than you have, but I can only wear one suit at a time. Certainly, I have more beds in my house than you have, but I can sleep in only one bed at a time. Of course, I can buy more food than you can, but I can only eat three meals a day. Yes, I have more cars in my garage than you have, but I can only drive one car at a time." He proved to them that basically they had everything that he had.

How true it is! Basically, we have everything that the millionaire has: we have the basic three meals a day, the same basic bed to sleep in, the same basic one suit at a time to wear, the same basic automobile to drive. Yes, basically, we have everything the "rich man" has. If only we would use what we have! Yes, we can be millionaires, if we will use what we have, and certainly *we can all be mental millionaires.*

A woman who found that she was going through life mean, sour, and difficult to live with, noticed that none of the neighbors had anything to do with her. Suddenly, it appeared that she had become the happiest woman in the entire neighborhood. The change was so noticeable that the neighbors decided to call on her and see why the sudden change of happiness came about. They asked her if she had come into money, and she said she had not. They asked her if any of her insurance policies had come due, and she said that they had not. "Well, then, what is it that makes you so happy?" She explained to them that she had noticed that none of the neighbors had anything to do with her, that the years were slipping by, that she was not a very nice person to have around, that she certainly was too mean and crabby to be happy, so she started a "Happiness Book."

Each night before she went to bed she would sit down and mark down all the things for which she could be thankful. She would start the list by being thankful for her two hands, for her two legs—most of us don't appreciate these until we see someone without them. She would mark down that she was thankful for her two eyes—most people don't appreciate their eyes until they see someone without them. She marked down that she was thankful for all the different parts of her body. Then she would mark down the furniture, the rugs, the dishes, the house, the beds, the clothes, etc., etc., etc., and by the time she was through making out the list, she said, "I went to bed so happy, I slept like a baby!"

Oh . . . If everyone would keep a Happiness Book, what a world this could be!

How great our lives would be if only we would develop the habit of being "thankful." We have so much to be thankful for in our lives. We live in the greatest country in the world, and that is something to be grateful for every day. Just think about it. If we opened the doors of the United States, it is very possible that every person in the world would want to come here to live. Yet, Americans, as a whole, walk around long-faced with worried looks, and grow more and more disgusted because they are always thinking of what they haven't got.

We start out and say to ourselves, "If I only had $100. . . ." Then, we save $100. Are we happy now? No. Now, "If I only had $200. . . ." Then, we save $200. Are we happy now? No. Now, "If I only had $300 . . ." and on down each time wanting more and more, all the time failing to take the time to be thankful. As long as we are thinking of what we don't have, we are unhappy—so it is that we go through life "eating speckled apples."

We start out life driving a Ford or a Chevrolet. Then, we complain because we want a better car, "If I only had a Dodge!" So, finally, we get a Dodge. We no sooner get the Dodge, we start to complain, "If I only had a Buick!" So, we get a Buick. We no sooner get the Buick, we start to complain, "If I only had a Cadillac?" So, we get a Cadillac. Are we happy now? How could we be? We never developed the habit of being thankful. Now, if we would be thankful for the Ford or Chevrolet, then we would enjoy the Ford or Chevrolet. If we are thankful for the Dodge, we will be happy while we are driving the Dodge. When we get the Buick, we will be happy while driving the Buick. Likewise, when we get the Cadillac, we will surely enjoy driving the Cadillac because "we have developed the habit of being thankful." So, in order to avoid the "speckled apples" of life, we must train ourselves to be thankful. If we will be thankful, we can't help being happy.

Now, the reason we must be thankful is that we will never be satisfied. The first principle of nature is "growth." Therefore, we must be growing. Nature will not let us stand still because as soon as we stand still, we start going backward. Because of this pushing forward (growing) of nature within us, we find ourselves restless and always anxious to be on the move. If we don't understand this, we are constantly discontented, and constantly unhappy. *The secret of happiness is always content (thankful) but never satisfied.*

Because we will never be satisfied, we must train ourselves to be thankful—which brings us to a very powerful principle:

>Being thankful . . . is the law of increase.
>Complaining . . . is the law of decrease.

So few people understand this great principle stated above. The average person, let us say, has only two dresses or two suits. What do they say, "Darn it . . . all I have is two dresses (or two suits)." They think that when they have twenty-two dresses or twenty-two suits they are going to be happy. No they won't! Then they'll want more—and that is good. But, we must:

First . . . be thankful for what we have,

then . . . ask and work for more.

You have two dresses, or two suits, then say to yourself, "I am thankful for these two dresses (or two suits), but I would like more." Then, you will be happy with what you have while you are searching and seeking for more. *This is the law*: Do this with all your possessions. You will find yourself so happy that people will wonder what happened to you. The above is so little understood by the average person that those of us who do understand it make people wonder how nicely we get along, although we do not have nearly as much of the material things of life as some people do.

In the meantime, we must be careful that we do not become satisfied for as soon as we do, we start to go backward. We think we are standing still. Then we start getting tired. Once we start getting tired of living, we start getting old, we start to lose our youth (explained fully in Lesson 12). That is why nature keeps pushing us, so that we don't become satisfied and old. We must keep growing; and in so doing, we must set goals for ourselves.

Years ago, we were taught to set a goal for our lives. But, if we failed to reach that goal, we became discouraged and the last years of life turned out miserably for many people. Today, we say set a goal or several goals for the immediate future. For example: suppose that you say you are going to read twenty books during the coming year, then at the end of the year you have read nineteen, now one more and you will have accomplished your goal. Every time you accomplish one of the smaller goals, it gives you confidence. So, have smaller goals that may take six months or a year. Keep getting new goals, it will keep you young and will make life very interesting for you. Then, have a big goal, a great big goal that may take your whole life. Maybe you may never even reach this goal, but it will keep you from becoming satisfied. So again, I remind you . . .

    The secret of happiness is
        Always content (thankful)
        But never satisfied.

Napoleon Hill, author of *Think and Grow Rich*, says, "A person must learn to laugh. If you can laugh, life cannot beat you. If you cannot laugh, then life becomes very difficult at times." It is very important to develop a sense of humor. We must be able to see the sunny side of life—and the funny side of life. We must learn to laugh at ourselves and not take ourselves so seriously. Unfortunately, we lose our sense of humor as we grow older. When we are children, we are constantly being reminded that life is no "cinch," that life is "no joke." We are reminded of it so often that before long, we begin to expect it—and it comes! We settle down and become so serious. We reach a point that we forget all about laughter.

Several years ago I went through one of the great European art galleries. Our guide showed and pointed out to us that it took two hundred years before the artists began to put a smile on the face of the Madonna. For centuries, ministers did not dare say anything funny in the churches. Today, even the ministry realizes that a good sermon can still have a little humor in it. We are slowly learning that we have made life such a serious business that we must change our ways a little and begin to laugh a little each day. Even the Good Book says, "A merry heart doeth good . . . like medicine." When will we learn what the Great Psychologist said, "Unless we become as little children, we shall not enter the Kingdom of Heaven?" Let us learn to laugh, to have a sense of humor, to see the funny side of life. It will make life happier, to be sure, and much less difficult.

A great religious leader had this to say about "joy":

For centuries, men have toiled to discover an elixir of life—something that will free man from all disease and distress and prolong the span of life. It is little wonder that these crusaders of humanity have failed to find this potion in the remote regions of the earth, for the elixir of life lies in man himself . . . *it is his power for joy.*

Be joyous and your difficulties will diminish in size; be joyous and you ward off illness; be joyous and your fears will lose their hold and your worries will lose their rancor; be joyous and sorrow will not crush you and suffering will not approach you.

Be joyous and the years will roll smoothly and peacefully by, leaving no painful marring gushes; be joyous and *you remain young all the days of your life.*

Be joyous and your days will be many on this earth. By keeping our hearts cheerful and joyous, we maintain a fountain of helpfulness both for ourselves and for others.

The greatest act of charity is not when one gives merely of his riches, but when one gives of himself to his fellowman. To impart courage and optimism, to inspire others with hope and with cheer, to create an atmosphere of serenity and joy, these are among the highest duties of man to man.

For joy is a tonic and a panacea, almost, for all ills of body and mind. When man is joyous, his health is sustained and preserved. Just as injurious parasites will not venture in an abode flooded with sunshine, so no corroding ailments will invade the body of one whose mind is *filled with joy*. When the mind is joyous, the entire being is lifted into a higher state; both mind and body are strengthened and invigorated.

The best way to insure health is *never to permit divine joy to become overshadowed*. As joy is a preventive, so it is also a cure. When the mind is charged with joy, the body is in possession of an antidote against any weakness that may have invaded it. Joy is the voice of God vibrating through the world. The Divine Mind is a great reservoir of joy. The Divine Mind within you is supplying you with an abundance of joy. Therefore, we need not appeal to Him with sighs, in order to bring forth, as it were His sympathy.

Come before Him with joy.

When you offer your prayer, express it in joy and in faith.

Read the last section over and over again. May I remind you that Florence Scovill Shinn, in her book *Your Word Is Your Wand*, states:

Nothing is too good to be true.
Nothing is too good to last.
Nothing is too wonderful to happen.

Repeat these over and over again. Read this lesson over and over again. Develop the habit of joy and happiness. You can. It's worth it.

In summary, here are the main points of this lesson:
1. You can only think of one thing at a time—make it a happy thought
2. You choose your thoughts . . . choose to think happy thoughts
3. There are only two natural fears . . . all others are man made
4. Why not eat good apples . . . instead of speckled apples?
5. We can all be *mental millionaires*
6. Start a *Happiness Book*
7. Always content (thankful), but never satisfied
8. Be thankful for what you have, then ask and work for more
9. The power of joy . . . joy is the voice of God

Lesson 10

Power of Mind Over Body

Dear Reader:
This lesson, psychologically, delivers a very profound message. Our mind power is very strong. What we believe, backed by faith, is manifested in our lives. This is both good and bad. When our belief system is one of right thinking backed by faith, positive results materialize in our lives. Conversely, when our belief system is one of wrong thinking backed by faith, negative results materialize in our lives. Our thoughts determine what course our lives follow. What our mind tells our body creates our physical outcomes and events. Thoughts work in tandem with manifestations.

Kohe gives several very simple, yet very convincing examples as to how this works. It may be termed self-hypnosis, autosuggestion, or even mind over matter, but nevertheless the results are the same. Our mind is the control center for our body. If we think we can, or we think we can't, we are correct every time. Shakespeare states it in another way when he says: "Our doubts are traitors, / And make us lose the good we oft might win / By fearing to attempt." When we learn to control our minds—our mental attitudes—we are well on the way to becoming Mental Millionaires.

Two important things to remember are that our minds cannot entertain two opposite thoughts simultaneously, and what we think about consistently over time we become. By knowing these two simple facts, it is easy to literally change our world by first changing our thoughts. Holding good thoughts conditions our mind for positive results in the future, and deciding whether we want the glass to be half full or half empty determines what attitude we assume as we travel this journey through life.

Kohe shows you one of many possible doors. Deciding to walk through the door is your choice. The door you select will determine your next opportunity. That, dear reader, will make all the difference in the world to you as you travel the distance. Stay the course.

—Judith Williamson

Something good can happen . . .
just as easily as something bad.
–YOUR GREATEST POWER

All of our lessons so far have been coming to you for the purpose of building you up generally and taking you along the road to becoming a "mental millionaire." Maybe you have begun to feel like a mental millionaire already. Many people find that it doesn't take long. Some people find that one idea may give them what they need to build them up. One lesson may do that for you. The "Power of the Imagination" (Lesson 7) is such a lesson. The lesson on "How to Control Your

Nerves" (Lesson 6) might do it for you. It may be the very first lesson on the "Power of Mental Pictures" (Lesson 1).

If it is Lesson 1, I would not be a bit surprised because it is the very best place to start to become a mental millionaire. However, you noticed that by making good mental pictures, your whole life begins to take on a new outlook. You noticed too, no doubt, that you begin to feel a certain power over your own life. You also began to realize that the mind is the important governing factor over your life. You can readily notice that the mind governs the body. The mind is the dominating factor of your life; and because it is, you might begin to wonder just how much power the mind does have over the body. So, from now on, that is what I am going to tell you about. This will prove to be very interesting and beneficial to you; but don't make the mistake that a lot of people make. You don't have to wait until the last lesson to become a mental millionaire. If you feel like one already, I am very happy about it. From now on, then, you will be building a reserve and that is what a lot of us need.

Throughout the past fifty years man has been trying to prove the power of mind over body. Some success has been achieved but not what it might be. So, we might spend ever so much time attempting to help you realize the power of mind over body. However, I have found that the easy way is to tell you stories which will help you once and for all to understand the power of mind over body.

A little girl found that her head was shaking constantly. The mother took the little girl to various doctors and they all told her the same thing—"There is nothing wrong with you." The little girl responded, "Now don't tell me . . . there is a string pulling my head back and forth and that string has to be cut out with an operation." All the doctors laughed and said that what the little girl needed was a good licking. However, the mother continued to try different doctors. Finally, one doctor who understood the little girl, and the power of mind over body, upon examination told the little girl that what she needed was an operation. Fine! She was brought into the hospital, placed upon the operating table, and given an anesthetic. As soon as the little girl fell asleep, the doctor cut away some of her hair, bandaged up her head, and in the meantime, took a piece of catgut and treated it in alcohol. Then, he sat by her bedside. As soon as she awoke, he said to her, "Here you are little girl, here is the string that was keeping your head moving back and forth." That did it! No longer was the little girl troubled with a shaking head. The idea had been cut out of her head, and she was all right again.

A salesman was traveling through a small town. He stopped off and went to a small hotel. That night he awoke and could not catch his breath. "Where's a window?" he cried. Coming to the first pane of glass (it was dark in his room), he broke the glass with his fist. The minute he heard the glass break, he felt relief. He began to breathe easier. He went back to bed and slept the whole night through. The next morning when he awoke, he looked around the room in order to locate the glass that he had broken the night before in order to let in air. Noticing the window, he saw that the glass was still intact. Puzzled, he glanced around the room still looking for a broken window pane. However, when his eyes fell upon the tall grandfather clock in the corner, he was surprised to see that he had broken the glass on the clock's face. Air? Certainly. The thought of air gave him the relief he needed.

Only recently there was a convention being held in one of the big hotels. The banquet of the convention was being held in the ballroom of the hotel. Almost everybody began to complain about how warm it was in the room. The manager of the hotel was present at the banquet. He was told to turn on the air-conditioning. He said he would take care of it right away. It wasn't long before everybody began to feel better. But, there was no air-conditioning in this hotel! The fact that the manager said that he would see to it that it would be turned on, turned the trick!

A married couple bought an electric heating blanket. When they went to bed at twelve o'clock, they turned it on. Two o'clock it was too hot, so they turned it off. Four o'clock in the morning, it was too cold, so they turned it on again.

Finally, at seven o'clock in the morning, when they were ready to go to work, they looked around and found that they had never inserted the plug of the blanket into the electric socket. Mind over body?

I would like to once again relate to you the story I told you in Lesson 1 (Power of Mental Pictures) of a man who was never sick. This man would go around kidding those who were sick. Tired of this, five coworkers decided to act out a scene with him. One day, when Joe walked in just as chipper as ever, one of them walked up to him and said, "Joe, is there something wrong? Don't you feel well, you look sick?"

Joe replied, "Who do you think you are kidding? I have never felt better in my life."

Shortly afterward, the second man in the plot came up to Joe and said, "For Heaven's sake Joe, what is wrong with you? You scare me. Don't you feel well?"

Joe replied, "I'm all right, but that is what Jack (the first man) said to me."

The third man came over later and said, "Joe, you look sick, sit down before you fall down, I better call a doctor."

Joe responded, "I don't know what is wrong with me. When I left home, I was feeling fine, but all you fellows keep telling me the same thing."

The fourth man used the same scare technique... then the fifth. By the time the fifth man was through with Joe, Joe went home a sick man.

In this story, it is easy to realize that the mind does control the body. Actually, there was nothing wrong with Joe; but when these five men continued to convince him that he was sick, Joe believed it and he went home sick. So, we must be careful. When we are well, we should be ever so thankful. What right do we have to go around kidding others and, not realizing it, actually hurting other people? Much damage is being done everyday by people who should know better. They never realize the power words have over a person's body. This is particularly true in the professions.

Two men went to see the doctor for an examination. "A" was in a run-down condition and "B" had tuberculosis. It was on a Friday and the doctor was anxious to get away for the weekend. He saw the two men in his office and said, "Gentlemen, I will examine you but I will have to mail you my diagnosis." They agreed, neither one knew what his difficulty was. The doctor examined them, called in his nurse, dictated the diagnosis of each man, and told her to mail them. She did. When the doctor came back from his weekend vacation, he found a "hurry-up" call from the man who was in a run-down condition ("A"). He rushed over to his home, and there he found "A" in bed, looking very pale, and as nervous as could be.

"What happened to you?" shouted the doctor. The man very meekly pointed to a letter on the dresser. The doctor picked it up and was astounded; he started to laugh. The letter told this man that he had tuberculosis; but the letter was not intended for him, it was the other man's letter! Evidently, what had happened was that the nurse had mixed up the letters when she put them into the envelopes for mailing. The man was relieved, but even then he was quite scared. The doctor told him that there was nothing wrong with him but that he was run-down and that what he needed was a vacation.

The doctor's curiosity was now aroused and he drove over to the man's home who actually had the tuberculosis. He rang the bell. The lady of the house answered the door. The doctor asked for Mr. "B." The landlady told him that he had received a letter from his doctor telling him that he was in a run-down condition and that what he needed was a vacation, so he went on a vacation. Now, what finally happened to him, I do not know. One thing I do know is that the fellow who did not have tuberculosis certainly was scared. Mind over body?

In the early days when Psychology first began to take hold, people naturally laughed, just as they laughed at the horseless carriage (the Ford car), the hot-pot on a wooden boat (Fulton's steamboat), the machine with the scissors (McCormick's Harvester). Mind over body? It's silly. Whoever heard of such nonsense?

A college professor, who was teaching psychology in the early days, had quite a little trouble with his class of twenty-four young men. So, he decided that he would really teach them a lesson. He invited them all to his home. He served them roast beef. They ate heartily, and even commented on how tasty and delicious it was. After the meat had been eaten, he said, "Well, boys, how did you like the roast beef?" In a chorus, they all said "Fine." Everyone went home very pleased with the dinner. Several weeks later, he invited them again to his home, and again served roast beef, and again they remarked how delicious it was. After they had eaten the meat, he asked them how they enjoyed it, and again they exclaimed in a chorus, "Fine."

"Well," said the professor, "I am so glad because what you have just eaten is the best kind of horse meat." All twenty-four of the young men took sick. Some fainted, some vomited, some began to run around all upset and confused. It was quite a sight. Finally, after all had been revived and back at their seats at the table, the professor said, "You see, you did not believe in my lectures of the power of mind over body, but you saw it work tonight. Tonight I told you that you had horse meat, and you reacted accordingly, but actually, you had the best roast beef that money could buy." And they all exclaimed, "Professor, thank goodness for that!" Then the professor went on and said, "Do you remember the last time you were here, that is when you really did have horse meat."

No longer did the professor have any more trouble with his lectures on Psychology.

There are hundreds of stories like this proving the power of mind over body. But, I hope I have given you enough to realize that this is true, that the mind does control the body, that thank goodness you control the mind, you do the choosing. I told you that in my book *Your Greatest Power*. Now, let me do a little experimental work, as best as I can, under the circumstances. These experiments should prove very profitable as well as very interesting. *Do it now,* while you are reading these pages, take a little time, please do what I tell you:

Place your left hand out in front of you.

Now stiffen it as much as you can.

Stretch out your arm and make it stiff.

Now tell yourself, as strongly as you can, that you can't move your hand.

Now tell your arm to relax.

Now move it.

Did you notice how stiff your arm became when you directed it to be that way? Then, did you notice how relaxed it became when you ordered your arm to relax? Who did it? You did, you tightened up your arm, through your thought, and you relaxed your arm through thought.

Now take a pencil.

Hold it as tightly as you can with both hands.

Now tell yourself that you can't lift it. You can't lift it.

Did you notice how heavy it became. Now tell yourself that you can lift it. Who did it? You did, you made the pencil heavy, through your thought, and then you made it light again through your thought.

Now clasp your hands.

Hold them out in front of you and clasp them so tightly that they begin to quiver.

Now tell yourself: "You can't pull them apart. You can't pull them apart. You can't pull them apart."

Now try to pull them apart, thinking that you can't. See what happens.

If you could not pull them apart, then it showed that you were thinking that you could not pull them apart. If you did pull them apart, then it showed that you were thinking that *you could* pull them apart. But, now you noticed that you could not think of both at the same time. You could not hold the thought that you could and couldn't at the same time.

This brings me to two of the "greatest principles" in the study of the human mind. Learn them, know them as well as you know your own name. Your whole life is centered upon these two principles. The whole key to psychology is in these two principles. The power of mind over body is easily understood as a result.

1. You cannot keep two ideas of opposite nature in your mind at the same time, the stronger one always wins.
2. Any idea completely filling the mind becomes true within reason, of course.

In other words, I come back to my original idea in the book *Your Greatest Power* that you must *choose* . . . between:

I can	or	I can't
I will succeed	or	I will fail
I will be well-to-do	or	I will always be poor
I am getting better	or	I am getting worse

You cannot think both. It is either one or the other. If you choose negative, you can expect negative results. If you choose positive, you will have positive results. Just as the mathematician said hundreds of years ago, one plus one is two, two plus two is four, so the psychologist says today—positive thoughts plus positive thoughts make a positive person, success thoughts plus success thoughts will make for success.

The guess work has been taken out of life, now. It is up to you to choose which it will be. The stronger thought is bound to win. Look around you and you will see hundreds of examples of just what we are talking about here.

You cannot hope for success while you are constantly thinking failure. You cannot hope for better financial life if you are constantly thinking poverty. You cannot hope for "I can" if you are always thinking "I can't." The stronger thought will always win. Ask yourself, pry into your own mind, into your thinking, "which is your stronger thought?" *Then you can foresee the results.*

Did you notice how easily you could change from "I can't" move my hand to "I can?" Contrary to general belief, mind control is not difficult. It is only that we have been told that it is. We have been told that "he who conquers himself, is greater than he who conquers a city" with the result that most people believe that mind control is difficult. Actually, it is very easy. It is so easy that it has been completely overlooked all these years. *Remember it is easy, very easy.*

We can take the easiest thing and make it difficult. You saw that when you attempted to pick up the pencil. When you told yourself that it was heavy, you could not pick up that little pencil, because you thought it was heavy. But, when you changed your mind and thought you could pick up the pencil, then you did without any trouble whatsoever. So, we must realize that we can control ourselves, that we can choose our own thoughts, that we can make a thing easy or difficult, according to the way we think.

Learn this lesson well. You will be a mental millionaire, the minute you do, and then you will go to becoming an even "greater" mental millionaire as you go along in these lessons.

Just as you make the pencil heavy, so we make life hard—by thinking that life is hard. Just as you make the pencil light, so we make life an enjoyable experience—by thinking this is the way life should be. So, we must constantly watch our thoughts—always, especially because most people do not understand what you understand, and they are too quick to convince you otherwise. If you let them, you will lose the privilege of being a mental millionaire. You would not let anyone take your money away from you—why let them take away your right to be a mental millionaire?

> *You either ride life or it rides you.*
> *Your mental attitude determines*
> *who is rider and who is "horse."*
>
> —Napoleon Hill

Lesson 11

Secret of Good Health

Dear Reader:
Maintenance of sound health is a topic that concerns everybody at every age. Regardless of whether you are 6 months or 60 years old, you will be unable to fully enjoy the other riches of life unless you have your health. Health is holistic. Mental health, physical health, and spiritual health are all interconnected much like the intricate strands in a spider's web. If one strand is cut in the spider's design, the remainder of the web lacks congruity, vitality, and usefulness. In simple language, it appears lopsided. A seamless web is to what we aspire when imaging our health in our mind's eye. Each element must correspond and support the other in making our web of life function at an optimum level. Peak life performances are said to occur when we are running on all cylinders. That means that we need to stay tuned up in order to maximize our potential.

Kohe believes that a good portion of ill health originates first in the mind. He substantiates this belief by credible research that is similar in its findings. Only in very recent times have the majority of physicians concurred that there is a mind/body connection that co-creates wellness or illness in an individual. The acceptance of this belief by the general population is now changing the face of modern medicine. People like Kohe understood it well in advance of modern findings.

It is not surprising that Kohe asks us to follow the procedures previously outlined for making auto-suggestions. Also, he reminds us to cultivate joy and not fear, to watch our initial response to whatever happens so that we can quickly locate the seed of an equal or equivalent benefit rather than focusing on a negative outcome, and to affirm that Infinite Intelligence is good and is working with us and not against us. These are learned strategies for maintenance of sound health and work just as effectively as a prescription. That, dear reader, is why you should become aware of the healing physician within you. Take the time to introduce yourself to this doctor who is always on call—your higher self.

—JUDITH WILLIAMSON

This ability to recognize this greatest power . . .
the power to choose . . . makes it possible for a person
to get the most out of life, while the other person
not recognizing this power makes life a burden.
–YOUR GREATEST POWER

There are three things that almost every person wants out of life—health, wealth, and happiness. When a person has these three things, he is willing to admit that he can have a Heaven on earth without waiting. I have already taken up the financial picture. In the "Secret of Happiness" (Lesson 9), I found that the power of joy is one of the best agencies for the elimination of sickness. Sickness cannot touch an individual whose body and mind are filled with joy.

We have learned in the book *Your Greatest Power* that when a person applies the thought of "God loves you," he can account for many immediate cures. He will find that when he stops fighting life—when he stops fighting God—he will feel better. He will have more energy than he could ever dream possible.

Children never seem to get tired of playing. Adults do not get tired playing—when they are winning! It is when they are losing, that they get tired. When a person is winning in life, he does not get so tired, and life looks pretty good. Then, he feels good, he does not worry about disease and he marches right along in a glorious manner.

For many centuries man has tried to find the cause for disease. In the last lesson of the "Power of Mind over Body," I found that the mind does control the body, that when a person takes an idea into his head about being sick, he doesn't feel well. So, at last, I have found that the mind does play a very important part in good health. The Mayo brothers found that out a long time ago in their clinic. The result was that they were able to help people who could get no help anywhere else.

The Mayo brothers, at their clinic in Rochester, Minnesota, at one time came out with the statement that disease was 90% mental. Some other experts in this field said that it was "all mental." However, I do know now that the very latest development in the field of medicine is the "psycho-somatic" method. Doctors have finally, after all these years, admitted that the mind does play an important part in health. They realize, now, that certain people will not respond to medicine alone. However, there are so many people who go to a doctor, and if the doctor does not give them any medicine, they think the doctor doesn't know his business.

Now we have Psychiatry—the branch of medicine dealing entirely with the mental life of a person. The psychiatrist goes back into the person's life and tries to find out what causes the difficulty. Once he is able to trace the trouble, the patient finds that he is feeling better. This is because the harmful thought has now been brought to the surface and is properly explained and understood. Consequently, the patient no longer has that unconscious reason for not feeling well.

If you are not a doctor, we call this same method "psychoanalysis." A person cannot practice psychiatry unless this person becomes a medical doctor first. However, a person does not need a degree in medicine to use psychoanalysis. This, an individual can learn to do for himself. For example: sometime ago a young man came to me who was always having headaches. Being in the army, there they tried to correct the headaches—no results. They had him treated by the splendid army psychiatrists for several months—no results. He came to me. I began to ask questions. I began to delve into his past life. Finally, I was able to discover the cause of his difficulty: he was going with a very lovely young lady whom he loved. He was engaged to her but he could not marry her because he was not able to support her. Why?—because he still had to support his own mother and father!

Upon further inquiry, I discovered that this young man was a printer. He even had his own printing shop! I said to him, "Don't you think you ought to be able to make a living in the printing business for both your parents and a wife?" He responded, "I don't see why not." The result—the headaches disappeared. Magic? No. One could see that the young man wanted to get married. Convinced that he was not able, he "unconsciously" had been disturbed. This disturbance was causing the headaches. Once I found a solution, the cure resulted.

You can work out some of these results in your own life. Go back into your past life and see if you can find what caused the trouble. Sometimes it takes weeks and months, just as with a psychiatrist. But, as you develop the knack of working out these difficulties, it will give you a world of satisfaction plus the beginning of "self-mastery."

Basically, what is disease?

dis   ease
dis means not . . . . . therefore, disease means
NOT   at   EASE

When you are not at ease about something, you do not feel well. Correct the thing that is causing the "not at ease" and presto, one feels better! Be honest with yourself, look into your heart and into your mind: what is causing you to be "not at ease?" Once you find it, tell it to God. He'll listen to you, forgive you; remember, to sin is human, to forgive is Divine. Go into your own room at home where you cannot be overheard and out loud tell God what you did for which you are sorry. Get it out of your system. If necessary, go for a ride in your car and talk out loud about your problems. Tell God to listen to you. He loves you and will help you—if only you ask him to help you! Then, don't do anything to make yourself "not at ease" and your health problem will be cut to a minimum.

Now, let us study "self-mastery"—through which good health is our reward.

Emil Coué, a Frenchman who became a druggist, noticed that people came to him for medicine, yet there was nothing wrong with them. He also noticed that certain medicine worked wonders with some people while it was worthless to others. Thus, he began to experiment. At first, he resorted to hypnotism, then finding it too difficult—for many people would not respond—he experimented further. He finally developed the system that is being used all over the world. Those who do not use it directly use it indirectly. His little book *Self-Mastery through Conscious Auto-Suggestion* tells of the system used and of the many remarkable and miraculous cures.

Each person has two minds: a conscious mind and a subconscious mind. The conscious mind is *you*, the outer self; the subconscious mind is the *inner self* which digests your food, keeps your heart beating, watches over you while you sleep, does your breathing for you, grows hair, grows nails, is the truly wonderful part of our make-up.

The subconscious mind was discovered in 1902 by Professor James of Harvard. But, it was Coué who first applied it to good health. Here is a chart to always remember:

Conscious mind . . . ***Outer self*—YOU**
  –is the boss
  –gives the orders
  –does the choosing

Subconscious mind . . . ***Inner self***
  –this mind works perfectly
  –it is creative

—it is always on duty, it never sleeps
—it takes care of all the inner functions of the body
—it is the servant of the conscious mind
—it believes what it is told, within reason, of course

Notice that the subconscious mind works perfectly. Your heart beats perfectly. Your lungs, liver, and the inner functions of the body work perfectly, unless through various wrong methods you have interfered with this perfect order. If one has used wrong methods to destroy the perfect working order of the subconscious mind, I shall show how to correct it so that one, too, can enjoy perfect health. Perfect health should be the rule and not the exception. The subconscious mind is always on duty. You knows that. You may go to sleep at night, but your body lives on. What takes care of it while you are sleeping is, of course, the subconscious mind. Not only do you realize that you are being taken care of by the subconscious mind while you are sleeping, but perhaps you have had the experience while driving a car of either avoiding hitting someone or another car because something inside of you pulled the wheel to one side.

I have had remarkable results with "conscious autosuggestion" in the matter of reducing. So many people wear themselves out on different diets, exercise, fasting and other methods of reducing. Yet, here is such a simple method which you may not believe, but *it works*. Take some food that ordinarily adds weight to your body. For example, when you eat bread, close your eyes, address your subconscious mind like this "Look subconscious mind, this bread is going to be tasty and delicious and *it is going to make me thinner.*" It will. Say it with every bite. I was concerned when one of my resident school students lost 17 pounds in one week. "How did you do it?" I asked. His answer was that he said the above sentence with every bite of food he ate that week. I thought the reduction was too much and advised he should do it just with the bread he ate. The result was that he continued to lose four to five pounds a week.

A woman who was very heavy had not eaten candy in fourteen years. She made the above suggestion to her subconscious mind, ate two pounds of candy the week after learning "conscious auto-suggestion," and lost one pound. She was thrilled!

Another very heavy woman found that she could eat strawberry shortcake without adding weight, simply by using "conscious auto-suggestion." By the same token, if you would like to add weight, you can do so, simply by using "conscious auto-suggestion." Thus, you take certain foods like bread or potatoes and you close your eyes and say to your subconscious mind: "This bread is going to be tasty and delicious and *will add weight.*" It will. Adding weight does not show up as fast as reducing, as a rule, but you will see results in thirty days. One resident school student did gain four pounds during the week after learning about "conscious auto-suggestion."

Test this method, you will find it works. Once you notice that it works, then you can let your weight go up or down or keep it on an even keel, to suit your own needs. If you stop to think about this method, you know it is true. All around you, what do you hear people saying—"everything I eat makes me fat" or "all I have to do is look at food and I put on weight," "candy makes me fat," "potatoes always make me heavier," "nothing makes me fat," "no matter how much I eat, I can't add a pound,"—isn't it true? There it is!

In the next lesson you will learn the "secret of youth." It lies in the fact that doctors have found that the body renews itself every seven years. Therefore, regardless of what your age, the oldest muscle in your body is only seven years old. Now, if you will make the right auto-suggestion, as you go along—"Day by day in every way I am getting better and better"—this powerful auto-suggestion, plus the fact that the body renews itself every seven years, gives you the secret of youth. It is the "bad" suggestion that gives the body that "old" skin and that "old" muscle, so we must be careful to make good auto-suggestions at all times.

Another very important time when one would make good auto-suggestions is at the time of a sudden happening:

    When something happens . . . always think of the best and not the worst

    Watch the first ten seconds . . . immediately after the difficulty so that you make a good suggestion instead of a bad one

As an example: one of my resident school students poured hot coffee over herself. As soon as she did, she started a flow of *good* suggestions. She started to tell her subconscious mind that "this coffee is making her skin stronger than ever before, it is making the skin tougher than ever before, it is making her feel fine, that the coffee is bringing new blood in the skin, that she is feeling good and that everything is working out for the good." She kept that up for several minutes—unbelievable results: no burns, no scalding, no ill effects. Hard to believe, I know, but she made good auto-suggestions. The subconscious mind believes what it is told—the result is what one might call a miracle. What is a miracle? *A miracle is an experience or happening which the average person does not understand.* Once you understand it, it is no miracle. I have had ever so many reports of people who ordinarily would have burned themselves, without ill effects. It is remarkable what "conscious auto-suggestion" will do.

Watch the first 10 seconds.......... after "it" happens

If one makes good suggestions
    during the first 10 seconds...... no ill effects

If one makes bad suggestions
    during the first 10 seconds...... bad results

Never forget this.
Several years ago, a bus loaded with people turned over. Everybody in the bus was hurt, but one man. He was asked why he wasn't hurt, and he replied, "I just sat still." How important it is *to keep calm in an emergency!* The circus clown, as one so well knows, falls and falls without hurting himself. Most people, especially adults, hurt themselves when they fall. Why doesn't the clown hurt himself?—he makes himself like an "old sock"; completely relaxed, he falls without injury. Let us keep that in mind.

There are other times when one must be careful to make positive auto-suggestions. In fact, it would be a wonderful idea—*if we always made positive suggestions*. This will take time, but keep working at it. Sometimes the subconscious mind is wide open. This means we must be careful what we "let fall" into the subconscious mind at that time. When a child or a person cries, the subconscious mind is wide open—make positive suggestions at that time, *never* negative.

So few people understand how the mind works, with the result being that these negative suggestions have caused untold harm and no one seems to know why. Be very careful what you say around a person who is sick. Although it seems that they do not hear what you say, the subconscious mind is wide open and picks up everything that is said, so be sure to say good things at that time!

Be most careful what you say to a person who is under the influence of liquor. So many young married couples ruin their married lives through lack of understanding this thought. John, who has been married only a few months, goes out with the boys and comes home drunk. Mary, his wife, gets all excited and starts to holler, making one negative statement after the other, such as: "Look at you, John, you're drunk"; "I suppose you will be drinking right along now"; "I suppose that every time you go out with the boys you will come home drunk"; "Just look at you, you make me sick." Then she wonders what happened to her wonderful Johnny! Bad suggestions!

What Mary should have done was something like this: "Listen John, from now on you are not going to touch that stuff"; "When the boys ask you to take a drink, you are going to decline"; "Something inside of you won't let you drink that stuff, it will be tasteless to you. Remember that, John." No bad effects—John will go for the longest time without being bothered by liquor.

One of my resident school students said, "Now I know what happened to my husband. He came home drunk one night, I was so disgusted, I started to holler, and I yelled out, "Next time you go out and get drunk, I hope it makes you sick." It made him so sick that he never drank anymore after that. Interesting?

Another time that we should be careful about negative suggestions is that period immediately following the sex act in marriage. So many times, when the act is not successful, the couple begins to argue. This is no time to argue. Negative statements made at this time are so harmful that they can ruin the happiest marriage. At this time, the subconscious mind is wide open. Be careful . . . don't argue. Instead, lay back and think of the things you want in life—the new car, the beautiful new home, or that vacation you have always wanted.

Make positive suggestions. Good health comes mainly from good auto-suggestions. Make them as often as possible. Herein is the secret of good health. Stay away from negative suggestions for they do not pay any dividends. For good health:

- Fill the mind and body with joy
- God loves you
- Watch out for dis (not at) ease
- Conscious auto-suggestion
- Control your weight through conscious auto-suggestion
- Watch the first 10 seconds
- Make positive suggestions especially when the subconscious mind is wide open

> *Most stumbling blocks
> are the handiwork
> of a negative mind.*
> —Napoleon Hill

Lesson 12

Secret of Youth

Dear Reader:
Why is it that some people seem to stay forever young and others are old before their time? Is it genetics, free radicals, or just a gradual wearing down that causes people to age, grow old, and die? In seeking the secret of youth it becomes apparent that the answer lies within each of us. Staying young is a matter of staying busy and being productive. When a person grows older and begins to enjoy the aging process, he is slowing down the life energy that maintains his youthful outlook and appearance. If a person allows life to wear him down, he will accelerate his aging. On the other hand, if a person stays in stride with life, life will reward him with youthfulness well into old age.

It is often said that we are only as old as we feel. Youthfulness is characterized by enthusiasm, energy, anticipation, and purpose. Young-minded individuals are driven to succeed and continually cultivate opportunities. Spirit is high, emotions soar, and rest is never complete. The capacity to duplicate these emotional feelings exists in each of us. However, as we age in years, oftentimes the inability to appreciate change for the growth process that it is, causes us to deteriorate. "When you're green you grow, when you're ripe you rot," is not just a saying about apples. Change is good for each of us because it moves us out of our comfort zone. It raises our level of awareness. It causes us to expand our horizons. And, it transforms us from the proverbial caterpillar to the butterfly.

Kohe states that if you keep interested in life, life will not tire you out. Learn the techniques delivered in this lesson and create for yourself your own Fountain of Youth. Then, dear reader, life cannot subdue you because you have discovered its secret.

—Judith Williamson

> If each one of us would make his own family life
> a pleasant and enjoyable experience, the whole world
> could be changed in a very short time.
> –YOUR GREATEST POWER

Ever since man has walked the face of the earth, he has been searching for the "secret of youth." All during these many centuries, man has felt that there was something outside himself that would give him eternal youth. Every now and then, someone appears on the scene with some potion, or some kind of water, with the promise that it will keep people young. The answer does not lie outside of ourselves, but inside. Some years ago, one of my resident school students did facial rejuvenation work. She would take a sixty-year-old woman, full of wrinkles, sagging skin, sunken eyes, looking every bit of sixty, and give her a facial rejuvenation job so she would look like thirty. I saw these women, I saw pictures of before and after, it was astounding! Had this student found the "secret of youth?"

This student revealed that before she would start one of these facial jobs, she would insist that they read many books on self-improvement, on positive thinking, on being more lovely in their thoughts than they had ever been before. Because, she went on to say, if these women did not change their thinking, the facial job alone would not be satisfactory. So, I begin to see that the "right mental attitude" has a lot to do with keeping our "youth."

In Lesson 7 (Power of the Imagination), you read about the man who was in jail for twenty years and came out looking not a day older than the day he went in. Did he find the "secret of youth?" Just about! If we would keep ourselves out of "mental dungeons," we certainly would go a long way in keeping our youth. Then, is it entirely mental? Not entirely, but a great part is. Mother Nature has come to our rescue in this problem as she has in so many others.

In working with thousands of people of all ages over a period of twenty-five years, I have come to the conclusion that *people don't really get old, they get tired.*

- People get tired of constantly trying to make a living.
- They get tired of constantly fighting colds and sickness.
- They get tired of being chased around and made to feel useless.
- They get tired of seeing so much misery in life.
- They get tired of reading all the bad news in the paper.
- They get tired of fighting for success, and not realizing it.
- They get tired of always worrying about their children.

- They get tired of husband and wife arguments.
- They get tired of shoveling snow and keeping the furnace going.
- They get tired of going to weddings and funerals.
- They get tired of fighting God.
- They get so tired that they are glad when old age comes along. Having lived the best they knew how, hoping that things in the next world will be different, that God will forgive them and allow them into Heaven, and that all their troubles will be over, they are ready and grateful to pass out of this life into the next.

Isn't it a pity that the above represents life to so many?

These people who look older than their true ages do not understand the Secret of Youth. However, when these very same people realize that life is not what I pointed out above, they begin to look younger. Enrico Caruso's question, "What is life... but a battle and a struggle and finishes with death?" is not a positive outlook. A person begins to grow younger with each passing day when he fully realizes that all stages of life can be rich and full, beautiful and interesting.

This "New Psychology" that you are now studying in these lessons is so new to many people. Most people live as I pointed out above. Now, let us see what life can really be like. Let us look at life as it can be:

- Nothing is too good to be true
- Nothing is too wonderful to happen
- Nothing is too good to last
- God loves you

- Good health through conscious auto-suggestion
- Good fortune through good choosing
- The successful person is the happy person
- Always content ... but never satisfied
- Happy marriage through understanding (Lesson 19)
- Subconscious mind giving you all the answers to your problems
- Knowing how to solve your problems through intuition
- Making a Heaven here on earth
- Disagree without being disagreeable
- Bringing up our children successfully (Lesson 13)
- Being ever thankful

When you live like the above, you want to live, you have so much life and spirit that you just want to keep on going, not for yourself alone but you begin to see how much good you can bring to those about you. As you become interested in other people, you forget yourself, your age, and everything else. The only thing that matters is helping the other fellow to live a better and more successful and happy life.

I have seen resident school students—70, 75, 80 and even 85 years of age—come in looking their ages. After they get some of the above ideas working in their minds, they begin to look younger, they have a new spirit for living, they want to go on, they don't want to die now, they lose their tiredness. *Now they want to live.* They forget their ages. They start to do a lot of things that they thought they would never be able to do. Yes, I might say that this is the real secret of youth. It could be, but I will tell you exactly what it is just a little later.

We must have the "forward look"—that is what keeps us young. We must look forward to a better life on earth. We must look forward to all the wonderful inventions that are making life easier for everyone. Look what television has done for the people up in years. It has changed their entire outlook on life—each night a show, a top comedian, a beautiful story, a new song, a different picture, travel scenes from all over the world. Actually, a new world has opened up to them. At the point where they started to get tired, now they are full of energy up to midnight or as long as there are good television programs on the air.

Life must be interesting, otherwise we get tired and with tiredness comes old age. Never forget . . .

The brain works best when it is most interested.

Frequently, a person who has been doing the same thing day in and day out needs a change. Sometimes, if a person wishes to stay young, he may have to change his employment or kind of business even though he has spent twenty-five or thirty years in the same work, maybe loving it all these years. But, if he feels himself getting tired of it, he may have to change or else he may find himself getting old.

A beauty expert once said to her customers, "*If you want to stay young, peg your age.*" Jack Benny has done that. As you may well know, Jack Benny's age is 39. Actually, he doesn't look any older. Even if he does, the fact that he keeps telling himself that he is only 39 makes it easier on his mental adjustments to life. Likewise, if we wish to keep our youth, we must *keep a youthful age*. If you are sixty, and you keep telling yourself that you are sixty, then you will act like sixty, your body will respond like sixty, your friends will constantly remind you that you are sixty, and before long, you will "feel" like sixty. However, if you peg your age at thirty (you don't have to go around telling people what you are doing), you will feel differently and act differently. Keep telling yourself the age you want to be—this is very important as you will learn just a little later. You may think you are kidding yourself, but you will see in a few moments that you are not. Before I finally give you the real secret of youth, I wish to present another thought.

At the present time we are living in a twelve-month calendar. Why? Because someone—maybe it was Caesar—said that "this is the way it is going to be." So, a person who is sixty years of age according to the twelve-month calendar has "lived" sixty cycles of the twelve-month calendar. Therefore, he is said to be sixty.

Suppose someone comes along and says, "I don't like the twelve-month calendar, I want a twenty-four-month calendar." Suppose he has the power to do just that. Then, how old is the sixty-year-old man?—now he is only thirty years old! So, it is easy to see that our age depends entirely upon our thinking. "Peg your age" if you want to stay young. If you don't want to do it, if it sounds silly, do what you want. Here, however, is the "real secret" of staying young.

Doctors have found that *the body renews itself every seven years*, that the body goes through a complete change every seven years. At first, this is hard to believe. Take a look at any of your old pictures and you will see that there is a change going on constantly. The body is constantly changing, but the oldest muscle in your body is only seven years old. So, regardless of what your age is, the body itself is only seven years old. Just as a bird sheds its feathers, so our body is constantly changing. We have seen a baby grow into childhood, the child grows into boyhood or girlhood, the boy or girl into adulthood, the adult into old age.

These changes are all going on, nature takes care of it, but nature needs help. If we help nature, then nature will do even a better job. How can we help nature? We found that out in the last lesson on the secret of good health and that is "conscious auto-suggestion." By constantly making good suggestions, we can retain good health, we can keep the body functioning properly.

When the body functions properly, how can old age take over the body? Day by day in every way we are getting better and better, not older and older. If we are not careful, we will feel that because we are over forty we . . .

- must take laxatives
- must wear bifocals
- cannot do the work we used to do
- are not as young as we used to be
- continue to make these bad suggestions.

The subconscious mind then picks up these suggestions and creates what we tell it to create. And . . . we create old age through bad auto-suggestions.

The secret of youth, therefore, is
- The body renews itself every seven years
- Conscious auto-suggestion

There it is... look it over for a few minutes... set it strongly in your mind.

Nature will do her work, she keeps changing the body. Now, you must do your work, you are the one making the auto-suggestions. Make them good and you will feel good. Keep interested in life and you will want to stay young. If you find yourself getting tired in your work—even though you have been in it for many years—and if you do not want to start making bad suggestions, *make a change*. Remember, the brain acts best when it is interested. If you cannot make a change in your work, then take frequent vacations. If you can, take a vacation for a few months. When you return, you will find your work is like new again. Get a hobby, take up painting, or ceramics, or cartooning, or something to give you that new interest, to keep your brain interested and young.

Above all, please remember that God loves you. We can get so tired fighting God. We can get so worn out trying to keep Him from hurting us and punishing us. God doesn't hurt us or punish us, rather we hurt ourselves with our own "bad choosing." God loves you. Think this thought and it will keep you young. When you realize that God loves you and helps you and others, you will forget yourself and in forgetting yourself, you will forget all about your calendar age. It isn't important how many years you have lived on this earth. What is important is how much good you are doing for yourself and those around you. That is how God measures your worth, not by your age but by your good works. (Did I repeat myself? I did it purposely.)

To keep young, remember the following:
1. God loves you
2. Peg your age
3. Keep interested so . . . you don't get tired
4. Make your own calendar
5. Body renews itself every seven years . . . you make good auto-suggestions

Lesson 13

The Secret of Dealing with Children

Dear Reader:

Jackie Kennedy once said that if you "bungle raising your children nothing else much matters in life." Every parent echoes this same sentiment. Even if our parents did a fantastic job in raising us, we still hope to do an even better job with our children. Children are our living memorials, walking testimonials to our values and beliefs. If their lives are not improved versions of our own, then perhaps we must admit that we have bungled the job. Since children have never been known to come with instruction manuals, perhaps taking the guesswork out of raising them would ease parental tensions somewhat. Kohe contends that one of our primary goals in rearing children for future generations should be to make each and every one of them Mental Millionaires. This, he feels, would set history on a positive course. I agree. Isn't it a beautiful thought to think that this generation's children could follow the Twelve Riches of Life on a road to peace and not war, that these riches would bond the nations of the world together in commonality rather than *tear them apart with differences, that peace would prevail and that love would rule? Just imagine! How long can we afford to bungle our most important job?*

Kohe believes that if children are treated with respect, told that they are loved by Infinite Intelligence, dealt with fairly and honorably, and held in high esteem by the parents, their lives will mirror the behaviors that have been extended to them. What goes around comes around, and those children who are the beneficiaries of good psychology will be the leaders who raise the world to a higher standard. Kohe's suggestions are easily applied and very reasonable. Try a few and if they make a difference, try a few more. What have you got to lose? That, dear reader, could make all the difference in the world to a child who is following in your footsteps.

—JUDITH WILLIAMSON

> In controlling our power to choose,
> we can make life interesting and worthwhile to
> ourselves and everyone else around us.
> –YOUR GREATEST POWER

There has been so much written on the subject of how to handle children that I was almost going to omit this lesson. In the field of psychology, there are a few outstanding principles that I felt must go into these lessons. Most people have children, and we must be able to guide them by helping them become a generation of "mental millionaires." After all, so much that we know we have learned from our parents. But, they knew nothing about psychology, or very little, and some of them did a mighty fine job of raising children. Now, if we can take the guesswork out of raising children, just imagine what the next generation could be.

The first step in dealing with children is to "have the right mental pictures about your child." I have had unusual success with mental pictures. One woman complained to me that her child was nervous and unmanageable. I suggested that she put a picture in her mind of the child being calm, peaceful, and very agreeable. It wasn't long before the child was exactly as the mother had pictured. Another complained about her child talking back and being most irritable. I suggested that the parent change the picture in her mind and, sure enough, the child began to change.

A very unusual case came to my attention some years ago. A woman had a daughter who was of marriageable age. She was going with a young man who did not share the same religion. When she became engaged to the young man, the mother was frantic. She asked me what to do and I said, "Put a picture in your mind of your daughter going with a very fine young man with whom she was very happy." She responded, "Is that all there is to it?" I answered, "Yes." She was amazed! She thought that I would give her a whole book of instructions. She did what I told her and six months later, she informed me that her daughter had broken up with the young man. Now, the daughter was going with a very nice young man who shared her religious beliefs, and she was very happy. The mother was astounded! Note that I did not tell the mother to do anything to hurt anybody, simply to keep the right picture and it worked. Too many times, as parents too well know, the more you threaten, the worse it becomes—rather, change the picture.

Another case came to my attention of a girl who was very good friends with a young lady whom the family did not like. They threatened to tell the young lady not to come to their home anymore, that they would call her parents and tell them to keep their daughter at home—but nothing worked. They, too, became frantic as the situation grew in proportion. Being familiar with the value of mental pictures, they began to picture their daughter being friendly with nice young ladies and being happy with new friends. It wasn't long before the daughter broke up with the objectionable young lady and started to chum around with some very lovely girls for whom the family had the highest respect. Mental pictures work wonders. Use it, you'll see.

The second principle in dealing with children is "suggest and request." It is very similar to the lesson on dealing with people (Lesson 3). Children like to receive suggestions and they also love to be praised. As I pointed out, "mix your praise with criticism" and always urge them on to better things in life. Do not expect them to be perfect or you will find yourself too critical. You can hope for perfection but always keep this approach in mind when you are prone to let only criticism govern your actions.

The third principle in dealing with children is "keeping a promise." Do not make a promise to a child that you cannot keep. If you make a promise and keep it, the child will always respect you for it. If you make a promise and don't keep it, you will have trouble most of the time. Then, too, remember an old adage—that the way a child is until seven, so he will be until seventy. So, watch the first seven years of a child's life with every degree of carefulness. If you promise a six-month-old baby that you will reprimand him if he spits out his food and then when he does just that, you respond by sitting back and laughing, you'll be sorry one of these days! On the other hand, if you promise to reprimand the baby if it spits out its food, then you reprimand him as promised, you will save yourself and the baby untold difficulties in the future.

The first seven years of a child's life are so very important. Yet, most parents do not enter into a training program for the child until adolescence; by that time, the damage has already been done. When a child reaches the age of seven, you often promise him a bicycle. At that time, the business is not good and you are unable to carry it through. Make some arrangements somehow or the child will never forget it. Keep your promises. Children, same as adults, like to have promises kept. Develop the habits that you want your child to have later in life—as early as possible during the first seven years of his life. If you want your child to be honest, truthful, friendly, sociable, cordial, reliable and dependable, start as soon as possible to develop these habits.

If you want your child to be sociable, then take the six-month-old baby visiting: get him used to meeting people, get him accustomed to having company. He will grow up that way. Start early on the characteristics that you want him to have. Don't make the mistake of thinking that these babies are too young to understand. They understand more than we are willing to give them credit for—in most cases they understand everything. Remember that the subconscious mind of a baby is fully developed at birth. The fact that his heart is beating, he is breathing, he is moving his bowels, and he is digesting his food is a sign of a normal developed subconscious mind.

Next, I come to the greatest and finest method of dealing with children. Although this method may seem a little strange and the results difficult to believe upon first hearing about it, the results are so quick and so astounding that you must believe in it and use it whenever necessary.

You realize by this time that each person has two minds: conscious and subconscious. When a person is sleeping, his conscious mind sleeps, but his subconscious mind never sleeps. Therefore, if you want to get something over to the child, then go directly to his subconscious mind—while he is sleeping. Go to the child's bedside, stand over him, and in a low voice tell the child what you expect of him, what you want him to do, what faults you want him to correct just as you would if he were awake. The big difference is that when awake, the child may or may not comply with your request. You may threaten or resort to arguing with the child, but even then your desires are still not achieved.

Talking to the child's subconscious mind is referred to as "night suggestion." This method has never failed and the results have been amazing. Many of the people that you have been reading about have tried everything imaginable. Many times, the doctors have given no hope. In other cases, large doctor bills were running up with still no results. "Night suggestion" will work when everything else fails. Use it and you will see results beyond your fondest dreams.

One of my resident school students lived on the streetcar line. His business was on the lower floor and he lived above the store. He had a six-year-old youngster who was constantly running across the streetcar tracks. Naturally, the parents were worried that someday he would be hurt. They threatened, they pleaded, they begged him not to cross the streetcar tracks but to no avail. Needless to say, the youngster continued to run across the tracks. The evening that I had this lesson in class, he returned home and told his wife all about it. She laughed, saying that it was silly to talk to a child while he is sleeping. He tried it anyway. He went to the child's bedside and started to talk to him like this:

"Johnny, tomorrow you will play in the backyard, you will enjoy playing in the backyard, you will have a lot of fun playing in the backyard, and you are going to keep yourself busy back there. You are not even going to think about going across the streetcar tracks. Remember, Johnny, you are going to have a lot of fun playing in the backyard." The very next day, Johnny did not go across the streetcar tracks. The wife was amazed. To think that what she thought was "silly" actually worked! It is unbelievable at times to see such results.

One woman had a son who used to tarry on his way home from school. She would worry each time her son was coming home. She was beside herself. This was making her nervous, yet she could not make him realize how important it was to come directly home and not be playing along the way. She thus resorted to "night suggestion." The first few times she used it, it did not work. However, after several days, the young man came directly home from school. She was thrilled with the results.

It is a thrill, when you hear all the trouble some people have with their children, to find a simple, easy way to correct a child; it would make any parent feel better.

Some time ago, a father who had a five-year-old daughter had a little son born into the family. The daughter was jealous. She would hit, pinch, and tear the hair of the little fellow. The two children couldn't be left alone for fear of the consequences. The father thus began the "night suggestion." He went to his daughter's bedside and started to talk to her. He said, "Now Mary, tomorrow you will be nice to your little brother. You will love him and kiss him and hug him. There is enough love for both of you. You must be nice to your little brother because soon you will both be playing together and having a lot of fun."

A week went by and no results. Two weeks went by and no results. The father was becoming discouraged. Finally, during the third week, he started to see results. The little girl was sweet to her brother now. She played with him, kissed him, and hugged him. The parents were thrilled with the little girl's new attitude.

Many times, the results of "night suggestion" are immediate. Other times, it may take a little longer. But, *it never fails*. So, if you don't get results right away, don't stop—you will get results.

In bed-wetting cases, I have had such a variety of reports that it is easy for me to understand that sometimes it takes longer in some cases than in others. Some bed-wetting cases stopped with the very first "night suggestion." Others took several weeks. But, *no failures*. Be patient for the rewards are *tremendous*. If you don't get results right away, you will. Maybe you have to change your wording. Sit down and write your suggestions out ahead of time. Examine them. Maybe you are too negative in your remarks. Keep your remarks positive— tell the child what you want him to do, not what you do not want your child to do. So many parents are so used to using negative statements to a child that they find it a little difficult to use positive suggestions. When you give your child "night suggestion," expect it to work. That always helps. Keep the picture in mind of what you really want when you make the "night suggestion."

Several years ago one of my resident school students had a son stricken with polio. She used "night suggestion." Each night, for months, she went to the child's bedside and told him that he would be walking straight, that he would resume his place in society, that his limbs would be getting stronger and stronger each day, and that before long he would be able to walk easily and normally. Results began to show. She continued with the "night suggestions." Before long, the youngster was walking without braces. Wonderful? Of course, it is. It works!

Another case—a child was born with crossed eyes. The mother began "night suggestion." Within three months, the child's eyes began to straighten. The mother was thrilled beyond her fondest hopes.

Another mother had taken her son to the doctor and he informed her that her child was going deaf, that he would lose his hearing in a short time, and that he should prepare him to study lip reading so that they would be able to talk to each other. Imagine such news! She was so upset; but being a mother, she prepared to follow the doctor's instructions. Then she learned about "night suggestion." Each night she went to her son's bedside and told him that his hearing was improving, that each day he would be hearing better and better. Yes, the child began to hear better and before long, his hearing was back to normal. Was the mother thrilled? Excited? You can judge for yourself. It is too bad that this method of child training is not more universally known. It would save millions of heartaches that come to parents in bringing up children.

A mother, living in a trailer, had a four-year-old son. He slept standing up! Can you imagine anything like that? How would you like to walk into your child's bedroom and find your child sleeping standing up? Doctors could do nothing. She told me about it. I explained "night suggestion" to her. Two evenings later, the child was sleeping in bed in a normal position. No longer was the mother frightened when she walked into his bedroom.

Another mother found that her son was stammering. She took him to a regular speech clinic and the clinic told her that the boy would never speak clearly. She should save her money. Nothing would help the boy. That's not good news for a mother, is it? I told her about "night suggestion" and showed her how to use it—as you have learned in these lessons. Within a few weeks, the boy showed results. The mother was so happy, especially since the speech clinic had told her that nothing could be done.

In sickness, with colds, "night suggestion" works wonderfully well. If your child has a cold, go the child's bedside at night and say "Tomorrow morning you will wake up feeling fine. God loves you and wants you to be well. Your nose will be clear. Your head will be clear. All the fever will be gone and you will wake up feeling fine. God loves you and wants you to be well." Time and again, a cold will be broken up immediately. Other times, it may take a little longer; but never as long as without the use of "night suggestion." Then, too, many a serious sickness can be prevented by "night suggestion." A cold may lead into something worse, but "night suggestion" prevents the cold from going into something more serious.

If at any time the child should awaken, do not let this disturb you. Simply say to the child that you were telling him to be a good child or that you were telling him to be well. Then, wait until the child has fallen to sleep again and carry out your suggestion. If the child is very sick, make the "night suggestion" as often during the night as you wish. If you find that you are talking too loudly and the child awakens, lower your voice, or even whisper. Experiment with it until you find the right voice and the right words to give you the results that you want. Remember, please, it is the duty of the parent to guide and protect the child, not to dominate or make the child do what you want it to do, regardless of results. As the child matures, teach the child to use suggestion, and then let the child make his own suggestions by himself. This is truly a healthy way to bring up a youngster.

Not only can you greatly benefit a child through "night suggestion" and then in later years teach the child to use suggestion for himself, but the child can learn to go directly to the subconscious mind by himself. If you remember Shirley Temple, she was considered by many to be a very unusual child. It is true. But Mrs. Temple understood "night suggestion." She sat by Shirley's bedside and went over her lines with her just before Shirley went to sleep and the next morning Shirley knew them. Therefore, contrary to general belief, one of the best times to study is just before going to sleep at night.

You may use this method and tell your youngsters about it. A child was failing in spelling. By studying just before going to sleep, no more trouble with spelling. Another youngster was failing in music. Taking the music lessons to bed with her, she began to read notes beautifully. She, herself, was surprised! Another youngster was having trouble with algebra. Taking her algebra lessons and studying in bed just before going to sleep, she had no more trouble with algebra. Another child was having trouble with geometry, but studying just before going to sleep, she was able to get along without failing in the subject. The dullest child can become a good student through studying before going to sleep at night. The results are amazing. Children who were failing in school, no longer had any trouble as soon as they began night study.

Adults can use this system as well. In fact, Mrs. Roosevelt, in her column "My Day," told that she went over her speeches at night just before going to sleep and the next morning, she knew her speech. Many students have reported similar results. If you want to learn a poem, a musical selection, a speech, anything that requires memorization, go over it just before going to sleep at night. You will be surprised how quickly you will learn what you want. It doesn't make any difference how old you are. The subconscious mind never gets old. You learned in a previous lesson that the body renews itself every seven years. So, although you may be forty years of age, the oldest bone in your body is only seven years old.

The fifth method of dealing successfully with children is the easiest and the one that will be the longest lasting. Keep telling your child that "God loves you." This is so important that the entire child's life can be changed. If you keep telling your child that "God will punish you," the results will be harmful. The child will start fighting God and may do so all of his life, as most people do. We have done untold harm to our children by telling them that God will punish us. It sometimes takes a full lifetime to get rid of this fear of God. If you will tell your child that "God loves you," as I have already explained in my book *Your Greatest Power*, your child will be good because it is natural to be good. If he wants to be good, because he is afraid of something or afraid that God will harm him, he will rebel too many times, and too often will do the wrong thing because he is fighting you and God.

Save yourself so much trouble, doctor bills, and heartaches by constantly telling your child "God loves you." He will be good for the sake of goodness and not because he is afraid. You remember the story in the book *Your Greatest Power* of the sick little boy, who although he was going to die, got well immediately upon learning that God loved him. You also remember the story of the mother whose child was always having colds until she started to tell her child that "God loves you." It will work for you too.

We parents have the opportunity *now* not only to make ourselves "mental millionaires" but we can also start our children on the road to becoming "mental millionaires."

Here in review are the five ways of dealing with children:

1. Make good mental pictures about your children
2. Suggest and request . . . mix praise with criticism
3. Keep your promises . . . watch carefully the first seven years of your child's life
4. Night suggestion
5. God loves you

Lesson 14

Power of Creation

Dear Reader:
In order to create the life we truly want, we must aspire to fulfill conditions that will cause us to experience both happiness and joy. Many readers are initially taken aback by the title of Napoleon Hill's all time motivational self-help classic Think and Grow Rich because of his supposed emphasis on finances. However, if you read beyond the cover, you realize that the riches Napoleon Hill speaks about are the Twelve Riches of Life. Financial richness appears last on the list. By emphasizing the word "rich," Napoleon Hill captures a person's attention, but the real lesson in personal growth begins later as Dr. Hill discusses the many ways riches can occur in a person's daily life through personal reflection and soul searching.

Kohe says that in order to bring about joy and happiness in our lives, we need to ask the subconscious mind what conditions will be satisfactory in meeting these ends. Add descriptive qualities to what you are seeking along with the particular thing you are seeking. For instance, say perhaps that you are looking for a warm, comfortable and cozy house wherein your family can relax, rather *than simply saying that you want a new house. Be specific as to the conditions, and this will help you clarify for yourself why you are seeking the thing in the first place. It could very well be that a new house is not the best means of fulfilling your request. Be open-minded and open-ended in your search for things, but be very specific in your search for qualities that these things are to possess.*

Do not limit your choices and always ask your subconscious mind to show you the way. Expect the best, believe you will receive it, and the rest is up to the Almighty Power of the universe to deliver your personal request to you right on your doorstep. Then, dear reader, you will see that your heart's greatest desire shows up right on schedule. You really knew that it would all along, didn't you?

—JUDITH WILLIAMSON

After the universal power gives man life . . . then it is up to man to choose to do with it as he sees fit.
–YOUR GREATEST POWER

As one has learned in my book *Your Greatest Power*, each person makes his life according to the way he chooses. Unfortunately, most people have been students of everything except life—learning to be lawyers, doctors, dentists, butchers, auto mechanics, etc. The first and primary job in life is that "we must make a living."

This primary quest—that of making a living—is so all encompassing that a person finds himself with little time to learn "how to live." Not only does a person spend so much time making a living, but he also begins to believe that "this is life." He thus becomes material minded, meaning that he is so interested in things that can be seen and felt that he forgets that there are also things which cannot be seen or felt. Therefore, if he does not have a lot of money, does not live in a big house, does not have a wife who wears fur coats, he feels that he has failed in life—failed to get things and to have things. Much of the trouble in the world stems from the struggle that exists between the "haves" and the "have nots."

All during these hundreds of years, man has failed to realize that there is something else besides "things"—there is a "mind." The power of mind is greater and more satisfying than the power of things. Slowly, the people of the world are beginning to realize this and are becoming more interested in this power and how it works. Then too, many people who never had any money before have now made money. They are able to buy cars, houses, fur coats, and everything that should make a person happy. Some have so much money that they don't know what to do with it all.

Not so long ago, there was an article in the paper telling about a millionaire who committed suicide. He had left a note saying that he had nothing to live for. It is a pity, to be sure. However, one begins to realize that cars, houses, furs, and diamonds are not satisfying. There is something which is definitely lacking—satisfaction! Oftentimes, a person's downfall is in believing that satisfaction comes with the obtainment of "things." However, when he gets them, he finds that things are not what he really wanted after all.

I frequently refer to God as the Creator and man as a little creator. Man creates according to the way he understands. If he understands the problems of life and how to solve them, he is a real creator; otherwise, he goes along creating and choosing as he sees best—which is only a part of the best that there is. In 1902, Professor James of Harvard University uncovered the complexities of the "subconscious mind" and brought his findings to the "thinking" world. This was an entirely new development in man's way of life. Certain things which were not understood before were now becoming clear. One is now able to solve the many mysteries of life.

Man has done most of his choosing with his conscious mind. For example, a man chooses to become a doctor — why?—because his uncle was a doctor or because he feels he will make more money as a doctor. He becomes a doctor and then secretly begins to wish he had become a lawyer. The lawyer secretly wishes he had become a doctor. Clearly, many people are unhappy in their work. These unhappy people want to do something other than they are currently doing. "Why is this?" we may ask.

Now, I know the answer. When a young man decides to become a lawyer, he wants it with his "conscious mind," the subconscious mind doesn't care what he is. The subconscious mind is interested in "conditions." Ask yourself what "conditions" you want from your work? To be happy, to be prosperous, and to be useful, are all desirable conditions. Actually, a person doesn't care what kind of work it is as long as he is content with fulfilling the conditions that he sets for himself.

To accomplish this, I suggest you "see yourself" in a work in which you are happy and prosperous. Ask the subconscious mind to lead you into such work. It will. Don't quit your job right away. The subconscious mind will answer this problem for you (see "How to Solve Your Problems," Lesson 17). If your child finds it necessary to make a choice for his life's work, help him locate a job or career that will allow him to be both happy and prosperous. Aptitude tests are available today at most colleges. These tests help a person determine what he is good at and what type of work will make him both happy and prosperous. When a person is happy with his work, he is more likely to also be prosperous at it since he is doing something that he already likes to do. Do not tell your son to be a doctor, or a lawyer, etc. Rather, tell them that you want them to be happy and prosperous. Next, let the subconscious mind direct them to a job, career, or profession that will fulfill these conditions. By using aptitude tests and the subconscious mind as aids to making a better choice, more positive career choices will follow.

Many people get married. They set their sights for certain types of men or women and if they don't marry these people, they are very much put out. As a rule, girls want to marry the tall, dark and handsome fellows, the men want to marry beautiful girls. In actuality, when the man does marry the beautiful girl, a year or so later he wishes he had never seen her. The girl does marry the tall, dark and handsome fellow, and a few years later wishes she had never married him. What is wrong with this picture? How have they failed in their choice?

Some time ago, there were three girls talking about the kind of men they would like to marry. One spoke up and said, "I want to marry a doctor, so that if I became ill, he could cure me for nothing!" The second girl spoke up and said, "I want to marry a lawyer, so that if I ever got into trouble, he could get me out of trouble for nothing." The third girl refused to speak. The other two insisted. So, she finally admitted that she would like to marry a minister so that she could be "good for nothing!" Silly? Of course it is. But that is just about how much judgment many people use. A parent doesn't want the child to marry a "good provider" —as most mothers want for their daughters—he may be a "good provider" and "mean" in every other way. A parent wants the daughter to marry a man that will keep her happy. A parent wants the son to marry a girl that will keep him happy. What more could one ask for?

The young man wants to marry the beautiful girl because he thinks that a beautiful girl will make him happy. Once in a while it works out that way; but in a majority of cases, it doesn't. What he really wants is a girl that will keep him happy. Keep this thought in mind, if you are single. The young lady wants to marry a tall, dark and handsome fellow because she thinks this is what she needs to make herself happy. Actually, she wants to marry a man that will keep her happy.

Keep this thought uppermost in your mind: you will attract that which you seek. If the young man wants beauty, he will be attracted to beauty. By the same token, if the young man wants to marry a girl that will keep him happy, he will be attracted to her.

We want happiness in marriage. That's a "condition." This condition is what the subconscious mind wants. The subconscious mind does not live for particular things, it lives in conditions. When we seek something without consulting the subconscious mind, we are liable to make a mistake and then be sorry for it later.

We want to buy a home. Immediately, we decide where we want to live. Sometimes we go so far as to decide in advance on what street we want to live as well. This may have been all right fifty years ago before the subconscious mind was discovered; but now, we must be careful not to use only the conscious mind in decision making of this kind. We just might get the house we want and then find that we never should have bought the house in the first place.

Let me clarify this by an example. A woman wanted to buy a home in a certain high-class neighborhood so that her children would grow up surrounded by wealth. She and her husband bought a lot and had a home built in the neighborhood she had chosen. She had not lived there very long before finding out that she had made a mistake. Her children were getting in with the "wrong crowd" of boys and girls and she began to worry as to the consequences.

Another woman was looking for a home on a certain street. Every time she saw an ad in the newspaper advertising a house on this particular street, she would go out and look. Fortunately, she did not buy a house there for it later became a thoroughfare—automobiles going back and forth all the time. Had she bought a house there, she constantly would have worried since she had a youngster who would always be in danger.

An interesting story is told regarding the Indians living on the reservations in Oklahoma. Oil was struck on these reservations and the Indians became ever so wealthy. Promoters moved in and started to sell the Indians everything under the sun. They even sold them on the idea of building huge, beautiful mansions. Thus, up came these mansions with all the modern conveniences—silver doorknobs, mirrors, bathrooms attached to each bedroom—and luxuries befitting a king! However, did the Indians move into these fabulous mansions?

No! Why? The Indians were happy living in their wigwams. Is it any wonder why Indians used to live so long? It was a common occurrence for an Indian to live to be a hundred years old or more and still be in the prime of life.

The Indian lived in "conditions." Maybe he didn't realize that he was living in "conditions," but that is exactly how he lived. He was not interested in cars, jewels, houses, and the things that supposedly make man happy, but in "conditions." When will we realize the value of "conditions?" We can do it now if we choose to do so.

In choosing a house, say to your subconscious mind: "I want a home that will keep me happy. Tell me where it is." It will tell you (see Lesson 17). It will help you get the right home. It may not be on a known street or a known section but you will be happy there. Only then will you realize that you have chosen not only with your conscious mind but have also consulted your subconscious mind. As soon as you put a picture in your mind of living in a home in which you will be happy, the subconscious mind starts to work. One day you get an idea to drive through a certain street, another day you have an urge to look into newspaper ads. The subconscious mind will lead you in the right direction. You will be surprised, but also very pleased and happy with your choice. Remember: you want a home that you can be happy in.

You want an automobile. Immediately, you decide that you want an Oldsmobile, or a Ford, or a Cadillac, or a Dodge, or a Packard, or whatever choice you may make. You no doubt will get the car on which you set your mind because you will not buy any other. You may be happy or not with the purchase, but does the subconscious mind really care what the name of the car is or the company that made it? The subconscious mind wants conditions. It wants a car that will give it conditions—conditions of happiness!

One traveling salesman found it necessary to buy a new car. He decided what he wanted (let me call it an "A Car"). He had been warned that an "A Car" is not easy riding and for a salesman, it would be too difficult for long trips. He refused to listen. He had his mind made up. He bought the "A car," drove it for about a month, and finally concluded that it was really too difficult for long trips. He then admitted to his wife that he had made a mistake. She asked, "What will you do now?" He told her that she could have the new car and that he would go out and buy a used car that would give him comfortable riding. This he did. Even though it was not a new car, he was very happy with it.

As you can readily see, he first made up his mind to buy a certain special-make car, got the car, and then found out it was not what he had really wanted. The second time around, he bought a condition—comfortable riding—and he was happy. Oh! When will we learn that conditions are more important than things for real living!

Let me take the average high school youngster, maybe you have one. You give him the choice of either buying a new car or a jalopy. Which one will he prefer? In nine out of ten cases, he will take the jalopy. Why? . . . because he will be happier with the jalopy. He won't have to worry about how many boys pack into the car, cigarette burns, and all the different things that would be of concern if he had a new car.

Children, as a rule, are much happier than adults. They lean more toward conditions than they do toward things. As they grow older, the parents make them "things" conscious. The child loses his happiness flavor and starts to become "grown-up" according to the standards of the day. It takes a lot of courage on the part of the individual to live with conditions instead of things. Sometimes people may even think one is "strange" or "different" until they begin to realize that the other is happier than they are, and then they find out who is really "strange!"

Take another example. You want to buy a suit and before you even step inside the store, you have already made up your mind that you want a gray suit or a brown suit. The salesman proceeds to show you a beautiful green suit—but no, you must have a gray suit. Finally, you buy the gray suit. Are you happy? Maybe, but usually you are not. You then wonder: "What's the matter with you? Where did you make a mistake?" Thousands of people buy suits and many different things, bring them home, and then never use them or wear them. They are ashamed to say they made a mistake . . . but where?

A person doesn't specifically want a gray suit or a brown suit. He wants a suit that makes him feel good, makes him feel rich—yes, conditions again! If a person buys clothes that make him feel rich, self-confident, and actually causes him to "vibrates," what more could he ask for? In wearing clothing that meets these conditions, a person will be at his best.

In order to get what you want—and be sure it is what you want—follow these three rules which are so very simple that they will make all the difference between ordinary living and living to the fullest:

1. Seek conditions along with the particular things
2. Do not limit yourself
3. Ask your subconscious mind what to do

RULE 1: SEEK CONDITIONS ALONG WITH THE PARTICULAR THINGS

Always add conditions. Why say you are going to the show tonight? You may go and see a very disappointing picture. Why not say: "You are going to see a very *delightful* picture tonight?" Why say you are going out to dinner tonight? You may have a very disgusting evening. Why not say to yourself: "You are going out tonight for a very *enjoyable* dinner?" Why say you are going to the ball game this afternoon? You may see a very poor game. Why not say to yourself: "You are going to see a very *interesting* ball game today?" Seek conditions along with the particular things—then you will get what you want, and it will be what you want.

RULE 2: DO NOT LIMIT YOURSELF

The greatest crime that people commit against themselves is the crime of limitation. Wherever one goes, one hears people limiting themselves. "It is too good to be true . . . It is too good to last . . . It is too wonderful to happen . . . I can't afford it . . . I'll never get it . . . It's just my luck, nothing good ever happens to me"—these can be multiplied by the hundreds. Almost every person has his own "pet limitations." Why do we do this? First, it is because we are taught limitations by our parents. How many times have we been told, "You can't have everything."? Second, it is because we were told that God doesn't want us to have everything, that God will punish us if we are not careful. Instead, we should have been told that God loves us and wants us to have everything.

We have grown up with misconceptions all around us. It isn't easy to shake off this limitation. That is why it is so important for those of us who understand better not to pass on this limitation to our children. A person has everything he needs, even though it may not be everything that he wants. We learned in an earlier lesson that it is good to always want more so that you do not become satisfied and complacent. To have everything you need is important because, as I said before, after your basic needs are met, everything else is "extra." You can get along with it or without it, if you have to. For example, the main thing in owning an automobile is that you are happy with it. This means that it runs nicely. It does not necessarily mean that the seats are covered with mink or that the steering wheel is made of gold or that the wheels are diamond studded. These are all "extras." You can get along without them just as easily as with them.

RULE 3: ASK YOUR SUBCONSCIOUS MIND WHAT TO DO

Remember: when making decisions without consulting the subconscious mind, you may get what you want but it may not really be what you want. Ask the subconscious mind what to do (explained fully in Lesson 17). In the meantime, each night before going to sleep, ask the subconscious mind what to do the next day. You'll notice that you are being told what to do. Once you recognize this guidance, you will find a new thrill in living. You know then that you are working together with your "inner self." In using the subconscious mind, you will begin to notice that you are getting what you want, are happy with it, are not disappointed with it, and you will sit back well pleased with yourself—and you should be—especially if you follow these rules.

Now, we know how to get what we want and have it be what we want. *Never forget these big three rules.* They make the difference between getting the most out of life and living to the fullest, or constantly making mistakes and spending most of our lives correcting these mistakes. Notice the people around you, especially those over forty, and what do you find? Most of these people are spending their lives correcting the mistakes that they made earlier in life. Isn't it a pity? However, we cannot blame these people. The subconscious mind was discovered in 1902. It is only since then that we have begun to understand the workings of the subconscious mind, so let us not be too critical of these people. But—we must be careful that we don't make the same mistakes; we should know better; we know the rules.

Lesson 15

How to Get What You Want—Part 1

Dear Reader:

This lesson and Lesson 16 deal with the subconscious mind on a more spiritual basis. Kohe interchangeably uses the words God and the subconscious mind. He does this purposefully in order to equate the two. We know that the subconscious mind and God are not one, but that the doorway to Infinite Intelligence is achieved through the subconscious mind backed by faith.

Napoleon Hill states: "The mind has been provided with a gateway of approach to Infinite Intelligence through what is known as the subconscious mind. From the vast reservoir of Infinite Intelligence, through the gateway of the subconscious mind, there flows into the conscious mind of man a continual stream of intelligence upon which we are dependent for our growth and development, and the unfolding of our innate powers. It is in this inflowing stream of intelligence that 'we live and move and have our being.'"

It is important to understand that the creative force of the universe operates through your mind when you align yourself to a *definite major purpose and back it with applied faith. No problem is insurmountable to God. God is within you. God is goodness personified. Nothing bad can happen to you when you take God into partnership with you. God is always with us because each of us is a manifestation of God's creative love for us. That, dear reader, explains why we are never without the presence of God. He is inside each of us and will guide us to greatness. Let your little light shine. You can do this by allowing God to throw the switch!*

—Judith Williamson

Therefore, the fact remains that inasmuch as we are going through life just once, we should choose to make life a confident one, instead of a timid one . . . that we should choose to make a calm life rather than one of restlessness . . . that we should choose to have poise rather than confusion . . . that we should choose to make the most of life for ourselves and everyone else around us . . . rather than spoil our own lives and those about us.

–Your Greatest Power

On the road to getting what you want, you have learned:
+ How to have self-confidence
+ How to deal with people
+ How to get ahead financially
+ How to handle troubles
+ How to control your nerves
+ How to use your imagination
+ How to be successful

- How to be happy
- How to stay well
- How to stay young

Now, what do you want? You feel that the lesson is not complete yet, that there is something missing, but—what is it?

I had the same experience as you are having. I knew all the above things; and yet, I felt that there was something missing. I studied the subconscious mind. I knew how to make it work for better health, answer my problems, help me in my work and in my life, but something was lacking. I felt short of something, felt alone, I did not feel I was living in a really satisfying manner. I found out why. Now you will find out, too. You will be delightfully surprised—you will reach a point of complete understanding for the mystery of life.

All through the centuries, man has been trying to find God. Each period of history has progressed according to mankind's attitude toward God. In prehistoric times man worshipped the sun, the stars, or whatever form or object that would give him some satisfaction. In ancient history, we are told that the Greeks had fourteen gods. They had a god of war, a god of love, a god of wine, and eleven other gods that they thought were necessary to make life complete. The Hebrews then came along and said that there is only one God. This was truly a great step forward, but it still did not give man the satisfaction that he wanted. Finally, there came a truly great psychologist on the scene—the Great Carpenter of Nazareth. He gave us the complete key. Still, man did not have the complete peace of mind that he wanted. Finally, it took the modern-day psychologist—after two thousand years—to find out exactly how the teachings of the Great Psychologist could be made applicable to everyday living and everlasting peace of mind.

As you now know, the subconscious mind was discovered by Professor James of Harvard in 1902. I have been studying the subconscious mind and the complete picture is found in these two lessons ("How to Get What You Want"—Part 1 and Part 2).

Over two thousand years ago when Jesus was explaining the subconscious mind, He referred to it as the "Father within," or "God." Now, I know what He was really talking about; now I know that we are not alone; now I know that God is with us—solving our problems, taking care of our hearts, lungs, breathing, and all the functions of the human body. Now, I can realize that God doesn't hurt us, that actually we hurt ourselves through our bad choosing. Now I know that God is with me and also with the person sitting next to me, God is greater than all the 6.5 billion souls living on this earth today combined. He is this many times as great as you and I! How do I come to this conclusion? There are over 6.5 billion people in this world; and yet, God is able to take care of all these people, to keep their hearts beating, to listen to each one's prayers, and to still keep the world operating in perfect order. God is not a man sitting up in the skies, at His desk, watching what is going on. God is in each one of us. You have a mind—big enough to do what is necessary for you, intelligent enough to make your life complete—but God is the great universal mind, capable of doing infinitely more than you and I or even the 6.5 billion souls combined.

Once you get this realization, you will find a new peace come over you. You will stop feeling that you are the important one in your life. Once you do, you will feel better, you will have more energy, you will be more at ease, you will stop "fighting" God, and life will run along smoother than you ever dreamed. You will find in the following lesson that God is always telling you what to do and that when you follow His instructions, everything works out beautifully. The only time you may ever have any trouble is when you do not listen to the "Father within," as Jesus explained the subconscious mind. Isn't that wonderful?

There is a very remarkable true story told about a young Australian woman who was an excellent swimmer. She was swimming about a mile off the coast of Australia when she felt something grab her. She noticed it was an octopus—an eight-armed sea animal. Evidently, she knew about the true power of God because instead of becoming frightened, she kept herself as calm as she could and she kept saying over and over to herself, "there is nothing but good around me, there is nothing but good around me, there is nothing but good around me, there is nothing but good around me" . . . and the octopus let go. She then swam back to shore. Remarkable?

Oh! If we could only realize that there is nothing but good around us, that there is nothing but God around us, that God is with us all the time, that God is for us, that God is ever at our service! You have learned in another lesson that one cannot keep two ideas of opposite nature in one's mind at the same time, the stronger one always wins. If you believe in sickness and in health, you will have both. If you believe in good fortune and in bad, you will have both. If you believe in good and evil, you will have both. If you believe in good luck and in bad, you will have both. But, if you will believe there is nothing but good around you, that is the way it will be. With all the negative thinking that is going around, it may not be easy to do what we know is right. But we can still begin to do what we are able to do, by starting within ourselves. Since others are not ready or willing to start, individually we must begin. You start it in your own family. Others will follow, you'll see.

To repeat, if we continue to believe and work on the principle that there is nothing but good around us, that is the way it will be in our lives. If enough of us would grasp that thought, we will all have our Heaven right here on earth!

E. Stanley Jones, the great missionary, tells an enlightening story in his book, *Abundant Living*. Many years ago when the Indians roamed all over America, they had a very interesting custom. When the son of the Indian Chief reached the age of ten, he was put to a test. He was taken into the forest just before nightfall and was to remain there until the next morning. If he failed to stay and ran out before dawn, he would never be able to replace his father as Chief when the time came. This little fellow was so scared, as one can well imagine, when he heard the wind in the trees, that he could hardly catch his breath. Everything upset him and everything disturbed him, but he remained in the forest all night long. Finally, when the dawn began to break through the trees, the little fellow looked around and there was his own father, the Indian Chief, standing behind a big tree, with a gun in his hands.

Oh, how this story applies to us! If we would only realize that God is always with us and behind us in everything we do, what could possibly frighten us? If we would constantly remind ourselves that God is always with us, and loves us, and wants us to have everything that is good, what a different kind of life we would lead! Would we worry as much as we do? Would we be anxious about tomorrow? Let us take God with us into the forest of life. Take Him with you, any time you are in doubt, or any time you feel insufficient for the task at hand. Be conscious of an ever-present God, and you will be conscious of an ever-present feeling that everything is going to be all right. *Keep it until it becomes a habit.* Remember: you have to undo all the negative thinking of your own past life.

A doctor friend of mine told me the following story. A minister came to him for a complete examination. The doctor had known this fellow, but the minister had never used him as a physician. After the examination, the doctor inquired whether or not the minister had seen other doctors. He answered, "Yes." Next, he asked what their findings had been. The minister stated that these doctors all concurred that his problem was cancer, and that he only had eight months or less to live. The minister then asked the doctor what he felt could be done for his illness. The doctor replied, "Reverend, I don't want to tell you your business, but go home, get on your knees and pray to God that He should destroy your cancer." The minister left the doctor's office and went home. Each day he prayed for one half hour, as the doctor had advised. Upon returning to be re-examined, the doctor found no improvement.

"Reverend, did you do what I told you?"

"Yes," replied the minister, "exactly as you told me."

"Reverend, again, I don't want to tell you your business, but you prayed to a God in the skies. I want you to go home and pray to the God within you. Come back in two weeks."

The minister did what he was told. Two weeks later when he returned to the doctor's office, upon examination the doctor found that the cancer had begun to break up. Eight months later, instead of being a dead man, the cancer was completely gone. Wonderful! The minister was alive and well. There is nothing to be afraid of! There is nothing too good to be true!

Yes, *with God the impossible becomes possible.* If we can do such wonderful things as we do, such as flying in the air, talking over wires, sending pictures through the air, watching games several hundred miles away as though they were in our own backyard, just imagine what we can do when we tap this Great Power that is 6.5 billion greater than our individual power! It is limitless! It is truly magnificent when one realizes that this power can be tapped by everyone anywhere in the world at the same time. Look what electricity has done for man—washing machines, radios, television sets, machines, motors, power plants, factories all working at the same time, all drawing on this great electric power. Just imagine how much greater God really is, when electricity is just one of God's accomplishments.

August Hashagen, in his wonderful little book *Let Us Have Love*, tells a delightful story of two sisters who owned a restaurant. They were on the verge of bankruptcy. One morning, they had a meeting with the dishwasher. The older sister said that they were having a lot of trouble and that she had decided to take in a partner. "Who is he? Does he have money? Will he be able to help us through?" These were the questions posed to her. In answer to the "Who is he?" question, the sister reached over, took a menu, wrote a word on the back of the menu and handed it over to the other two. The word was "God."

"Oh," burst out the dishwasher, "I know everything is going to be all right now."

They had no sooner gotten up from the table where they had their little meeting, when the sheriff walked in. "Sorry girls," he said, "but I'll have to close you up."

"Oh," said the younger sister, "you won't have to now, we have a new partner."

"Does he have money?" inquired the sheriff.

The younger sister reached for the menu, turned it over, and handed it to the sheriff. The sheriff read it. He was astounded! He said, "Well, I guess I'll have to wait a little longer."

Business began to pick up, almost like magic, people came to help them out. Everything was fine. They changed the name of the restaurant from the "Two Sisters" to the "Three Partners." Wonderful? Yes, when man works with God everything is wonderful. It is when we think that we are the big "so and so's" that we get ourselves into trouble. *Take God into partnership.* He will help you at every turn. God never fails a person who takes him into partnership.

In these lessons on "How to Get What You Want," you will come across this remarkable little thought, "The Lord will Provide." Yes, the Lord will provide. He will provide ideas, health, money, success, happiness, whatever you want. You are familiar with the Bible quotation "When you pray, believe that you receive." When you turn on an electric switch, you expect the lights to go on, and they do. When you ask God for something, expect it—and you'll get it. If a little switch is able to bring light into your home, then certainly a little faith (right thinking) switch will turn on the God Power to help you to get what you want. The fact that the switch is there shows that there is possible light, so the fact that we are "able to choose" shows that we can choose to have God help us, and expect that

He will do it. The electric power plant is available to burn all the lights one has in his home and the homes of millions of others. So the God Power is available to us and to the millions who care to use it. However, too many people are burning 25-watt bulbs when they could just as well burn 75-watt bulbs or even 300-watt bulbs. So, we find so many people have only 25-watt faith in God instead of 75-watt faith, or even 300-watt faith when they need it.

Here is another story that will help you to understand God better and how He works. A man owned a growing business in New York City. In fact, the business was growing so fast that he was unable to take care of it himself. So he decided that he would take in a partner. He began to think of different people whom he thought he might be able to take into the business to make things easier. He considered upon Gallagher. After weighing the pros and cons, giving every possible thought about Gallagher, he came to the conclusion that Gallagher was not his man. Then he thought about Brown. Brown would be a good man to have in the business. He weighed Brown's possibilities back and forth and finally decided that Brown was not the man either. Then he thought that surely Jones would be just the man he wanted. He talked with Jones and told him all about his plans for expansion and growth. After lengthy talks with Jones, he decided that Jones was not his man.

Taylor, the man in this story, kept asking and wondering what to do. He just could not seem to find the right person for the partnership. One morning he woke up, and almost like magic, said "I know what I will do, I will take the Lord into partnership!" So, he changed the name of the company from "Taylor Co." to "Lord and Taylor Co." It is one of the finest and one of the largest department stores in the city of New York. Almost everyone who does not know this story thinks that Lord is the name of a man. It isn't. He took God into business and made God a partner. Many more businessmen are now doing the same thing. We are on our way to the kind of life some of us have dreamed about.

Do you want your troubles to come to an end? Then, take the Lord into partnership. Take Him with you wherever you go. Take Him with you in everything you do. He won't limit you. Jesus said, "I came that they may have life, and have it abundantly" [John 10:10]. People think that when they take God into partnership in everything they do, they are limiting themselves. How would God limit you? He certainly will let you do anything you "choose" to do. He won't limit your good times for He wants you to be happy. He won't limit your vacations, your parties, for he wants you to have fun. Someone counted up to 800 times in the Bible where God said that He wants you to be happy. Certainly, if He said it 800 times, He really means it.

Where, then, is God limiting you? Is it in your sex life? In Lesson 19, "How to Become a Mental Millionaire," I will discuss this fully. However, if God did not want you to enjoy the sex life, He never would have made sex so strong that men and women want to marry and make love to each other. Of course, common sense tells us that promiscuous lovemaking is harmful and frequently brings about serious diseases and trouble. But lovemaking in the married life is perfectly normal and right—if we think right. In fact, one outstanding psychologist said that God is a Lover. Then certainly if we use the God power within us to be lovers in the married life, is that limitation? (Some of you reading this paragraph may disagree with me, but sex is always a difficult subject to handle on the written page.) God is with you during the sex act; and if you are making love to your wife or your husband, God is with you. Where is the limitation? God loves you, and you being a part of Him, must love your fellowman as well as yourself. This is easier said than done, but it is something interesting to work towards.

So, now, the mystery is solved! We all know now that we are not put on this earth to sink or swim. We are not put on this earth to suffer so that in the next world we would be happy. We don't have to wait to meet our Maker in the next world. We need not be afraid of anything outside ourselves. God is with us, working with us, loving us, telling us what to do—if we would only listen! God is our Partner. Will we be His partners? Will we be a worthwhile partner, or will we try to get by on the least possible amount of help? Will we see to it that God will be proud of us?

It is up to us. God gave us the power to choose, the greatest power He could possibly have given us. We can choose to be His partner or we can choose to go on struggling and fighting Him. Eventually, you will be His partner—why not now?

You can't fight God. I did for many years, but I couldn't win. He is too big and too powerful. You may think you can fight Him—forget it, you can't win. When you cannot fight something, what is the sensible thing to do?—work with it, cooperate with it. It's easier, believe me.

Man has tried to fight the elements, but he has not succeeded. By learning how to work with these elements, man has saved himself all the trouble that he used to have. Man fought electricity because he was afraid of it. Once electricity was harnessed, look at all the pleasures we have gained! Now, let us work with God. Take Him into partnership, in everything you do, you'll love it. You'll begin to look younger and feel better. Your mental, emotional, physical, financial, social and spiritual problems will fade when you really use "the Lord will provide." Your heaven on earth is here, will you claim it?

Always keep the following in mind:
1. God is with you . . . through the Father within [subconscious mind]
2. There is nothing but good around you
3. God (the Father) is always behind you [story of Indian boy]
4. Minister got rid of terrible disease . . . through God Power within
5. Take God into partnership [story of Two Sisters]
6. Take God into partnership [story of Lord and Taylor Co.]

Lesson 16

How to Get What You Want—Part 2

Dear Reader:

In striving to be the very best we can be in this lifetime, Kohe speaks at length of the importance of seeing the spiritual aspect in all of life. Judging life strictly from what we can glean from our five senses is insufficient. Happiness and joy require a spiritual partnership with Infinite Intelligence that enables us as individuals to tap into all the goodness and abundance that is readily available for each and every one of us as children of the Almighty.

We must never forget, however, that these gifts require a contribution on our part. Emerson speaks of it, Hill speaks of it, Stone speaks of it, Shakespeare speaks of it and all successful people know that rewards follow service. There is no getting without giving. Likewise with spiritual abundance, we have been told to make our life a prayer, to take God into partnership, and to always think positively. These requirements are the giving that is necessary before the getting.

Prayers of gratitude are said to be the best and most effective prayers. Being grateful for what we have, supplies us with endorphin—like thoughts that color our world positively. Knowing that we are blessed with abundance, does not deter additional abundance from coming into our lives. Rather, it alerts the Universe to our receptivity for all good things. There is a difference between looking for a handout and looking to make a difference. When we give to get, we send the wrong message. Giving is its own reward. An old Chinese saying states: "Flowers leave some of their fragrance on the hands that bestow them." Bestow goodness and you are doubly gifted. That, dear reader, is why we give to give rather than give to get.

—JUDITH WILLIAMSON

Keep thinking good thoughts. Keep thoughts that will help you, not harm you. It is important, because through this greatest power . . . the power to choose . . . life becomes what you think and choose it to be.

–YOUR GREATEST POWER

A minister found that there was something else he wanted besides being a leader of his church. He wanted to have an orphan home for children. So, he talked it over with some of his associates and together they decided that they would leave the church and start an orphanage. Together they prayed that someone would donate the building for the housing of their orphanage. Before long, someone did donate a suitable building. Then they prayed for dishes, for beds, for linens, and all the different necessities for an orphanage. Everything they wanted they got through *prayer alone*. During the course of his lifetime, Mueller (the minister in this story) and his co-workers prayed for and received over $5 million. Fantastic? But, true! Mueller in his book, *Trusting in God for $5,000,000.00*, said the following:

> *The point is this: I saw more clearly than ever that the first and primary business to which I ought to attend every day was to have my soul happy in the Lord. The first thing to be concerned about was not how much I might serve the Lord, nor how I might glorify the Lord, but how I might get my soul in a happy state and how my inner man might be nourished. For I might seek to see the truth before the converted, I might seek to benefit believers, I might seek to relieve the distress, I might in other ways seek to behave myself as it becomes a child of God in this world; and yet, not being happy in the Lord and not being nourished and strengthened in my inner man day by day, all this might not be attended to in the right spirit.*

Commit this passage to memory. Make a copy of it and put it where you will be constantly reminded.

What a remarkable way to live! Is it any wonder that Mueller was so successful? He did not wait for Sunday. His religion was not a once-a-week proposition. He not only asked God to help him when he wanted it, he saw to it that day by day his "inner man was properly nourished and happy."

That is what we have to do. Each day, we must seek to have our "inner selves" happy in the Lord so that the work that we do is done right.

- Jesus said: "Pray without ceasing."
- The psychologist says: "Always keep your thoughts positive."

Our minds are working constantly, so we must direct them constantly.

- *Reverse every wrong thought* that comes into your mind
- *Substitute good thoughts* for those that are harmful
- *God is your Partner* so consider Him in all that you do

"Have Faith" we are told. What is faith?—right thinking. If you are thinking right about your company, you have faith in the company for which you work. If you have faith in yourself, then you are thinking right about yourself. If you have faith in your automobile, then you are thinking right about God. If you have faith in God, then you are thinking right about God. If you are thinking right about your prayers, then you have faith that your prayers will be answered.

Too many people have the bad habit of praying only when necessary instead of doing what Mueller did, praying everyday, especially to have his "inner man nourished day by day." One must build himself up in prayer. As a rule, one does not start working at the top, one starts at the bottom. Maybe a person starts at a job at $25 per week. So, it is a good idea to start praying for such things that you are sure of getting. For example, on your way home from work, pray that your wife or mother should have a very delicious supper waiting for you. You come home, and here is your favorite dish! Well, that prayer was answered. That gives you confidence. Then pray that you will see a very enjoyable picture that evening. You go to the show and you see a very pleasant picture. There is another prayer that was answered. More confidence ensues. Keep doing this way until you have confidence to ask for bigger things. Then you will have the faith (you will be thinking right) about the big things—and you will get them.

Lincoln said, "I will prepare myself and someday my time will come." It did. Do the same with your prayers. In fact, the records show that Lincoln prayed at a time when the North was losing the war. He was down on his hands and knees praying. He was there quite some time when all of a sudden he felt very still and quiet. He rose from his position. He knew that his prayer was being answered. Before long, news came that the tide had turned and the North was winning again.

You don't have to get down on your knees and pray; you can pray anywhere, anytime. You can pray for anything you want, the very fact that you want it shows that it is already there for you to have. Build yourself up in Your Prayer Power, just as you build yourself up for anything else. Expect it, when you ask God for something, He has it. He can give it to you. He would not be God if He was not big enough to give it to you.

I have found, from experience, that the best kind of prayer is to "ask for guidance." Every night when you go to sleep, ask God, or ask your subconscious mind, to tell you what to do. Then, you will know what to do. You will be told what to do. And—if you are constantly told what to do, you will have what you want, and you will be doing what you want to do. So many people make an investment and then start to pray that it will work out all right. But, if they had asked God what to do, if they had consulted their subconscious mind, they would not have had to pray for they would have known that it was right.

After a period of time, you will notice that you are being guided. You are being told what to do. Your Partner is constantly telling you what to do. If He tells you, then it must be right. You cannot go wrong. Consider the story of the father who was consistently missing his bus while the daughter was always just on time to catch it. The daughter was asking for divine assistance while the father continually complained. When you practice asking for guidance each night, you will begin to see divine intervention at work. Continue to keep this up.

This brings us to one of the most discussed and argumentative subjects in the field of psychology (and among most religions). It is frequently one of the most difficult matters to get straightened out in one's mind. The problem is: *how to harmonize our thinking about the material and the spiritual.* If we could get this straightened out once and for all, we could save ourselves so many inner conflicts. We could also save a lot of wear and tear on the nerves when we find ourselves in a discussion with others.

Food is material—we can see it, we can feel it, we can eat it. A minister in a small southern town decided that man could live on the spiritual things alone. So, he stopped eating. He went along nicely for thirty days, then he started getting weak and then he died.

Clothing is material—we can see it, we can feel it, we can wear it. If we try to go down the street without any clothing on, people will really think there is something wrong with us. In the colder climates of the world, if a man tries to get along without clothing, he will freeze to death. Material—yes —but we can't get along without it.

Housing is material—we can see it, we can touch it, we can own it. Prehistoric man lived in caves. Most of the people of Biblical days lived in tents. The present-day man lives in houses. Material—yes—but can we get along without them? One cannot live in the fields. One cannot live in tents in this present day. What is wrong in living in a house? In the colder climates of the world, if people were not properly sheltered, they would die. The same thing is true in the hot climates of the world. They must be able to shelter themselves from the constant rays of the sun.

Medicine is material. If it were not for medicine, the world would be in a sorry plight today. Millions upon millions of people owe their lives to medicine. No one will deny the value of penicillin and sulfa drugs in our present-day living. Everybody cannot make their minds work so well that they can get along without medicine. Someday, yes, but in the meantime, these people need help.

Money is material—we can see it, we can feel it, we can use it. This business of money has caused most of the arguments in the material—spiritual debate. Most of the churches tell us not to be interested in money. However, they take up a collection every service. If they don't take up a collection, then they have collection boxes, or dues, or even a 10% tithe—which is very good. Therefore, if money is material, and we can get along without it, why do churches want it? I am not against giving—I give my 10% and more when possible—but let us be consistent. Let us not preach one thing and live another. We need money, let's face it! Then why tell people you want it on the one hand and denounce it from the pulpit on the other?

We need churches where people can meet, gather, and have Sunday school for our youngsters. It takes money—even the good minister has to live and has to be paid.

In view of all this, why all the argument about the material and the spiritual? Of course, we all have made the mistake of paying too much attention to the material way of life. Almost anyone, with a little common sense, will admit that. Money is not evil any more than food is evil. We must have food to live; man has tried to live without it and has failed. We need money as a means of "exchange," that is how it came into being in the first place. The "love of money" is what causes the trouble. Also, if a person doesn't care what he does to obtain money, money itself is not to blame.

What is there that is evil in itself? Nothing? Think about it.

Money is not evil in itself. If we use it for evil purposes, then it is the use and not the money. Food is not evil in itself. If we use it to such an extent that we become sick, is the food to blame? Houses are not evil in themselves. If somebody takes a house and uses it for evil purposes, is the house to blame? Sex . . . is sex evil? If it were not for sex, the human race would have died out long ago. How, then, would children come into the world? Is sex to blame for people's misuse of it, for their making it filthy, for their making gluttons of themselves, and worse than this for failing to understand it properly?

To what conclusions can we rightfully come?

- God is our Partner
- God is spiritual—which means the highest form of thought
- Let us concentrate on the spiritual

By concentrating on the highest form of thought, the material needs of this world will take their place where they belong. The material things of life will serve the body with the basic needs of food, shelter, and clothing. Meanwhile, we must work day by day to keep our souls in a happy state by nourishing our inner self.

The great Psychologist said: "Store up your treasures in Heaven, where thieves cannot break in and moth and rust cannot destroy."

Lesson 17

How to Solve Your Problems

Dear Reader:
This lesson focuses on developing your intuition, your sixth sense, to help you with problem solving. Kohe reminds us that Infinite Intelligence is accessible through our subconscious minds. As we train ourselves to seek guidance through the subconscious mind, we sharpen our discernment skills as we progress. Full-blown intuition is not something that comes to us ready made, but rather becomes fine-tuned and enhanced over time. Hunches, feelings, and an ambivalent sense about something that is to take place, is not mature intuition.

Your intuitive skills can and should be developed. They help you in the decision-making process. They enable you to assess subconsciously things that you may not even consciously have tuned in to using your basic senses. There is a reason that you may have a foreboding or anticipation about an upcoming event. Something indirectly is causing these feelings. At bedtime, when you ask your subconscious mind to guide you as you go to sleep, you will find that decisions become struggle free, worry evaporates, and the results are more often positive than not. As you sharpen this skill, your percentage for success will escalate too.

Sometimes you have a strong urge to do something that may take you outside of your daily routine. If the thought persists, and if it is positive, do it. Take the day off, visit the bookstore, drop a card to a friend, contact a colleague whom you have not spoken with for awhile, and sit back and wait to see what the Universe has in store for you. Time and time again, the action taken will reap wonderful, unexpected rewards. That, dear reader, is what Napoleon Hill meant when he said that "Your ship won't come in unless you first send it out." Do not be afraid of intuition. Sharpen it and add it to your tool kit for success.

—JUDITH WILLIAMSON

All over the world people choose to believe
that if it isn't one thing, it's another.
–YOUR GREATEST POWER

Although you went through grammar school, high school, and even college, were you ever taught how to solve your problems? Arithmetic problems yes, but the problems of life—No! Why? We have not gotten around to it yet. Most people learn to solve their problems in the University of Hard Knocks. Yet, one mistake can ruin a person's entire life. One mistake can cost a person ten or fifteen years of fruitless living. One mistake can frequently so affect a person's life that one may never recover from it. You have seen it. I hope that you have been spared the awful cost that some people have to pay.

Here in this lesson you will be given a complete and thorough understanding of how to solve your problems. I feel sure that after reading it, you will say as thousands of people have said before you, "If I had only known it sooner." Keep in mind some of your own experiences and those of your friends and relatives, and you will see just why things happened as they did.

God loves us. We have found that out. He loves us so much that He has given us not only the power to choose, but He has given us a power whereby we may choose correctly and in such a way that it is almost impossible to make a mistake—the power of intuition. Through this power we are able to take every trick in the game of life. As we become familiar with this power of intuition, we can truly say this is our "Aladdin's Lamp."

In Lesson 16 you found that God is with you all the time and that God, being the Universal Mind, operates through your subconscious mind, which is the God within you. Therefore, the main reason we are here is to help God do some of the things He cannot do Himself. God can make trees but He cannot make chairs—man must do that. God can grow wool on the back of a sheep, but He cannot make clothes—man must do that.

Actually, man is "mind." Without a mind, man is nothing. God is Universal Mind; God works through us. Where the Good Book says "Thou shall love the Lord thy God with all thy heart and with all thy soul," we might say today, "You shall love your mind with all your heart and all your soul."

God is constantly telling us what to do. Of course, we can choose to do it or not. You and I have the last word. But,

He tells us. Universal Mind is expressing itself through our minds. He tells us through intuition. Therefore, we must be familiar with the way intuition works. When we know how it works, we are free from "worry," we cannot make any serious mistakes, we cannot fail, and, as a result, life becomes a glorious adventure.

Follow intuition. Every night before you go to sleep, ask your subconscious mind, the God within you, to tell you what to do the next day. It will. You will see yourself being guided. You will be amazed and astounded with some of the things that will happen to you. Many a miracle will occur in your life. The tension of living will be cut way down.

Previously, I related the story of a father and a daughter who were having a conversation. The father had said, "Every time I run for the bus, I just miss it." The daughter had replied, "That's strange, Daddy, every time I go for the bus, it's just coming." So, intuition is always on the job and always waiting to be recognized and used.

Before entering into any worthwhile proposition, give it the intuition test. If it tests out as a hunch, then leave it alone or you may be headed for a little trouble. If your proposition tests out to be intuition, go ahead, you can't lose. Any businessman will tell you that after a period of years, you learn what is right and what is wrong. In using intuition, you become adept at making the right decisions. In using intuition, you lose one of the greatest destroyers of mankind—hurry. We hurry into trouble, we try to hurry out of trouble, we hurry through the day, we hurry through the years, we hurry through life. With intuition, we live life through at a sensible, beautiful tempo. There is no hurry.

Stop to think about it. Your heart doesn't beat a hundred miles an hour one minute and ten miles an hour the next, it goes steadily along. So, life should go steadily along. God is in no hurry. According to religionists, the world is several thousand years old and according to scientists, the world is seven million years old. Whether the world is thousands or millions of years old is not important, the important part is that "God is in no hurry." So let us live as we go. Why hurry into trouble? Why hurry into difficulty? Take your time. Work out your problems through intuition and *then* you are on the right track. As you have learned in an earlier lesson, you will never be satisfied anyway, so why the hurry?

Mainly, use intuition to solve the biggest problems of life so that you don't make any too-costly mistakes. Then, apply intuition in the smaller things of life. For example, if you go into a restaurant and you can't make up your mind as to what to eat, ask your subconscious mind. How do you feel? It will help you with the little things, as well as the big things.

Remember always that you will make the final choice.

After a while, following intuition will become a game instead of a chore. You will find life not only very interesting but you will find yourself actually playing the "game of life." Instead of life being something difficult to master, it will become a glorious experience that the future will bring to us as long as we remain positive.

Keep practicing intuition. You may not always be right, but keep working at it. It takes the hard work out of everything you do. Someone once said, "Work hard, but don't make it hard work." Don't make hard work out of life. You don't have to anymore, not with the knowledge that you have gained in these lessons. Through intuition, all the hard work is taken out of life. Follow intuition and live life like the lilies. See how beautiful they grow, yet Solomon in all his glory cannot compare.

Ask each night to be guided the next day.

There is something about truth that makes it easily recognizable by all who are searching for it with open minds.

—Napoleon Hill

Lesson 18

Solving the Mystery of "Why Are We Here?"

Dear Reader:

Sooner or later at some point in our life we all ask the same question, "Why am I here?" This question of existence did not originate with us nor will it end with us. Different religions have even prepared various pronouncements that answer this question for us. Still, deciding if the answer meets our own belief system is one decision each and every one of us must determine for ourselves. One approach to answering such a question, is to consider how noteworthy individuals responded in the past. Solomon is a well-respected individual from the Old Testament and Kohe believes that his findings merit repeating.

Solomon, considered to be one of the wisest men to have ever lived, determined that the answer to the question has six parts. His beliefs and experiences determined the direction of his life, and they can determine the direction yours takes too. Solomon believed that God is always a good God, that God loves you and me, and that all negativity is man made. God is our Great Companion as we *journey through life and everything works toward the good when we choose to align with God. This belief should be trusted and internalized, not questioned and debated. Cheerfulness is essential in our daily approach to life. Kindness should be extended to others. Dishonesty should be scorned, and talent should be developed.*

In defining a definite major purpose, Napoleon Hill states that any purpose that you desire to achieve, backed by faith, and not violating the rights of another human being, is a good one to pursue. Satisfaction is in the doing and in the journey, not solely in the accomplishment. That, dear reader, encompasses the wisdom of Solomon and the homespun philosophy of Dr. Hill. You are given great leeway in pursuing your life's dream. Begin it. You can't lose with God as your Great Companion.

—Judith Williamson

If each of us will start to choose to improve himself, we can change our own little worlds, the little world that each and every one of us lives in. That's the most important one for us. That is the one we can do something about.

–YOUR GREATEST POWER

Ever since man has walked the face of the earth, he has asked the question, "What are we here for?" Many times this problem becomes so perplexing for some people that they do not know which way to turn. Many have changed religions, thinking that they would find the answer in the next religion. Some have even changed their religion more than once hoping to find the answer. Too many people, after searching for a while, throw up their hands and give up in disgust, coming to the conclusion that life is a matter of accumulation. "How much can I accumulate?"—that is the final answer for too many men and women.

From time to time a speaker or lecturer will attempt to answer this question from the platform. One experience I had along this line was as follows: One speaker said, "We are here to have pleasure" and went on to explain that that is why we like to eat, drink, and take vacations. He went on to say that that is the main reason people hate to die—they hate to leave the pleasures of life behind.

Another speaker said, "We are here to work and to have faith" and went on to show that man is a "working animal," that he is happier when he has something to do, that without work he would be lost, that faith is necessary because without it life would be too difficult.

Then another speaker said, "We are here to be friendly and to find the work in which we can be happy" and went on to explain that because man spends so much of his time working, he should at least be engaged in work which would make him happy. He also stressed the fact that inasmuch as we are going through life only once, we should be friendly as we go along. He contended that if we were happy in our work and we were friendly, that would pretty much take care of our purpose on this earth.

Strangely enough, a man who lived several thousand years ago asked the very same question, "What are we here for?" This man was none other than the wise King Solomon. However, he was more fortunate than most of us. He had the wherewithal to try out his ideas. He, too, thought at first that we were here just to have pleasure and so he put on some parties that lasted for months at a time. He imported the richest and the sweetest of wines, the tastiest and finest of foods, the most alluring and attractive women that could be found. After a few months of nothing but wine, women, and song, Solomon came to the conclusion that this was not it. Becoming tired of having nothing but pleasure, he turned into other directions.

Solomon decided that if we are not here just to have pleasure, we must be here to work. So, he began to work. He started to build roads, buildings, and warehouses—he worked and worked and worked. It took him a long time to find out what you and I have found out, that "All work and no play makes Jack a dull boy."

"Well," Solomon said, "if we are not here to have pleasure, and we are not here to work, then we are here to study. There is so much that one must learn. There are so many things that we do not know and with which we are not familiar that we must spend all of our time in study." So, he began to study and study and study. He finally found the answer. It is in your Good Book—I will give it to you here—I call it the "Philosophy of Solomon." There are many wonderful philosophies of life, but I feel that this is the most complete:

1. To feel and know that there is a Great Companion back of the Universe working with you, loving you, and trying with all His might to prosper every righteous enterprise, and to aid every righteous effort; to know that He never dies and that you, being a part of Him, will never die either
2. To go cheerfully, trustingly through life
3. Doing what simple kindness you can to those about you

4. Building a worthy success
5. Scorning dishonest advantage
6. Having time always to be friendly and kind

I recommend you *learn this philosophy by heart* because many times in the years to come, you will ask yourself the question, "What are we here for?" You may forget this during the busy moments of the day and it may slip your mind. You may become so disturbed at times that you may entirely overlook the fact that you did have a healthy philosophy of life at one time. Then, too, if you have gone the greater part of your life without some kind of philosophy of life, it is easy to slip back into the "old ways."

Now, let me discuss each part of this great philosophy:

POINT 1: "PARTNER WITH THE GREAT COMPANION"

Solomon starts out by saying: "To feel and know that there is a great Companion back of the Universe working with you, loving you, and trying with all His might to prosper every righteous enterprise, and to aid every righteous effort."

He calls God a "Great Companion." From Lesson 16, you found out that this is so, that God is always with you. What better name can you think for God than a "Great Companion?" Really, God is not someone you should be afraid of or hide from, rather He is someone with whom to live and work, a "Pal" to take with you wherever you go. Can one think of anything more wonderful than that? God is so great that He can be with you and still be with me and with billions and billions of other people. He can listen to your prayers and my prayers and those of others, regardless of what their language may be.

So many people make the mistake of believing that when they know something, "they are all set." It isn't enough to know something, "you must also feel it. Then you have it." You know things with your conscious mind; but when you feel it, you know it in your subconscious mind. As we learned in Lesson 7, "Power of the Imagination," a thought doesn't mean anything until it becomes creative.

Solomon says that God is working with you. You know that now. He keeps your heart beating, your blood circulating, tells you what to do, answers your problems, works with you all the time. Now, a very important part—God loves you! You learned that in the book *Your Greatest Power*. You can't tell yourself that too often, that God loves you. Where people got the idea that God hates people is really surprising. Certainly Jesus said that "God is Love." In the Old Testament, Solomon also said that "God loves you"; so from where did the "hate of God" come? The answer simply lies in man's foolish choosing. Man simply believed that God hated him; and through his harmful choice of thought, made billions upon billions of people unhappy. Let us not continue this mistake.

Solomon also said that the Great Companion is helping us with every righteous enterprise and doing so with all His might. That is why the "righteous" always win out—because the Great Companion is constantly improving the world. Whether we realize it or not, the world is better today than it was several thousand years ago. Man is more educated, more knowledgeable about how nature works, able to better understand his fellowmen. Machinery has enabled man to have a better way of life. Now that man realizes that he is part of the Great Companion, he is working with God to make this world a better place in which to live.

Every once in a while, however, something happens to make man lose his faith and trust in God. Some years ago it was Haley's Comet that was going to destroy the earth, sometime later it looked like it was Hitler who would succeed, now we have the atom bomb. Millions of people in the world have sleepless nights worrying about the possible destruction of the world through the atom bomb. Let us never forget that the Great Companion who runs this world will not destroy it. God loves us—would He destroy us? God needs us—would He destroy the world? If you would only remember that the Great Companion is constantly working with us and for us, you would be a confirmed *optimist*. Go back over your history for the past few thousand years and you will readily see that the world is getting better, although we do slip once in a while.

Now, as to the very important question of death, most people worry about what is going to happen after life is over. Too many people go to pieces when their beloved ones pass on—of course, it isn't easy. So far, no one has ever come back from the beyond. Whatever we have been told up to now is purely speculation. No one really knows! We don't know either what is going on on the other side; but one thing we do know, as Solomon said, "To know that He (God) never dies and that you being a part of Him will never die either." Therefore, God is with you now and will be with you on the other side (whatever it is), so why do we have to be afraid of death? In other words, if God is in New York, He is also in Los Angeles. If God is with your beloved one now on this earth, He will certainly be with your beloved one on the next earth. So, let us not be so afraid of death. When a beloved one passes on, let us not say he died but that he went with the Great Companion into the next life. Please remember this.

Most people do not have a "Psychology of Death," and this is very important otherwise it may hit us too hard mentally. Then, too, those who do not understand what we do will frequently make our life miserable because we don't go around with a long face the way they expect us to do. When you choose correctly, and you understand who you are, you don't have to be ashamed of your conduct, nor do you have to go around explaining to everybody just how you feel.

POINT 2: "TO GO CHEERFULLY, TRUSTINGLY THROUGH LIFE"

Solomon did not say to go cheerfully through life on pay day, or on Saturday night, or whenever everything was going along nicely. He said "through life" which means all the time. In my book *Your Greatest Power*, you learned that you can choose to be happy all the time, if you want to so choose. Solomon said the same thing. He did not say to go through life trustingly only when your pockets are full of money, but all the time. Jesus said the same thing in another way—"The Lord will provide." The more you study, the more you will find out that all great thinkers thought very much alike, with different words and different ideas, but basically the same (that is why if one reads a great deal of Psychology and Philosophy one seems to be reading the same things more than once). My experience has been that each writer says it just a little differently. If the full meaning was not grasped with one writer, the next writer might make it a little clearer and simpler to understand. However, you have the final "say-so." Will you choose to go through life cheerfully and trustingly? You will, if you apply the lessons I've been teaching you. You won't if you choose to live without directing your thoughts for the best results.

POINT 3: "DOING WHAT SIMPLE KINDNESS YOU CAN TO THOSE ABOUT YOU"

How very important this is. It was Elbert Hubbard, author of *A Message to Garcia*, who said, "What we need in this world is not more religion, what we need is more kindness." If you are kind, who cares what your religion is? If you are unkind, then can you excuse it by saying you are religious? Solomon's point does not mean you should make a fool of yourself.

Too many parents are being so good to their children that they cause these children to grow up spoiled and irresponsible. We must realize, and many of us must learn, that "when you are too good, you are no good." Therefore, let us be kind, but not to the degree that we spoil the very things we wish to preserve.

Along this line, a very powerful story is told of a little boy who was watching a butterfly work its way out of the cocoon of the caterpillar. The butterfly struggled and fought to work its way out; and when it did, it flew away. The little boy vowed that the next time he saw this happen, he would help the little butterfly. It was not long before he saw another butterfly working its way out of a cocoon. He was very careful not to hurt the beautiful butterfly. He did everything he could to help the struggling butterfly, and finally it was free—but it could not fly!

We must be careful not to do so much for those around us that in so doing, we make them weak instead of strong. We must not take all the struggle out of the lives of our children or they will not be able to "fly" through life. Let us give them understanding so they will be strong. Doing everything for them is not the answer. We must help them, of course, but we must mainly help them to help themselves. Take the author of *Acres of Diamonds*, Russell H. Conwell, as an example. He helped young men to help themselves through college. This is the important feature.

POINT 4: "BUILDING A WORTHY SUCCESS"

Solomon was not so foolish as to eliminate the element of success. What is success? I contend that the most successful person in the world is the happiest person. After one has money and power, what does one want next?—happiness. Isn't this true? If one is happy, one is successful. Everybody can be happy; therefore, everybody can be successful. Happy people do not hurt anybody. Happy people are not envious or jealous. They don't have to be.

Another success attitude I might propose is this: to work together with the Father within. If one cooperates with the Great Companion, one must succeed in whatever one undertakes—one cannot fail. Regardless of what one's personal attitude toward success may be, one will find that these two that I have proposed will certainly fit into one's program of success.

POINT 5: "SCORNING DISHONEST ADVANTAGE"

I feel that this is more or less self-explanatory. One knows when one is dishonest. One knows when one is doing something one shouldn't. One can judge quite well whether or not one has been honest in one's contact with others. Keep being careful about this for it is important to your own welfare. To be honest is one of the great laws of life.

POINT 6: "HAVING TIME ALWAYS TO BE FRIENDLY AND KIND"

This is very difficult at times to put to practice, but it can be done. Always having time to be friendly and kind, means just what it says—always—not just when you feel like it but even when you don't feel like it. This is what makes it so hard. Our old prejudices keep coming up. These old thoughts keep pecking away at us; and unless we are constantly on guard, from time to time we will violate this principle. Sometimes we are unkind in the most unusual way.

Most of us are poor receivers. It is true that the Good Book says, "Tis better to give than to receive." It is important to be good receivers as well as good givers. How many times when we are given something, we say "Oh, you shouldn't have done it." How unkind!—when someone goes out of his way to think of you, buy something for you. Instead of being gracious and say "Oh, you are so sweet and so thoughtful," we say "You shouldn't have done it." How many wives, when given a gift by their husband, will immediately become suspicious, or even go so far as to criticize the gift, causing the husband to feel he has committed a crime in being nice. Is it any wonder that after a few years of married life the husband stops buying gifts and forgetting all about anniversaries and birthdays!

In doing favors for people, it is important to learn to be gracious and to be kind to those who wish to be nice to us.

Remember that you are not the only one who likes to do favors, other people want to do favors as well. Let them. They enjoy doing things for others. It is very important that you learn to be a good receiver. Remember also that if we can't help one another, what good are we? God is in you, and in me, and in the other fellow. When you are good to the other fellow, you are good to yourself. When you let the other fellow be good to you, it becomes an endless chain of well-wishing.

Too many "would-be wonderful people" have been stopped by some bad receiver. Before long these people, who were so willing to help, decide that it isn't worthwhile and are willing to let well enough alone. Too often, we hear people say, "Why is he being so nice?" or "What's he getting out of it?" Let us not be suspicious of the good people who want to help us. Wherever possible, attempt to recognize the true well-wisher from the make-believe type. Let us not destroy those good people who want to be good to others. Let us be good receivers, as well as good doers.

Memorize the philosophy of Solomon.

> *If you are truly at peace with yourself, you'll never be at war with others.*
>
> —Napoleon Hill

Lesson 19

How to Become a Mental Millionaire

Dear Reader:

I am deferring to J. Martin Kohe with the inclusion of this lesson. As a psychologist, he is qualified to make the observations and conclusions that he has made regarding the significance of understanding sex in the process of becoming a Mental Millionaire. In reading his findings, I concur with his observations and also agree that a timely explanation regarding the stages of sexual development need to be introduced at appropriate times in a person's life.

You have probably heard the statement that we as spiritual beings have a physical experience. In this physical manifestation, certain aspects of our growth and development are predetermined by the human experience. We are born, mature, grow old, and then cease to exist. This, ultimately, is the process for all living things. Part of this process is sex and the better we understand it the better we can cope with it and adjust for its impact in our lives. If you would rather not follow Kohe's teachings on this subject, that is your prerogative. However, I do suggest that you become educated in this area so that you can understand the impact that it will have in your life. Simply denying sex as a component of the human experience is not accurate thinking. Think accurately, arm yourself with the facts, and then use these facts to strengthen your status as you reach to become a Mental Millionaire.

Kohe says that there are five areas we must understand and address during our journey to Mental Millionaire status: you, others, God, money, and sex. That, dear reader, allows me to remind you again that we are spiritual beings having a physical experience. Learn to see both sides of your reality so that you can understand more fully why we are here and how we operate.

—Judith Williamson

If these people involved would use this greatest power given to man . . . the power to choose . . . we would find ourselves in an altogether different style of living.
–YOUR GREATEST POWER

You have now come a long way in your development of becoming a mental millionaire. You have almost all the necessary steps to accomplish this. I contend, after a quarter of a century of working with thousands of people, that there are five steps necessary to becoming a mental millionaire. Four of these steps I have already covered, leaving one remaining. Depending upon your age, this fifth step may not be important because you have simply charged it off to experience. Some of you have been very fortunate for you have gained an understanding which has prevented any difficulty from arising in this direction. But, there are a large number of you who are still confused with this fifth step. For those of you who are parents, or who are in a position to advise those in need of proper guidance, I feel that this lesson is very important. It can be used either for ourselves or in helping others. In any event, whatever the case, make the most of it and "choose" to use it sensibly. Here are the five steps in becoming a mental millionaire:

1. YOU—understanding yourself
2. OTHERS—understanding others
3. GOD—having a working understanding of God
4. MONEY—understanding money, how to gain it and keep it
5. SEX—understanding sex

The fifth step I feel is so important because we must face it with our children, in marriage with ourselves, and in properly advising others.

Let me tell you a story about a minister named Oliver Butterfield. Oliver one day came to the rude awakening that most of the people whom he had married were already either divorced or getting along miserably in their married lives. He couldn't understand it. He finally decided to find out what was the trouble. He began to ask questions commencing with the next couple who came to him to be married. He asked the young lady what she knew about sex in marriage and she answered that being a woman, she knew very little. He then posed the same question to the young man who also admitted knowing very little. With such a finding, Oliver decided to explain to both the young man and the young lady what they should know. The result was a "happy" marriage. He continued to do that with every couple that came to him; consequently, every couple that he married was "happily married."

Oliver was so delighted with his findings that he gave up the ministry and devoted all of his time to sex education. He wrote one of the finest books on the subject entitled *Sex in Marriage*. In this book he explains just about everything a young couple should know when entering into wedlock.

I was so impressed with Oliver's findings that I, too, began to tell young couples who were about to be married what was necessary for them to know to be happily married. The end result is that every couple I talked to before their marriage is getting along beautifully. To those with whom I was unable to talk, I saw to it that they had a copy of this wonderful book, also achieving similar results.

So, it is clear to see why I feel this subject is so important. "Knowledge is power." You have heard that before. If we have the power of understanding the Sex Laws, we then have made the choice to obtain this knowledge and save ourselves the trouble of divorce, separation, and unhappy marriages. If our married lives are unhappy, our children look upon marriage with the same conclusion. They, too, marry and find difficulty in marriage and explain it away by saying, "Well, my parents had the same trouble, I suppose that is the way marriage is." A poor choice, to be sure; but how were they to understand otherwise?

I have talked to so many young people on this subject. I have found so much misery that has been caused by this subject. I have found that "proper understanding" can eliminate almost all of these difficulties. However, most people have no place to which to go to get this information. Too many people were brought up with the wrong ideas about sex. Others think that there is "nothing to it." So, one picks up the papers and finds statistics showing that there are almost as many divorces as there are marriages. What an awful disgrace!—especially when one sees the young couple before marriage being so in love with each other. One wonders why? It is indeed a pity.

Educators thus decided to do something about this situation. They started to teach sex in various ways. In many high schools throughout the country they taught sex completely—from the beginning to, and including, sex in marriage. The result was that many illegitimate children were born to high school students who had taken these classes. Consequently, sex education in the high schools was stopped—this rightfully so.

The law is: sex should be taught according to the age of the individual. Sex is not a one-lesson course; it is a constant education.

FIRST STAGE: CHILD

The little child must have a sex vocabulary so that the parent can speak freely with the youngster without embarrassment. Teach the child the proper names for the sex organs. Having a sex vocabulary, the parent can answer most questions easily.

SECOND STAGE: ADOLESCENCE

The little girl is now becoming a young lady. The parent must explain menstruation and how it works so that the young lady has no trouble with nature's functioning (more about this later). The young boy is now becoming a young man. The parent must explain the demands that nature makes upon him. If possible, do the explaining before rather than after he enters this stage.

THIRD STAGE: COURTSHIP
Here we must explain to the young lady and the young man that sex relations are the privileges of marriage, that they will be married many years, that they may have the pleasures of the sex life all during their married life. Why spoil it now? There are so many other ways for a young couple to enjoy themselves during courtship.

FOURTH STAGE: MARRIAGE
Here Butterfield's book will give the married couple the necessary information.

FIFTH STAGE: MENOPAUSE
Here the woman enters the age in which she no longer will menstruate, which means she can no longer have children (more about this later).

We can readily see that it is impossible to teach sex all at one time. There would be too much confusion and too many people would be misled. It is due to this misleading that little or no sex education has been brought into the lives of those who need it. However, if we understand that sex education is to be given in different stages, then the problem eases itself and we make ourselves ready for the next stage of new information. Furthermore, when we realize that we must enter these different stages, and prepare for them, we won't be shocked by them, we won't be caught unawares, we won't suffer from them; instead, we will come through each stage with success.

We choose, thereby, to make even our sex lives a happy experience instead of a miserable one.

The Law of Nature is "to grow." Nature, therefore, wants man to grow. When a man stands still, or stops growing—as we have learned in a previous lesson—he is dissatisfied and starts to move backwards. Consequently, woman has been made attractive to man and man has been made attractive to woman. Man marries woman and has children.

Nature goes on century after century because man continues to bring new life into the world. Due to this attraction between man and woman, the sex factor has become an important part of almost everyone's life. Some people fight it. As you have learned before, you can't fight anything, you have to understand it. Fighting sex doesn't help. It has been forbidden, cursed, and outlawed, and yet, man and woman find a way—because nature is stronger than man. So, remember: we can't fight it, we have to understand it.

We must understand that woman has been chosen to help God with his Creation. Woman bears the child—the child is formed in her womb. When the child is in the womb, the child must be fed. How is it fed? It is fed through "pure blood." When there is no child in the womb, the blood must be eliminated. How is the blood eliminated? The blood is eliminated through what is known as the "menstrual flow." We realize now that the blood that is eliminated is pure blood, not bad blood as so many people think. (Mothers, don't tell your daughter who is about to menstruate that this is bad blood, tell her that this is pure blood which ordinarily would be used to feed the child during pregnancy. Furthermore, please don't tell your daughter that she will be sick every month. If you do, she will be sick every month. Rather, tell her that she will "be busy" every month, that it is a natural and normal function and will not trouble her in any way. If this is explained properly, you can save your daughter untold difficulty, and trouble.)

Because the body of the female is so constructed as to be able to have children, and because nature has endowed the woman with the privilege of bearing children, a certain physiological change goes on in the woman's body that not very many people understand. Very few women understand it, and even fewer men understand it.

Here is a sample "sex calendar" of woman. It may vary in different cases, to be sure. It may not work exactly as we will show you, but it will work approximately close enough to make it very helpful and practical:

1 2 3 4 5 6 7 8 9 10 11 12 13 14 15 16 17 18 19 20 21 22 23 24 25 26 27 28

| 1 | 2 | 3 | 4 | 5 |

Section 1 represents the period of 3 or 4 days in which the woman has her menstrual flow (the pure blood that would be used to feed the child if there were a child in the womb).

Section 2 represents the several days (in the above case, 6) following the time of menstruation in which the woman finds herself rather passionate.

Section 3 represents the several days following the passionate period (in this case 8) in which the body of the woman is receptive.

Section 4 represents the several days (in the above case, 6) in which the body of the woman is now "cooled off."

Section 5 represents the few days before the menstrual flow begins again in which the woman finds herself in the "crabby period."

This tremendous physiological change which takes place is so little known among men and women that it is no wonder that the marriage state has become the "battlefield" state. In understanding the "sex calendar" of the female, let's see what happens: A woman is married. The first few months of marriage are so filled with love and companionship that things work along fairly well. Then things begin to settle down. The woman runs into her "crabby period" just before her menstruation is about to begin. She starts to argue with her husband. She may call him all kinds of names. She may even throw things at him. He is alarmed! He can't understand what happened. Then she menstruates. She now enters her period when she would like to be loved and to have some attention paid to her. But, her husband is still angry from the way she treated him just a few days earlier. He doesn't come near her. She says, "My husband doesn't understand me" (you have heard this before). Then the days go by, and by this time, he would like some attention, but now he finds her "cooled off." She pushes him away. She doesn't want his attention now. So he says, "I don't understand women." And—he is right! He doesn't understand women.

Now, we understand what is happening. Let us assume now that both the husband and the wife understand the "sex calendar." The wife finds herself in her "crabby period." She starts to argue with her husband. Her husband says, "Dear, I will not argue with you now, this is your crabby period. You can say anything you want, I'll understand." She then admits that this is her "crabby period," calms down, and realizes this to be the situation with no bad effects and without entering into any tongue lashing. Before long, as the woman understands herself, she will admit that she is in her "crabby period" and will learn to keep better watch over herself at this time. Then, she menstruates and approaches the passionate stage. The husband knows this now and he is ready to keep her happy at this time. Just as the young couple looks forward to being together on "Saturday night" during courtship, so the married couple can look forward to this "passionate period" of the woman each month. The honeymoon is never over—with understanding. Without understanding, it is only a matter of time before trouble starts. Almost every argument in the married life can be "patched up" during this "passionate period" of the "sex calendar."

Now that the couple understands, when the husband approaches his wife during her "cooling off" period, he will not let his imagination run away with him. He will not make such statements as "I suppose the insurance man is a better man than I am," and a lot of other not-so-complimentary remarks. He will understand that the reason his wife is not interested in "love making" at this time is due to her "cooling off" period. He will adjust himself to her, and that is what a husband should do. The wife has enough to occupy her, plus her adjustment period every few days, and then the "busy period" each month. If he will adjust himself to her, he will never regret it. He will be supremely happy, the honeymoon will never stop, and he will be most pleased with his marriage. And more than anything else, he will not be jealous for he will understand his wife's cycle. It's easy to understand now, isn't it? It's a pity on how few people understand this.

Mothers should explain the "sex calendar" to their daughters when they start to date young men, help them to understand themselves so that their friendships with these young men will not be lost during these "crabby periods," and teach them to learn to adjust themselves so they will not develop "sour" personalities. More important than anything else, the young lady must not allow any "special privileges" during her "passionate period" since at this time she may be so aroused that she could not control herself and the next thing you know is that she is permitting young men the privileges to which they are not entitled before marriage. Too many young women "go astray" during their "passionate periods." They must recognize what is going on in their bodies and control themselves accordingly.

Now I enter into the fifth stage of sex that is known as "menopause." This is the time in which the menstrual flow stops. This stage takes place at different times with different women. Most women, however, find theirs to stop between the ages of forty-five and fifty. Oh, how the imagination takes over in the case of most women! Most women fight the menopause for they are afraid that it is a sign of getting old. However, this is not true. You know from an early lesson that the body renews itself every seven years. Therefore, the body is actually only seven years old—at any time. Menopause does not mean "getting old," but rather means that one is no longer able to bear children.

Another reason that women are afraid is the belief that the pleasure of the sex act would be lost. Here again, it works just the opposite. She will find more enjoyment in it now because the worry of becoming pregnant is gone—now there is no blood to feed the child. Women who understand this lesson will now enjoy their sex more than ever before, and that one should not fight menopause rather they should let it come naturally. When one finds that the menstrual period is becoming irregular, one should tell the doctor so that he will help the patient through this period by perhaps prescribing some shots or pills. With the "right mental outlook," one will come through this without any real difficulty. These women you hear about who are having so much trouble do not understand what you now understand.

Do men have a "menopause?" I am of the opinion that men do not go through a menopause. Some authorities seem to think so, but I do not see how. This subject regarding men is so new that I will not be too positive at this time. However, I am of the opinion that what happens is this: A man is married. He doesn't understand the "sex calendar" of the woman. His wife enters into "menopause." At this time, it is very hard to live with her because her imaginations seem to run away with her. As a consequence, he is not able to come near her—"She is too mean, how can he?" He is not able to be aroused, is too fine a man to seek another woman, becomes discouraged in thinking that he has lost his "manhood," becomes moody, becomes disgusted—he too is going through a change, not sexual but purely psychological. If the woman understands her position during this period, she could prevent her husband from going through a similar psychological "menopause." Yes, you can't fight it, you have to understand it.

I have completed going over the five stages. One can easily understand why I have included the understanding of sex in the five steps to becoming a mental millionaire. It would be very easy for me to eliminate this "understanding sex" lesson entirely. However, I hope that you will agree with me that this step is very important towards making life worthwhile. If you are past the stage where this sex lesson means anything to you, surely it will come in handy in advising those close to you and those whom you feel would be so much better off with this understanding.

Remember that God loves us. He loves us so much that He put love into the hearts of every one of us. He loves us so much that He has given man and woman the privilege of helping Him in His creative work. The more love we have in our hearts, the more lovable children we will bring into the world. The more lovable children we bring into the world, the more lovable the entire world will become. Let us cooperate with our Great Companion.

Lesson 20

Power of Grace

Dear Reader:
This last lesson is as powerful as the very first lesson on imaging our dreams as vivid mental pictures. Seeing our dream fulfilled in our mind's eye is the best way to imprint it on our subconscious mind for progression toward fulfillment in real time. Then, letting it go and letting God by placing yourself "under Grace" is the very next step. After you have done all you can do to bring about your objective, are comfortable that you have given it your best shot, and know that doing anything else would simply be redundant, then—and only then—is the time to let go and let God.

This "letting go" attests to the power and glory that you give to Infinite Intelligence. God has been called the Great Teacher, and being a teacher I know that when a student puts forth their best effort, regardless of the outcome or grade, the teacher approves. So, too, it is with God. We do our best and leave the rest to Infinite Intelligence. That is all that is expected. God then aligns with us in our best interest and works toward the good that we both want.

This power of divine grace is inside each one of us. We can call it up and use it at will. It slows us down, eases our worry, reduces our self-blame, encourages us to keep on the path, and assists us in getting the job done even when we are too tired to pick up a pencil. By placing yourself and others "under grace" you are acknowledging the divinity within each and every living person. You are also calling up God to assist in achieving the best possible outcome for all concerned, including yourself. That, dear reader, is how the world is made a better place in which to live. You can perform your own miracles each and every day. Just apply what you have learned in this course daily; and as soon as you do, you can claim your status as a true Mental Millionaire.

—Judith Williamson

This greatest power . . . the power to choose . . .
will make life for him what he always wanted it to be;
not to depend upon something outside of himself,
but to depend on that great power within himself,
this god-given power which makes him a man.

–YOUR GREATEST POWER

I am now in the last lesson of this course on "How to Become a Mental Millionaire." This is not only the last lesson, but also I might say the most important. It is the most important because it is the easiest to apply and the most to be used. It applies to everything one does in life. This lesson will give us the "one big magic wand" to make our lives complete. It is the lesson that will eliminate worry and anxiety more than any one of the other lessons. It goes beyond the laws of life—it is the heavenly life—that which we all want and to which we are entitled.

Up to this point of our lessons, we realize that there is a Heaven that we reach after this life is over. We do not know much about it except that it will be nice, of course, and that we will accept it when it comes. We realize also that we can and do have a Heaven right here and now. If we choose to wait until life is over, then that is the way it will be; but, we can choose to believe that this life is Heaven too. Just as so many people have made a "Hell" for themselves here on earth, so we can make a "Heaven" for ourselves. Why wait? In becoming a "mental millionaire," we are making a Heaven for ourselves now. Let me prove to you that this Heaven—now—is true and possible.

Sometime ago I came across the following story: A young minister was having some very wonderful experiences. It seems that people who came near him seemed to have a strong feeling of peace; those who were ailing seemed to be cured "instantaneously." Reports were going around that this young minister had some strange power or that he was doing some of the same wonderful things that Jesus did when He walked the streets of the Holy Land. People of the community began to talk about it more and more. It wasn't long before the Bishop of the district heard about this and summoned the young minister for a report.

"What is this I have been hearing about you?" the Bishop inquired.

"It is nothing," said the young minister.

"There must be," insisted the Bishop. "What are you doing to these people? You must be using some strange power."

The young minister insisted that he was doing nothing wrong. The Bishop proceeded to compel him to tell of his experiences. The young minister said, "All that I have been doing is to keep telling myself, over and over, 'Thy will be done on earth as it is in Heaven.'"

Yes, in the Lord's Prayer it says "Thy will be done on earth as it is in Heaven," which is proof enough that the Creator wanted a Heaven on earth for His people now as well as later. Why have we missed it? There are many reasons, but suffice it to say that we have missed this "Heaven on earth" probably because when the scientific astronomers began to scour the skies with their great telescopes, they could not find God up in the skies, nor could they find what we refer to as "Heaven."

Similarly, I came across another very powerful story about three wise men who were discussing the question: "Where should we put God?" One wise man said, "Let us put God in the skies, man will never find Him there." The other two wise men responded, "No, man is sure to find Him there."

The second wise man spoke up and said, "Let us put God at the bottom of the ocean." The other two wise men responded, "No, man will surely find Him there."

The third wise spoke up and said, "Let us put God within man, he will never find Him there."

And so . . . for centuries man has failed to find the God within himself and has failed to recognize his Heaven on earth, as the Lord's Prayer states.

Jesus also said, "Unless you become little children, you shall not enter the Kingdom of Heaven." Most of us refuse to be like little children; we have to "grow up" and be very serious, long-faced, troubled adults. How often have we been told, "Don't be a child!" Maybe it is about time that we should be "as children," as Jesus said, so that we could have our Heaven now, and another one later, if that is to be.

Along this line, I would like to tell you a humorous story about a worker who was making a lot of money working in a war plant. This worker went to Mexico for a vacation. While there, he noticed an Indian sitting on a fence, whittling a piece of wood. The Indian was very strong and the war worker thought the Indian should be working. Approaching the Indian, he said, "Why don't you work?"

"What for?" the Indian responded.

"Then you will be able to save some of what you earn."

"What for?" the Indian continued to respond.

"Well, then later on you will be able to take it easy."

The Indian replied, "Ugh! me take it easy NOW."

Just a story . . . but how true! Most people don't want a Heaven now. They want to wait. They will take their Heaven later on, but why not *now*?

Take a look at the average person: He starts to work, works all of his life—until he retires—then if he isn't careful, he dies shortly after his retirement. When did he live? He never had time to live! He had plenty of time for trouble, for work, but never time to live. Work is good for us, man seems to be a working entity, but *let us live as we go*. Let us enjoy this life as we go. Let us have Heaven now. Then, although we work everyday, it will be so pleasant, everybody around us will be so pleasant, everyone with whom we deal will be so pleasant, our work will be such a pleasure. Result—Heaven will become a reality for all of us NOW. Surely, it will take time, but we can start, it will grow more and more until it becomes a living fact.

This Heavenly life seems to slip away from us at a time when we just about have it within our grasp. We have to keep working at it, keep reminding ourselves that Heaven is within our reach so that it doesn't get away from us. The one way that will help you to keep this Heaven now, more than any other way I know, is to use and understand the "power of grace."

Very few people understand the "power of grace." I will now acquaint you with it. Use it, and you will find it to be the greatest lesson you have ever learned. For example: when you have an insurance policy due on the first of March, and fail to pay it, do you lose your insurance? No, of course not, the insurance company gives you a thirty-day grace period in which to make your payment. When you buy something in a department store on credit, you are supposed to pay your bill on the first of the month following the purchase. If you fail to pay this bill, do you lose your credit? No, of course not, you are given an additional ten-days grace in which to pay.

If the insurance company gives you a grace period and the department store gives you a grace period, don't you think that God will give you a grace period? Of course, He will and does—if you will only ask for it! How do you ask for it? I will explain.

Most students build up a "worry" as to what will happen if they fail to follow their intuition. It can be a worry, but not after you understand the "power of grace." Suppose that you have a feeling, an intuitive feeling, to buy a certain piece of property but for some reason or other, you could not get yourself to go ahead with the deal. Now you began to worry. You start to wonder what was wrong with you, why you didn't buy the property, and before long, you have yourself in a "dither." Instead of filling your mind with all kinds of possibilities, you simply say, "I am under Grace." Now you lose your fear and you are no longer worried. *It is now back in God's hands.* You have actually asked God to give you another chance. It finally turns out that although you missed buying a good piece of property, another chance comes along and you find that "your Heaven has not been disturbed," everything is all right again.

The "power of grace" is like a great mental eraser. It erases the errors that we make due to foolishness or lack of confidence. As we become more familiar with the "grace power," we become more careful, we make fewer mistakes, we worry less, and we lose the "feeling of overconfidence" entirely. We know that: "I of myself am not smart, I am successful because of the God Power in me, and the grace power that God has given me."

Suppose you have a feeling, an intuitive feeling, not to take a certain automobile trip but your friends convince you to go. You go, reluctantly, and without "grace" you might worry all the time that you are on this trip. The trip is almost over and nothing contrary has happened. You then start to become overconfident because nothing has happened. You become careless. Forty miles from home, you run into another car and you damage your car. You say to yourself, "I knew I shouldn't have taken that trip!"

To state this another way: You have a feeling that you should not take this trip, but your friends insist. Say to yourself over and over again, "I am under grace." You are now taking God with you, you are no longer afraid, you do not become overconfident, you are careful all the time, and you are constantly reminding yourself that you are "under grace." Nothing happens, the trip will be enjoyable, and you are surprised. Yes, you will have many surprises as you use the "power of grace."

Everybody wants to change somebody. You certainly know certain people whom you would like to change. But, is it easy? Not always. With the use of the "power of grace," you will see many, many miracles. One of my resident students told me the following story: Her mother-in-law, whom she couldn't stand, was living with her. They argued constantly. Needless to say, the home was in constant turmoil. She thus began to put her mother-in-law "under grace," and the result was that her mother-in-law became as nice as she could be, no longer gave her any trouble, and stopped her arguing. She could hardly believe this was the same woman!

Sometime later, my student told me that her mother-in-law had moved in with one of her other children. Reading this, you wonder whether it is a true story or not—it is! I could tell you many, many more. Why did it work out this way? When you expect people to be mean and to argue with you, something always happens that will cause this. You misinterpret what they say and everything is exaggerated, causing difficulty and misunderstanding. However, when you put the other person "under grace," actually you are seeing the very best in that person; you are seeing the "God within" that person. The "God within" that person will not cause any trouble.

It takes months and years to develop the habit of seeing the "God within" other people. However, when someone is placed "under grace," it only takes a second before the results begin to show. Heaven now can be quickly realized since with the "power of grace" life moves along much more smoothly. This can be difficult to believe, especially when you see everyone else around you having one trouble or another, but it is true.

There are so many stories that I could tell you that I could actually fill a book with just this lesson. This specific one, I must tell you: A fifty-year-old woman found it necessary to work. Her boss was a mean one, and the worst part of it was that he liked to cuss and swear. She would beg him to stop and he would respond, "If you don't like it, go and get yourself another job." This would always put her in her place. Then she started to use the "power of grace." Every time she saw him or thought about him, she would put him "under grace." Result—in one week's time, he stopped swearing. She could hardly believe it! She was amazed and astounded!

One will, indeed, see many miracles as one puts the "power of grace" into practice.

As you learned in a previous lesson, you cannot keep two ideas of opposite nature in your mind at the same time. You cannot think of a person being mean and "under grace" at the same time. It will be either one or the other. If you think and see the other person "under grace," he must be pleasant because God always works, otherwise God would not be God. When you call on God, you must expect God to help you. When you use the "under grace," you don't question it, you just know it. The results are so quick and so certain. Remember, with God the impossible becomes possible.

You cannot worry and keep "under grace" at the same time. You cannot worry about someone and keep this person "under grace" at the same time. You cannot be concerned about certain happenings and keep these happenings "under grace" at the same time. Consequently, as you use the "power of grace," you will notice that you don't worry as much as before. You will be trusting God more and more. As you trust God, life becomes so much easier. You begin to feel more at ease with life. You begin to realize that now "you can have a Heaven right here and now."

Regarding children, I used to say, "When they are little, they are little trouble. When they are big, they are big trouble." This is 1900 psychology. Keep your children "under grace" when they are small, keep them "under grace" when they are big, and you will be amazed as to the small amount of trouble that they will give you. One woman who had two little "devils" in her home reported that when she started to put her children "under grace," she could hardly believe that they were her same youngsters. Parents of grown children have reported such miraculous results that if you didn't know these people and the "power of grace," you could hardly believe their stories.

Many, many of my resident school students went through the war without a scratch. They were in the service but came out beautifully. These men reported that they constantly kept themselves "under grace." One young man told of how he was in transit across the Atlantic Ocean, German planes were flying overhead, firing on the ships below, submarines were sending out their torpedoes, but nothing happened to him and the men around him. Hard to believe? Of course, it is. Always remember that "with God the impossible becomes possible."

The "power of grace" is the "miracle power" that God has given to his children (man). Parents of growing daughters always seem to be worried. Their daughter is out on a date. Should they stay up until all hours waiting for her to return? One can, if one wants, but one will find it easier to put the daughter "under grace" and go to sleep. If one can't trust one's daughter with God, what hope is there?

In a previous lesson, you came across the thought, "Cast your burden upon the Lord, and He will sustain you." This is the crux of living a Heavenly life. However, this takes time! It may even take a lifetime to learn to trust the Lord with everything that transpires in one's life. Using the "power of grace," one is actually doing the same thing and it is so much easier and with no doubt. Results are so quick and certain that it doesn't take long to trust this "power of grace." In the meantime, one is gaining a greater faith in God.

When you go on an automobile trip, put yourself "under grace." This means that you are asking God to go along with you and keep you safe. When you go up in an airplane, be sure to also put yourself "under grace"; now you know that God is with you and you need not be afraid. I know of people who refused to go up in an airplane until they learned about the "power of grace." Whenever you travel, put yourself "under grace," you will enjoy the trip so much more than you would otherwise. You may not believe this now, but when you put yourself "under grace," you will have very few bad days due to bad weather. This sounds preposterous, I know, but I also know that it works. You'll see.

May it never happen, but if you should ever have to undergo an operation, put yourself "under grace" and you will come through with flying colors. One time a great surgeon was found praying before an operation. Someone saw him and asked, "Doctor, do you mean that you pray before an operation?" The doctor replied, "Yes, it is very difficult at times to tell where the work of the surgeon ends and the work of

God begins." If any member of your family should also have to undergo an operation, put this person "under grace," and you will see wonderful things happen. During the whole ordeal, you will not worry about the results for you have now placed the results in God's hands.

Sometime ago, one of my resident students told me that her child was very sick. The doctors gave very little hope that her child would pull through. She, being a mother, said to God, "God, if you want her, then you take her; otherwise, I would like to have her live." Next day, the child was better and she recovered from her sickness.

There are hundreds of stories like this. *We must learn to let go.* Man gets the idea that he is so important and yet, he cannot keep his own heart beating. Man must realize that there is something bigger than he is to handle life. The more we trust this Great Something we call God, the more Heavenly Life we are able to live. Through the "power of grace," we are able to reach that station in life. As you may have come across this thought, "The Lord shall fight for you and you shall hold your peace," God helps us at every turn in life; and even when we don't listen, He gives us another chance through the "power of grace." God loves us so much that He not only gives us everything we want from a material point of view, but in giving us a Heavenly Life, He makes our lives truly complete.

If you have people working for you, put them "under grace." You will save yourself many hours of difficulty and anguish. If you are a salesman, put your customer "under grace," it will make selling so much easier for you. If you are in the field of entertainment and you find that you have to appear before small and large audiences, put yourself "under grace," put your audience "under grace." You will thus reduce your nervousness to the very smallest degree. You will find your performances going over more easily and better. You will avoid all the strain that goes with public speaking. It means—now—that you are not speaking alone, that God is speaking with you, that you are not singing alone, that God is singing with you.

When you are in a hurry, this is a time that you can test "under grace," without too much difficulty. One of my resident school students told me the following experience: One night after he had learned about the "power of grace," he had to go somewhere and was late. The very minute he sat at the wheel of the car, he started to say that he was "under grace." He kept repeating and repeating, "I am under grace." As a result, he never hit one red light, did not have a "stupid" driver pull out in front of him, did not have any streetcars interfere with his driving, and then upon reaching the place, he found a parking place without any trouble. Too good to be true? Try it, and you'll see. However, there is one thing for which you have to be careful.

Sometime ago I was going out of town by plane. I had to drive to the airport. Starting out, I started to say "under grace," "under grace," and kept hitting every red light. So, I stopped to think and asked, "What's the trouble?" I began to realize that the trouble was that I was saying "under grace" for a "purpose." In other words, I said to God I was going to say "under grace, if you will keep the lights from getting red and I get to the airport on time." The idea is this: when you ask God to help you, you must realize that God will help you for the very fact that you asked Him. If He didn't act, then God would not be God. Therefore, you must say, "under grace" and stop—don't put any conditions into it—"under grace" period. You told God what you wanted; then leave it up to Him. Don't make any propositions afterwards. Let go. You asked God and know He'll take care of it, there is no doubt about His doing it. Say the words "under grace," if you have to, in order to keep your mind from continuing to take control of the problem.

Through the "power of grace," you will come into the Heavenly Life. Things will run along smoothly for you, so smoothly that your friends will begin to wonder what has happened to you. They will see such a change come over you that they will think you are using some strange power—yes, you are using a power but not a "strange" power—"God power." You are using this "God power" in the finest way possible—through the "power of grace." Don't be a bit surprised if some of your friends tell you that you are getting younger looking. Why not? God is ageless, tireless, and endless. You, being a part of Him, can demonstrate some of these great characteristics.

Heavenly Life is yours. You have learned in these lessons how to do it. Keep everlastingly at it. Keep these lessons handy and go over them every day. Spend at least fifteen minutes a day with God—don't wait for Sunday. Money, ambition, success, all have their places, but to be a "mental millionaire," you must pay attention to your mind and keep God ever present in your mind. Result—a Heavenly Life! What more could one ask?

> The art of being grateful for the blessings you already possess is of itself the most profound form of worship, an incomparable gem of prayer.
> —Napoleon Hill

Appendix 1

Our Human Barometer or How To Control Your Thoughts

A Word with the Author

No doubt you have heard of the use of a barometer. A barometer is used for the purpose of indicating the atmospheric pressure and conditions. It has always been the belief of the writer that each human being should be able to either own or develop a barometer in order to indicate the condition or pressure of his everyday existence.

The writer has been very fortunate in finally developing a "Human Barometer" so that any individual with a little common sense and practical use may be able to tell exactly how his system is generating.

"Our Human Barometer," which is fully described in the following pages, will bring to you the use of one of the greatest discoveries in human existence. No doubt, you will find many of the experiences related similar to your own. Some of these experiences have baffled science and medicine for many years.

You will be convinced after reading "Our Human Barometer," and applying it, that you will be able to open your eyes to a greater and freer life. Many facts which have caused great harm and even human destruction may be eliminated through the experience of "Our Human Barometer."

It is the simple purpose of the writer to bring to those who desire the understanding which will free them from the very serious thoughts, which too frequently cause hours and years of difficulty and even self-destruction.

Would you like to have more life, pep and energy? Do you find that you tire easily? Would you like to go all winter without a cold? Have you ever had wild or crazy ideas run through your head? Have you ever thought that you were going out of your mind? Have you had trouble falling asleep at times? Have you awakened after a very fine night's rest and then found yourself to be extremely tired? Have you frequently found yourself to be so overjoyed that you wanted to jump around and slap people on the back? Have you at times found yourself unusually irritable for no reason at all? Have you ever had a feeling that you were going to have an accident or serious trouble? If you have ever had any of these experiences, you will find the reason for them in "Our Human Barometer."

Isn't it a fact that we overlook the simplest things in life, yet we find that it is the simple things that mean so much to us? Everyone, regardless of age or position in life, can take advantage of "Our Human Barometer." But, how many really will? Too many people will complain bitterly about their experiences and yet will refuse to listen to new ideas.

A story is told of how monkeys are caught in the wilds of Africa. Some of you may have seen the picture of Frank Buck in *Bring Them Back Alive*. In this picture, we are shown the way monkeys are caught through a trick used by the captor. We see Frank Buck taking a coconut, cutting a hole in one side of it and fastening it to a rope on the other side. The open side is just large enough for the little monkey to put his hand through. Inside of the coconut is placed some special rice for which these little monkeys go crazy. When the monkeys smell this rice, they are attracted to the coconut. They then slip their hands into the hole in order to retrieve it. Once they have a handful, they are unable to pull their hands out of the shell. If the monkey would let go of the rice, he would be able to get his hand out and would be free, but because he wants the rice so badly, he loses his freedom and is captured.

Isn't this what most of us do in life? We hang on to certain negative, serious, destructive thoughts and conditions that we could be easily rid of by simply accepting new and constructive ideas. All that is necessary is to let go of the old ideas and accept the new. Unfortunately, we fail to realize that by accepting new ideas and new discoveries in the field of "Psychology or Mind Training," we hold back the good things of life. People throughout the ages have prayed for certain things, and then they hold both of their hands so tightly fisted that good things cannot get into their hands even though these good things would readily come to them. Remember the story about the monkeys. The reason I am giving you the precaution is this: this lesson in "Our Human Barometer and How to

Use It" is so simple and so wondrous that a person—because of resistance to change—may deprive himself of the benefit that can be derived from using this method.

Before I enter into this subject, let me spend a few minutes on the importance of breathing. The importance of breathing cannot be overestimated. When a child is born, what we have is a little boy; and as soon as the body begins to take in air or oxygen, we have life. Likewise, when a person is in the state of dying, the last thing that he does is to stop breathing; and then the body without any air, has no life.

$$Body + Air = Life$$
$$Body - Air = No\ Life$$

With this clarity, you can readily understand the importance of deep breathing. Many people complain of tiring easily. For example, I will cite one of the cases at my local school: A young lady about twenty-five years of age complained bitterly of a constant tired feeling. In fact, she said that about three or four o'clock in the afternoon she would either have to lie down or go home from work.

Within two weeks after learning the importance of deep breathing, this girl reported back that she could work until seven or eight o'clock in the evening without feeling tired. In other words, breathing or oxygen is to the body what electricity is to the electric bulb. An electric bulb will not burn without electricity and so we get no light from the bulb. The body does not have the life that it should have when it does not take in sufficient oxygen. Let me compare the body with an automobile tire:

Tire − Air = Flat
Body − Air = Tired or Flat

So, we find the simple principle of breathing deeply will eliminate practically all tired feelings. This may sound too good to be true, but after using this suggestion for a period of time, you will agree with me.

So many people are what is known as "mouth breathers," and others are found to breathe somewhat deeper as you will note in the chart on the following page. These are known as "No. 2 breathers," or just a little deeper than the "mouth breathers." Still, others are known as "chest breathers." Then, we have some who will breathe a little deeper but the proper breath should reach the abdomen. This is designated on the chart as "No. 5 breather." In this way, one is able to reach the "solar plexus" and give more life to the body. The "solar plexus" is at the seat of the nervous center and when we exercise it through deep breathing, it tends to give us more life, more pep and energy.

You will never see a nervous person who is a deep breather. The nerves in the nervous system live on oxygen. When the nerves do not get sufficient oxygen in the system, there is a tendency for the person to display a certain degree of nervousness. As a rule, whenever you see a nervous person, you find that he is also a shallow breather. It is almost impossible for a person to be nervous and be a deep breather at the same time. Frequently, worry, trouble, difficulties, hardships will also affect the system and the intake of oxygen will automatically be reduced, even though the individual affected will not be conscious of it. The reduction in the amount of oxygen intake, quite naturally results in nervousness.

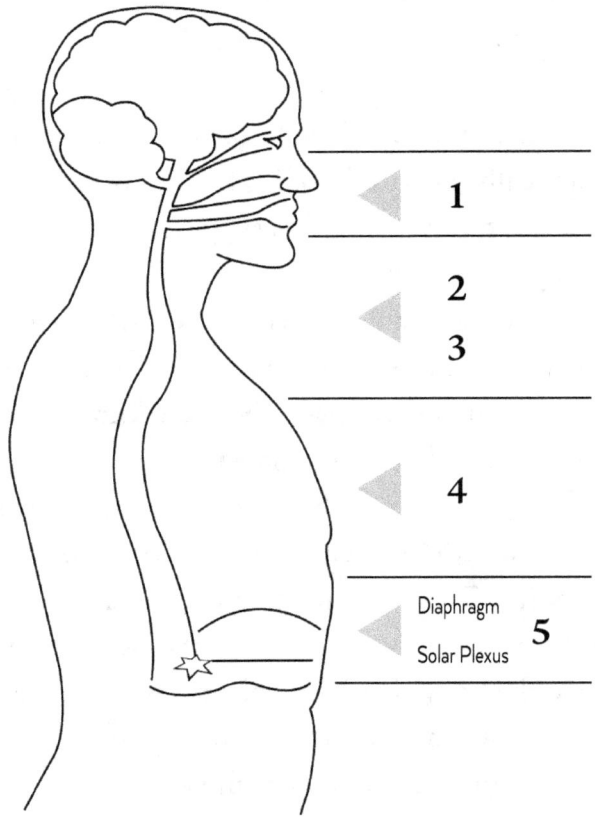

The proper way to breathe is slowly, through the nose, inhaling until one reaches the solar plexus or the abdomen and then exhaling slowly through the mouth. This should be done very slowly, as rapid breathing is not very effective. Then, too, in the winter the rapid breathing is liable to cause an uncomfortable sensation in the nostrils because of extreme cold air suddenly being rushed into the system. If one breathes slowly in the wintertime, he will have a chance to warm the oxygen before it goes into the system. When one is speaking or if one is interested in public speaking, it will be necessary for him to breathe through the mouth. This method of breathing is better than not breathing at all. Other times the oxygen should be inhaled through the nose and exhaled through the mouth.

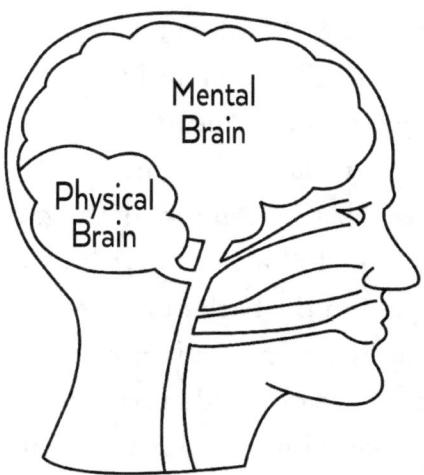

Haven't you often heard a woman say that she feels much better after a good cry? Psychologically speaking, the reason is more definite. As you will notice in the first chart, we have two brains—the mental brain and the physical brain. The reason a woman feels better after a good cry is that she unconsciously begins to breathe deeply and this flow of oxygen mixes with the blood and goes into the brain, causing a relaxed feeling. Any time you feel discouraged or blue, it makes no difference what the reason may be, you can always eliminate this discouragement through a good session of deep breathing.

I have found from experience that the reason so few people breathe deeply is due to the fact that they become dizzy as a result of it. If you are not a habitual deep breather, be careful that you do not create a feeling of dizziness in your system. If you find that after taking two or three deep breaths you become dizzy, *better stop and then later in the day or the next day, start again.* After a period of a few weeks, you will find that you can breathe just as deeply as you want, without causing any serious effect. Then, once you build the habit of breathing deeply, you will find yourself full of energy, full of life and pep, and you will seldom feel tired.

An interesting case that came to my attention several years ago was that of a young lady who came into my school to take one of my courses. Without any knowledge on my part, the young lady related the following story: "For years I have been troubled with a pain in the back of my head. For four years, I had taken medical treatments and tried to get rid of this pain. The last doctor that I visited told me that it was of no use, that pills and medicine could not help me. He told me to save my money and forget about it. I was under the impression that I would have to go through life with this pain in the back of my head. I enrolled in your resident school in order to gain self-confidence and then you gave your lecture on the value of proper breathing. Within one week after using your method, I found that the pain in the back of my head had started to leave and within two weeks after that, the pain was completely gone." The reason is obvious and apparent to a person who understands the value of deep breathing.

The physical brain, as indicated on the chart, is located in the back of the head. When a person is a shallow breather or a "No. 1 Breather," he does not get sufficient blood into the brain and so a heavy feeling may result. When this same individual begins to breathe deeply and a fresh supply of blood is being constantly sent into the brain, then the heaviness disappears as though by magic. So, if you at any time have a heavy feeling in the back of your head, you can easily rid yourself of it though breathing deeply. The young lady I spoke about in the preceding paragraph, spent a lot of money trying to overcome this difficulty; and yet with this simple process of breathing, as provided by nature, she was able to gain freedom from this apparent affliction.

With the "psychology of deep breathing," we also find an apparently new feeling of courage. In my vast experience of dealing with salesmen, I have found the following to be true of the average salesman: When first starting out and being new in the selling field, he would walk up to a door or a store and then walk away, afraid to go in because he was lacking the courage to meet his new prospect. So, many salesmen who have adopted the habit of deep breathing have found new courage in themselves. By breathing deeply before approaching the prospect, they found they could enter into the customer's area without any hesitation. Whenever you have to face someone whom you are afraid of, take several deep breaths before seeing this individual and the deep breathing will give you a greater courage to meet your prospect. Whenever you hesitate seeing a person due to fear, remember that a number of deep breaths will develop enough courage so as to eliminate this particular state of mind.

When climbing the steps, reverse the normal method of breathing. Instead of breathing deeply, or as we say inwardly, exhale as you go up the steps. Do this—you'll see just what I mean—keep breathing outwardly. It is much like blowing out a lighted candle. Keep blowing outwardly as you go up the steps or climb a hill. This may seem strange, but it works! Even people with heart trouble have found that they can climb steps when they use this exhaling, or "blowing out," method.

Now let me enter into the working of "Our Human Barometer" which may appear at first to be a little strange to you. After you have learned to use it, it will become a part of your everyday life and will be a God-send to you. One young lady, upon hearing about "Our Human Barometer," exclaimed, "I thought that the writer was rather silly, and even absurd and ridiculous. Yet, after using the following method for a period of only one week, I found that everything the writer said was true." So, with you as well, I ask your indulgence for a short time until you are able to put into practice the simple and yet truly marvelous principle of breathing.

We have, as everyone knows, two nostrils—the left nostril and the right nostril. The left nostril is known as the negative nostril and the right nostril is known as the positive nostril. We know that the earth is constantly moving and as the position of the earth and the sun change, atmospheric conditions change. These atmospheric conditions not only change the weather and conditions of the air, but even change our mental status and the functioning of our mind. When these atmospheric conditions take place, unbeknown to us, it affects the flow of the left or the right nostril. Most people go through life without ever recognizing the operation of this very important function. In fact, if people would understand the operation of this "Human Barometer," many ailments could be eliminated and serious fears could be eradicated.

Unbeknown to the average individual, there is a decided and distinctive change going on in the body. Without the knowledge of the "Human Barometer," one is unable to understand this situation. One may be extremely happy one minute and for no reason at all, find himself very much depressed the next. This is caused by the change in the human system which can be recognized through the flow of the left or the right nostril.

Have you ever awakened one morning, after a full night's sleep, to find yourself very tired? Apparently, there is no reason for this tiredness. You slept well and nothing particularly worried you or bothered you, and yet you found that you were so tired you could hardly move! No doubt, you have often wondered about this and wished that you might find a way to overcome this feeling.

Under these circumstances, you will find that your left nostril is very empty. You cannot see it with the naked eye or even with a microscope, but you can feel it. You can feel that your left nostril seems to have absolutely no air in it. If you will close the right nostril and breathe in through the left nostril alone, you will notice how unusually easy it is to breathe in through the left nostril. When you find your left nostril empty, *place the left hand on the right nostril and inhale through the left nostril slowly and yet so deeply that you must raise your head—now hold the breath, to the count of five—then place the right hand on the left nostril and exhale only through the right nostril.*

The mouth is not used in this particular method. If you will persist in the use of this exercise, going through the motions as described from three to ten times, you will find that this tired feeling will be completely eliminated, and you will once more be your natural self. When using this exercise, wherever possible, quiet yourself and close your eyes. In this way, you will get immediate results. Students so often ask this question, "Why must I breathe in through the left nostril and exhale through the right?" The reason is that the oxygen taken in through the left nostril, after it enters into the blood system, becomes positive and the oxygen that is exhaled through the right nostril is negative. In that way, the body retains all of the positive air which is so necessary to keep our "Human Barometer" equally balanced. The reason for the extremely tired feeling is attributed to the empty left nostril, which means that all of the positive air has left the body and the body is very tired and very negative.

Students also ask this question, "Why is it necessary to place the left hand on the right nostril when inhaling, and the right hand on the left nostril when exhaling?" If you have studied physics in school, you will remember that every magnet has a negative and a positive pole. The human body is constructed in much the same fashion. When we place the left hand on the right nostril, we are making a complete circuit, and in that way we are easily able to control our bodies. By placing the right hand on the left nostril when exhaling, once more we complete the circuit. By making a complete circuit in exhaling and inhaling, we have complete control of our bodies, and we find that we are able to use the "Human Barometer" to our complete satisfaction. This particular method, as described above, may appear rather silly and even crude to some readers, but I promise that if you will persist in the use of this exercise, you will find a greater joy in life than you ever dreamed possible.

Some people laugh at what they do not understand. This could be at certain unexplainable facts that have baffled scientists for ages, or for which no answers have yet been found. However, the use of the left nostril breath or exercise will become more and more popular and due to its use and positive results, hundreds of mysteries will be solved.

The average individual would like to be calm, cheerful, and have courage at all times. Usually, where there is a lack of calmness or cheerfulness, you will find that the left nostril is empty. If you will use the following ideas together with the filling up exercises of the left nostril, you will get immediate and satisfactory results. If you desire to be calm when you are nervous about something, say to yourself audibly, or by moving the lips (when exhaling through the right nostril, after inhaling through the left) the words, "I am calm." If you are depressed, say the words, "I am cheerful" on the exhale. If you need to undertake a very serious task and you fear that you do not have the courage to go ahead, fill the left nostril and on the exhale say to yourself, "I am fearless and courageous." After several of these breaths, together with these statements made to yourself, you will find yourself cheerful, calm, or fearless and courageous, if you need to be. Of course, we understand that what I am trying to point out to you here may seem too good to be true; but after using the knowledge gained in the "Human Barometer," you will realize that everything I report to you is true, workable and practical. Here is a statement that should be worth a great deal to you . . .

> It is impossible to have negative thoughts of a very serious nature running through your mind, unless the left nostril is empty.

Have you ever had the feeling that you were going to have an accident? Have you ever had the feeling that something very serious was going to happen to either you or one of your loved ones? Feelings of this nature can be easily eliminated. Whenever you have the feeling or the thought in your mind that you are going to have an accident or that something serious is going to happen to you or one of your loved ones, you will find that these thoughts run through your mind only when your left nostril is empty. If you will take a minute or two or even five, to fill up the nostril as directed, this fear of accident will leave you.

So many times after we have laid our plans well, we get the feeling that we are liable to fail. So many students and scholars who have studied diligently and conscientiously still enter into the examination room afraid of failure. The very fact that they have studied hard and have spent a reasonable length of time in preparation should have made it easy for them to enter into the examination, but the thought of the examination will so frequently upset the mental balance of the individual that it causes the left nostril to become empty. All of the positive air of the body has left, and the result is—the student finds himself very negative and afraid of failure. This is one of the reasons that accounts for the brilliant student failing on an examination. The brilliant student, as a rule, if he is not careful, becomes very sensitive about the examination and causes such a disturbance in the body that he loses the ability to keep calm and cool while taking the examination. This situation can readily be eliminated by using the exercise necessary to fill up the left nostril.

Have you ever had crazy or wild ideas go through your mind? Have you ever had the feeling that you would go out of your mind? If you have, there is no reason to become alarmed any longer. The next time you find these crazy or wild ideas running through your mind, don't become alarmed, just quiet yourself for a few minutes and fill the left nostril. You will find that as soon as you have filled your left nostril, these thoughts will stop going through your mind and you will feel at ease and become perfectly calm. I have experienced many cases where students thought they were going out of their mind. Some of them had hallucinations, some of them were on the verge of being taken away to the insane asylum. These cases have all been set on the right track by understanding how the "Human Barometer" works. Once they learn to control themselves through the use of the left nostril, they do not become alarmed any more and instead of going into a rage, are able to calm themselves and have destructive thoughts pass away.

One young man with whom I came in contact was on the verge of being sent to an asylum when he was brought to me for attention. The young man had the idea that his mother was putting poison in his food and that his brother, with whom he shared a bedroom, was going to kill him during the night. When this young man walked on the street, it appeared to him that everybody was looking at him. It also appeared that he was seeing three and four people where there should have been only one. I proceeded to teach this young man the art of controlling himself through the use of his left nostril. I explained how to adjust his "Human Barometer" to keep himself calm and free from crazy thoughts and ideas. The young man was relieved almost instantly. Today, he is perfectly normal and is no longer afraid of wild and crazy ideas. He is no longer afraid of going out of his mind and no longer feels that he may someday find himself in an asylum.

I am convinced that the time will come when all people will understand the workings of the "Human Barometer" and how to control themselves through the left nostril so that the insane asylums will be empty and the need for them will no longer be required. I sincerely hope that if you know anyone who is having these wild and crazy ideas running through their minds that you will let them read this lesson or advise them to purchase a copy.

Some people frequently get the feeling that they are going to die. Many times perfectly normal, healthy people will wake up in the middle of the night with the feeling of death coming over them. This feeling infrequently arises during the day. It may also come to one who is already ill; yet, it is a feeling which one does not easily forget. If this feeling should come to you, do not become alarmed or worried, but instead test out your left nostril; and if you find that it is empty, fill it up as I have explained. The feeling will immediately pass away after several breaths and you will remain calm and positive. You will then be able to go back to sleep saying, "Well, it was just another time that my left nostril was very empty." There is nothing to worry about if you understand, but as one of our great teachers of olden times said, "Many people are destroyed because of lack of knowledge." When we understand, we no longer become worried and upset. However, the use of the "Human Barometer" is so comparatively new that very few people understand it and are able to get the joy out of its use.

Frequently, women more than men, get the feeling that they are going to faint. I hope that the women will use the knowledge gained in this lesson to prevent this fainting spell from happening to them. When a woman hears some very bad news or sees a scene that is sickening, if she is not careful, an overpowering feeling of weakness may come over her and she may feel that she is going to faint. Instead of the lady permitting herself to go into a faint, if she will just take hold of herself and fill the left nostril, the feeling will pass away and she will remain normal and calm. If you recall reading a few pages back, I said that "it is impossible to have negative thoughts of a very serious nature running through your mind unless the left nostril is empty." The fear of fainting is a negative thought. By filling the left nostril, the feeling and the thought are eliminated.

I have known people who have been troubled with epilepsy (fits) who have been able to eliminate these spells completely through the controlling of the "Human Barometer." A person who gets these spells, almost always gets a very weak feeling before the actual spell. If this individual, upon getting this feeling, instead of filling his mind with the fear that he is going to have a spell, will test his left nostril, he will find that his left nostril is very empty. If he fills it, the feeling will pass away and the spell will be eliminated. Some forms of epilepsy can be controlled and eliminated without a great deal of extra difficulty—if the person involved will remember this method.

Sometimes, when everything is going along lovely and things seem bright and rosy, you may get the feeling that things may not work out so well in the future. You begin to see all kinds of serious difficulties that may arise in times to come. You begin to feel that the security you have wrapped around yourself may be blown away like a leaf. If these thoughts come to you often enough, they will tend to break up your feeling of security to such an extent that before long you will find yourself in the very position that you so strongly fear. Next time you get a feeling of uncertainty about the future, and it seems to disturb and bother you, remember—"It is impossible to have negative thoughts of a very serious nature running through your mind unless the left nostril is empty." Fill the left nostril and the feeling of fear about the future will leave you.

We may think about the future, the present and the past and it will not cause any real mental disturbance unless the left nostril is empty. Sometimes it may be that something in the past that has happened will cause a strong mental disturbance when you think about it. Suppose, for instance, that you lost a loved one and the thought of this always seems to break you down when you think of it. It may be that you start to think of some wrong that you have done in the past that you have already corrected or were going to correct. These thoughts come only when the left nostril is empty. If you will take time to fill up the left nostril, the thoughts regarding certain incidents of the past will leave you. *Read this again.*

During the winter, you may find a cold coming on. There are some people who are troubled with colds even in the summertime. Generally, when you find a cold coming on, especially if the cold is in the nose, you will find that it is the left nostril that is running. You will find that the mucous is coming through the left nostril only. Clear the nose with your handkerchief as much as possible and inhale through your left nostril. You will find that this will pass the cold away. I have had reports from many of my students who have been able to go all winter long without a cold by using this knowledge gained in the "Human Barometer."

My students are able to control themselves and their colds. You, too, if you will use the left nostril breath when you feel a cold coming on, will be able to protect yourself especially during the winter. Once in a great while, you may find that the mucous comes from the right nostril. In that case, clear the nostril with a handkerchief and then fill up the right nostril in the same fashion. Instead of breathing in through the left nostril, you breathe in through the right nostril, after having placed the right hand on the left nostril, then exhale through the left by placing the left hand on the right nostril. This method is used only when you find the mucous running from the right nostril, otherwise, always inhale through the left nostril and exhale through the right.

Students frequently ask the question, "What happens if the right nostril is very empty in cases where there are no colds?" What happens is that you will feel like jumping around and slapping people on the back and that you just don't seem to be able to settle yourself peaceably. Oftentimes, even though you have had a complete meal, you still feel hungry and it seems that you have an unusual appetite that you are unable to curb, you will find that your right nostril is empty. When you are overjoyed and feel like jumping to the ceiling, you will find that your right nostril is empty.

At this time, I wish to caution you against something which is too often overlooked. It is just as harmful to be too overjoyed as it is to be depressed. When a person is overjoyed, he becomes careless, negligent and wants to be slapping people on the back and doesn't care what he does. Nature demands that we should always strike an even balance. She does not want us to be depressed and yet she cannot afford to have us overjoyed. So many times, people who have become overjoyed as a result of an unusually good happening, turn right around and get themselves into trouble because of the careless attitude brought on by over-joyousness. When you find yourself overjoyed, you had better fill up your right nostril, because you are sure to find it empty. Fill it up as directed and keep yourself calm and happy as well. It is much better to be calm than to permit some over-enjoyment to get you into trouble.

Very often the following happens: a husband will get a raise in pay and then goes home to tell his wife about it. Both of them, quite naturally, are very happy about it. They decide to celebrate on their good fortune and the result is that they may indulge in too much liquor. The husband may become too familiar with another man's wife. The wife may become too familiar with another woman's husband and before long, the evening ends in a brawl and a serious setback has resulted. By all means, enjoy your good fortune, but the wise individual enjoys it more or less calmly rather than having it end in disaster.

A husband and wife may be getting along very well—everything seems to be working along smoothly—then, all of a sudden, the husband or the wife may become unusually irritable. The wife seems to get on the nerves of the husband and the husband seems to get on the nerves of the wife. They cannot figure out what has happened. They are surprised at each other's actions. They are afraid that their happy union has lasted too long and cannot continue. Nothing serious has happened between these two but they cannot understand why they should feel the way they do about one another. The answer once more is the "Human Barometer." The left nostril is empty. If the husband and wife will fill up their respective left nostrils, they will find their old calmness coming over them again and their love for one another will be the same as it always has been.

One of my students reports the following incident: "My wife and I were getting along very well. One night we went to a show together and enjoyed it immensely. After the show, we went into a restaurant to get a bite to eat. While we were waiting for the waiter to bring our orders, it seemed that everything my wife said to me irritated me and everything I said to my wife irritated her. This was the first time anything like that had happened in our short married life. At first, I was bewildered and didn't know what to make of it. Then I reminded myself that it was my left nostril that was empty. I filled mine and asked my wife to do the same. The result was that an irritable situation came to a very quick end and we left the restaurant in the best of spirits." Here is a situation that frequently breaks up many a happy married couple and could have been eliminated by the knowledge of the "Human Barometer."

All forms of irritation can be traced to an empty left nostril. Frequently, while driving down a street, it seems that everybody gets in the way. Ordinarily, you may not understand it, but you will find that if you are irritated about these people getting in your way, your left nostril is empty. Fill it up the best you can while you are driving along under these circumstances. Of course, you will not be able to close your eyes, but filling up the nostril will help to end this irritation. Sometimes your children, whom you love dearly, may seem to irritate you and get on your nerves. When they do, you will find that your left nostril is empty. Fill it and they will not seem to bother you much. If you happen to be a teacher and you find that your pupils irritate you, fill your left nostril, and you will find that this period of irritation will leave. If you are an employer and you find that your employees seem to be getting on your nerves, you can usually trace it to a left nostril. If you are an employee and your boss is not of an irritable nature but seems to be getting on your nerves, try out your left nostril. I can cite ever so many cases, as those mentioned before, which are usually due to an empty left nostril.

Sometimes, you may find it extremely difficult to fall asleep. You roll around—you count sheep—you do everything possible to try to go to sleep but you find you are not successful. If you will only take the time and have the patience to fill up your left nostril several times, you will find that you will be able to fall asleep without any trouble.

If you are a student of speech, you may find that before you get up to speak, you are extremely nervous. If you are, you will find that your left nostril is empty. Fill it up, and then you will be able to go ahead with a much greater calmness. If you attend a lecture and you feel that you would like to ask the lecturer a question but your heart beats so rapidly that you are unable to do so, if you will fill up your left nostril first and on the exhale say, "I am courageous," you will have no difficulty asking the question. If you find it necessary to call upon someone whose position in life or finance is greater than yours and you fear to make this call, if you will fill up your left nostril before going to see them, you will lose this fear.

Many students complain about being unable to control their mind properly. It seems that their minds wander and they don't know what to do about it. Whenever you find your mind wandering, if you will test out your left nostril, you will find that it is empty. Fill it, and you will once more be able to control your mind the way you desire. I cannot say too much about the value and the use of the "Human Barometer." In fact, I know of a case of a man who has had hay fever for many, many years. Whenever he felt that he was going to have a re-occurrence, he was able to check it by the use of the left nostril. You may be able to figure out many other ways of using the left nostril in your own experience. Students, who once know about it, cannot get along without the use of this knowledge any longer.

Troubled with headaches? Almost everyone is. One can deal with most headaches with the use of the left nostril. I know people who never take aspirin. What does the aspirin do? Actually, it changes the flow of the nostrils. Therefore, use the method of filling the left nostril and the headache will disappear. Even the so-called incurable migraine headaches have shown signs of improvement, and in many cases have been completely eliminated by the use of the left nostril breath. If the person who is troubled with migraines will be very careful, he will start to fill the left nostril just as soon as he feels the headache coming on. This is important. When there is a small leak in the roof of your house, for example, it is easily repaired and very little damage is done. However, when there is a big hole in the roof, then there is a lot of damage and it is not easily repaired. So it is with certain types of headaches. They must be dealt with just as soon as there is a sign of a headache coming. Then, the problem is easy to solve. Keep ever watchful. The guarding of oneself through the application of the left nostril breath will pay untold dividends and will make life worth living.

Sometimes—I hope it never happens to you—both the left and the right nostrils go empty at the same time. It may never happen to you, yet it may. When it does happen, the individual feels like ending his life by jumping off a bridge. It is a terrible sensation. It makes one feel helpless. But *be alert.* Don't become panicky. I realize this is not easy at a time like this, but keep calm anyway. Sit down, or if possible, lie down. Relax as much as you possibly can. Now, fill the left nostril five times, rest, then fill the right nostril five times, then rest. Do this several times. It may take an entire morning to get to feel the way you want, but it is worth it. Take your time. This terrible feeling will pass, and life will begin to look good again. This may never happen to you, I certainly hope it doesn't. Nevertheless, now that you understand it, you will be prepared. Preparation is like the old proverb, "A stitch in times saves nine."

We cannot control the weather. We cannot control the stars. We cannot control the unseen forces that weave their way into our lives, but we can control ourselves and in that way, we control our lives and our experiences. We can become complete masters of ourselves, if we so desire. The main thought to bear in mind is first to gain the knowledge, and secondly to apply it. Reread this lesson several times. Apply the knowledge gained herein and before long you will become very familiar with what is meant by an empty left nostril. Before long, you will come to realize that it will only take a moment to change an irritable condition. You will realize that the many crazy, wild, and negative thoughts can be prevented from getting the best of you. You are indeed a fortunate person to have gained the knowledge set forth in these pages. I have had students say that they would not sell the knowledge gained in this lesson for any amount of money. I know of others who have been prevented from becoming mentally unbalanced by applying this knowledge. I have also seen many serious ailments corrected through this technique. Remember that knowledge by itself is not power, rather, the use of knowledge is power. This technique will only work wonders for you if you use it.

It is impossible to have negative thoughts of a very serious nature running through your mind, unless the left nostril is empty.

Appendix 2

The Secret of Dealing with Trouble

I learned to read and write when I went to school. I learned that two and two are four. I learned many things that are of great importance; and now, through the medium of this lesson, you will learn one of the greatest lessons in life.

There is nothing in one's life that is such a burden, and always seems to be present, as "troubles." As the common saying goes, "Everyone has his troubles." This statement is so well received that I have become accustomed to accepting the idea that troubles are a necessary part of one's life. To make the statement that one can go through life without troubles, would subject one's self to ridicule and harsh statements on the part of friends and relatives. This would be a Heaven on earth if one could live without troubles. Troubles seem to have caused millions of people to live in utter misery, often causing them to take their own lives.

The sad part about it is that people who live good, clean, moral, and honest lives can be continually in trouble. It is tragic when one stops to think about it, that these same people who do no wrong to anyone, who don't violate the laws of the city, state, or national governments, who don't become involved in other people's business, who go to church, who help their fellowman—that these people should live under conditions of poverty and discouragement, steeped in worry and trouble. The main reason is that these people do not understand the psychology of trouble. It is startling to find the large number of people who are becoming atheists, because of the fact that they cannot understand how God could bring them such trouble. (Be sure to read this entire lesson before drawing conclusions.)

The Greatest Psychologist who ever lived said, "*Whosoever doeth good, what wrong can come to him?*" You, who are living good and clean lives, who are doing no wrong to anyone, why should any wrong come to you? Some people think that by going to church, that by giving to charities, that by helping their fellowman, that they are being good. Yes, that is true, but that in itself will not offset trouble. The really pathetic part about most people is that they are good and yet seem to be filled with troubles. Going to church, helping one's fellowman, being of service to others, is all well and good, but one must go a step further. When the Master Psychologist said, "Whosoever doeth good, what wrong can come to him?" He meant exactly what He said, but with one exception. What it really means is "Whosoever doeth good ideas choose—what wrong can come to him?"

Most of the people in this world have troubles. If it isn't one thing, it's another. Oh, but if someone should dare to say that he can live without trouble, he would be laughed at and ridiculed. When an individual chooses to believe that he can live without troubles, he is considered stupid, and consequently he succumbs to the general belief that a person must have his troubles because that is the way it is. No matter how good a person may be, no matter how much he may contribute to charity, and no matter how much he goes to church, if he still persists in believing that one must have troubles, then that is what is going to happen to him. But if he is wise and chooses good ideas, and believes that he can live without troubles, then the entire picture changes for the better.

A young man kept his car in a garage. It so happened that there was a stretch of garages behind a public building. The only light at night was a bulb hanging down from a canopy without any protection whatsoever. Frequently, when this young man would come home rather late at night, the bulb would be either burned out or smashed to bits by the wind. The young man was frightened to death. He rushed in to open the garage door; he hurriedly sat himself behind the wheel, drove himself into the garage, excitedly locked the garage door and ran out to the main street. This young man did this quite frequently, and one night when he drove in, the light was out, but he realized the importance of the statement that "Whosoever doeth good, what wrong can come to him?" He began to review his past life. He realized that he had not done any harm to anyone, that he had not stolen, that he had not violated any laws. "Why should I be afraid?" he said. With this thought in mind, the young man drove into the garage, closed the garage door, and without hurrying, walked out to the main street. As long as he kept the thought "Whosoever doeth good, what wrong can come to him?" he was not afraid. As long as he was filled with fear-thoughts, he was frightened that something might happen.

Here is a very true case, and a very simple example of what is going through the minds of millions of people living today. When millions of people begin to understand the secret of dealing with trouble, then they will no longer believe that one must have his trouble, or that something must happen to spoil our lives. Choose the right ideas and you will eliminate much trouble from your life. Choose the wrong ideas and life will become a burden and you may be filled with one trouble or another as long as you continue to believe that one must have his trouble.

Truly speaking, your troubles, difficulties, hardships, and disappointments are not truly such. They do not come into our lives to tear us down and make us weaker but to build us up and make us stronger. If we do not whine and complain, we shall be given strength to overcome all of these. If you are disappointed in obtaining that something upon which you had your heart and soul set, it is only because you have unconsciously set a force in motion which will bring you something bigger and better. Always look for the lesson in your so-called trouble. Disraeli said that "All of my successes have been built on my failures." Ella Wheeler Wilcox said, "Always think success no matter what happens."

Here is the secret of dealing with trouble. Troubles don't come into our lives to tear us down and make us weaker but to build us up and make us stronger. Why should we go through life always afraid that something might happen to destroy our lives and peace of mind? The purpose of trouble is not to spoil one's life, but to give life more joy. If something bigger and better is coming our way as a result of various troubles, why, then, should we fill our minds with the fear that something may happen to spoil our lives and destroy our peace of mind? Every trouble that comes your way is not your enemy, but your teacher. It is trying to teach you something which probably could come to you in no other way. If you will always feel that any trouble which has arisen, or may arise in the future, is only another lesson which you are to learn, which will make you stronger and bigger, you will have learned life's greatest lesson.

Disraeli, England's greatest Prime Minister, knew very well the secret of dealing with troubles when he said, "All of my successes have been built on my failures." It is no crime to fail. Don't ever let anyone tell you that; but the main trick is to *build a success on that failure*. So many people in life fill their minds with failure so much that they make success a very difficult task. They believe success is only for the privileged few, but unless one has some kind of psychology of trouble, such as you are discovering in this lesson, or such as Disraeli had, then life becomes hard. The fear that trouble may intervene to spoil and upset our lives completely, fills our minds and does its disastrous work—as it has for centuries past. Build a success on your failures, and there is nothing to stop you from going forward and making progress. Allow your failures to keep you down and you may as well throw up your hands and resign yourself to living a very ordinary or mediocre life.

Every great man who has ever accomplished anything in life has developed some kind of method of dealing with troubles. Without this method, these men could never accomplish very much. Each great man has developed his own psychology of trouble; but today, every person who can read and write can become familiar with the secret of dealing with trouble and make his ambitions in life really worth living.

We all know of the many and great disappointments of Lincoln. He started out in life a very disappointed boy. He lost his mother when he was only ten years old. He was disappointed in his schooling and obtained only one year of academic training. He went into business and here, too, he was disappointed, spending many years of his life to pay off the debts incurred while in business for a few months. He ran for office and no matter what office he ran for, he was disappointed. He met lovely Ann Rutledge, became engaged to her and was very happy for a while. According to some writers, she was the only bright spot in his life and she died. For about a year, Lincoln was absolutely worthless to himself, to his clients, and to his community. Many times townspeople found him crying over the grave of Ann Rutledge, in the worst kind of weather. Frequently, he felt like committing suicide, so they had to watch him.

Yes, Lincoln went on from one disappointment to another. In fact, he was a failure until he was fifty years old, and then he was elected to the presidency of the United States and became one of the greatest and most beloved presidents we have ever had. Even during the Civil War, his disappointments were many. At one time during the Civil War when the capital of the country, Washington, D.C., was almost captured, he was at another extreme point in his life. Shortly after this close call, the North defeated the South, and the war was over. We all know the disappointing way in which he met his death—and yet all through his struggles and disappointments, Lincoln made this statement: "I have been so well acquainted with disappointments, that if I have another, it won't make any difference." He also said, "This too will pass."

Lincoln and Disraeli both must have understood the psychology of trouble. No man can go through life and reach the heights that these two men did without knowing the psychology of trouble. You will notice in Lincoln's life especially every time he was disappointed, there was something bigger and better coming his way. Today, he lives with a stronger and more powerful influence upon mankind than ever before. Every school boy looks up to Lincoln. Millions of adults have been influenced and are continuing to be influenced by his life and the lessons it teaches. Lincoln knew how to handle disappointments and he also knew that "This too will pass." Sometimes, in our dark moments, when our troubles seem to come from all sides and we seem to feel that somehow they will not end, and when we feel that there is no hope, remember what Lincoln said—"This too will pass." It is keeping thoughts like this in our minds that help us to make life a game instead of a battle.

And now, let us apply the "psychology of trouble" to a number of troubles that we have in life, showing you how you may apply the secret of dealing with trouble to the various troubles which you may have. If they should come your way, you will be prepared to deal with them so that you will be able to cash in on your troubles instead of having them spoil your life and your peace of mind.

One of the most common types of trouble is the loss of a job. A story is told of a young man who was laid off from work. He was married. He was afraid to go home and tell his wife. On his way home, he stopped and leaned against a telegraph pole trying to think of an excuse to tell his wife. While standing there, he picked up a piece of wire and began dreamingly to twist the piece of wire. Before untying it, he twisted the wire into the now-famous paper clip. Of course, you know that fortunes have been made as a result of this little invention. Surely some of you will say, "He was simply lucky." It is easy to see the lesson in this loss of a job. Had he not lost his job, he would have had no occasion to stop and lean against the pole. Then the opportunity of finding this invention may have never presented itself. In order to completely understand the loss of a job, I present the story of Sam Jones, which is a more common experience to the average person than the one where the fellow invents a paper clip.

Sam was selling chewing tobacco in the southern part of the United States. His sales had fallen off greatly. One day the Sales Manager called him into his office and said, "Sam, if you can't bring your sales back to normal, I will have to let you go. I will give you a thirty-day trial period; if at the end of that time you have not increased your sales to a proper point of normalcy, you will be through."

Sam went to work the following day. He plugged and fought as hard as he knew how. He schemed, planned, and thought of new ideas on how to increase his sales. At the end of the thirty days, although his sales had increased considerably, they were not brought back to a point of normalcy.

The Sales Manager called Sam in and told him that he was sorry but he would have to let him go. The Sales Manager said, "You are no salesman. If you were, you certainly would be able to bring your sales back to normalcy." Sam left the selling field and went to work in a very ordinary form of employment. Not that there is anything wrong with ordinary type of employment, but the possibilities of earning large salaries were not there. Thus, we conclude that Sam did not understand the psychology of trouble.

In the clip story, we say that the man was lucky; so was Sam Jones, but Sam did not know it. The former knew that he had found something valuable but Sam did not understand that the best thing that could have ever happened to him was the loss of his job. The truth of the matter is that Sam was selling a product that was on the down-grade. People were not chewing tobacco as they had in the past years. Jones, or any other salesman, could not have brought the sales back to normalcy. But, Sam did not understand the psychology of trouble. Instead of trying to find the lesson that the loss of his job was trying to teach him, he became openly discouraged, agreed with the Sales Manager that he was no longer any good as a salesman, left the selling field, and is now working at a very ordinary job.

Almost all losses of jobs are blessings in disguise. If you will only analyze some of the losses of jobs you have had in the past, according to the psychology of trouble, you will find that this idea is true although, on the surface, it may not have looked that way. Always look for the lesson in the loss of anything. Try to determine in the best way possible, just what lesson your trouble is trying to teach you. Remember, there is always something bigger and better coming your way. Trouble does not come into your life to tear you down and make you weaker but to build you up and make you stronger. Once you start to apply the psychology of trouble to your difficulties and troubles, you will find a new ray of hope and understanding in life. As I said before, you will have learned the greatest lesson in life.

One of the most pathetic cases that we are forced to face is dealing with the loss of a loved one, a problem that is quite common and always carries with it a great deal of distress and disturbance. There are thousands of people walking the streets today who are really "living corpses." So many people fail to realize that when a loved one passes on, there isn't very much that one can do about it, except to look for the lesson in this particular trouble.

Let me go back for a moment to the case of Lincoln, in losing his beloved Ann Rutledge. After a year of despondency, Lincoln began to live a normal life. Shortly after that, he met Mary Todd and married her. Mary Todd was just as much responsible for Lincoln becoming President of the United States as Lincoln was. Sometime before the Civil War, a group of men came to Lincoln and said, "Lincoln, we would like to have you run for Governor of Illinois." Mr. Lincoln replied, "Gentlemen, I am highly honored and I shall be glad to run for governor; but before I give you my final word, I would like to talk it over with Mrs. Lincoln." When she heard the proposition, she emphatically responded, "You will run for president or nothing."

If Lincoln had run for Governor of Illinois, it would have been an entirely different story. Ann Rutledge was sweet and loving and kind. She probably would have said, "Mr. Lincoln, if you want to run for Governor of Illinois, go ahead. After all, you know what is best." But, not Mary Todd! She was determined that her husband should become President of this great United States. Yes, it does seem that at times we cannot understand why nature does certain things as she does, but as in this case, when properly understood, we can understand that there is something bigger and better coming our way. If we could only understand and apply this fact, it would change our outlook entirely!

A young man who was very high up in politics told me this story. He said, "I lost my oldest brother when I was a rather young man. Our entire family was upset about it. They could not understand why this had to happen." Today, this young man says that if his oldest brother had lived, he would not have reached the position that he had at such a very early age. He added, "When my brother died, all the responsibility of the family was thrown on my shoulders. I had to make good and in making good, I have been able to reach an unusual position in our city government because of the loss of my brother."

Sometimes it is hard to see the lesson in a trouble that comes our way. Sometimes, one is able to see the lesson in the trouble immediately and sometimes it may take months, or even years. However, when a person begins to understand that there is something bigger and better coming his way as a result of a single calamity that appears, he is able to live free from the fear of trouble. Even though a particular trouble could not have been avoided, the person is still able to keep his composure and to overcome the trouble by holding on to this belief.

There was a man who was very honest, truthful, and had a congenial character. This man's wife died. He became frantic. He suffered greatly and consequently ruined his health. He could not understand why God would ever want to take his wife away from him. He began to study the various forms of psychology to determine, if possible, why God took his wife away. He could not find the answer. He was at the point of losing his mind, much the same as Lincoln, and about to become an atheist and deny that there was any such thing as a God. He said that no God, no righteous God of any kind, would want to do a thing like that to him. After about a year had passed, this man had given up all hope. After a year of brain-storming and brain-racking experiences, he gave up the struggle. Then one day the lesson in trouble came to him.

He noticed that his two little children were always ill while the mother lived, yet had never been ill a single day after the mother died. Then he began to understand. In this case, although this woman was a godly and righteous woman who had made an excellent wife, she was sickly. Every time she took her two children into her arms she conveyed this sick magnetism to these children. These children would possibly have never been well as long as their mother lived, or until they had reached maturity. This is one of the most pathetic cases that I know, yet it stands the sound reasoning of the psychology of trouble. It is sometimes very hard to understand the death of a loved one but with confident and sound reasoning, before long, the lesson which is to be taught becomes visible and apparent so that we are able to go about our business with a faith that is unwavering. Naturally, after the above experience, this man had a greater faith in God than ever before.

Another point in fact is about a young lady who was living very happily with her mother and her brother. The three of them were inseparable. All three liked the same things, did the same things, went everywhere together, and enjoyed each other's company immensely. Then something happened to this young lady—both mother and brother died within a year's time. She became frantic. She could not understand why it had to happen. She began to lose interest in living and in people. She had a splendid job, but she lost interest in her work. One day a fellow worker said to her, "Young lady, better be careful. It is true that you lost your mother and your brother, but if you continue to keep up your work the way you have been in the past few months, you will be out of a job, and jobs are scarce." The young lady then became familiar with the "psychology of trouble" through my training at our resident school. She began to change, to see things differently, and to understand. Life once more began to look bright and she was able to control her emotions and to live a normal and happy life instead of living steeped in the miseries of the past.

When a loved one has gone to the beyond, there isn't anything we can do about it except to look for the lesson in the trouble. We can simply carry on as they—those who have passed on—would probably want us. Look for the lesson and you will find that your so-called trouble will make you stronger and not tear you down.

Another trouble or experience that is very common is the automobile accident. In many cases, automobile accidents seem to have no significance. On careful and proper interpretation, we find that here, too, the "psychology of trouble" plays a large part. Analyze some of the accidents which you may have had and ask yourself if it could not have been much worse.

Here is a case of a young man who had never in any way caused harm or done anyone wrong. He purchased a new car and about a month later, while driving directly behind another car, struck that car. He destroyed that car's two fenders and did damage to his own car. He, too, began to question why

God brought this accident to him. He had not deserved this happening. It was only after becoming familiar with the "psychology of trouble" that he began to understand and learn the lesson that God was trying to teach him. First of all, this being his initial driving experience in the rain, he learned that he must drive at a slower speed. Second, he should always avoid driving directly behind another car, for in doing so his view might be obstructed. Third, he should also drive either to one side or the other of the car in front of him so that he could see clearly and anticipate what that person in the car ahead of him might do. Finally, he should continue to drive more cautiously when it is raining.

This accident cost the young man fifty dollars and many days of grief and anxiety. Yet, he would not sell the experience for many hundreds of dollars. It taught him how to apply the "psychology of trouble" and gave him a finer and a greater sense of security while driving. Knowing the "psychology of trouble," you will respond by saying to yourself: "Let it happen—if it does, I will be shown the lesson in this particular trouble." With this attitude in mind, you will not attract trouble to yourself.

Another young man, shortly after receiving a promotion in his work, had an accident. He could not understand why he should have had that accident. He had not harmed anybody nor had done anything wrong. He could not figure out why he was being punished. Trouble, however, does not mean punishment—*trouble means education.* Trouble means there is something bigger and better coming your way, something to build you up and make you stronger, not to tear you down and make you weaker.

In discussing his case with the writer, this young man found that the lesson in his trouble was "overconfidence." Overconfidence is as much responsible for automobile accidents as any other thing. A person has a stroke of good luck and, in the course of this good fortune, becomes overconfident. The overconfidence leads to carelessness and then, of course, accidents occur. Nature has a very simple way of doing things. Nature does not want us to be under-confident and yet does not want us to be overconfident. Overconfidence has caused more harm than under-confidence. Therefore, when everything is running along nicely and smoothly for you, do not become overconfident because if you do, something may happen to keep you on an even keel. This young man finally agreed that the accident was due to overconfidence and not to have been punished by some unseen force or by some revengeful God. Remember, overconfidence leads to carelessness.

If you have had any automobile accidents, stop to analyze them and you will find that in every case, these accidents did not come about in order to tear you down and make you weaker but to build you up and make you stronger. If a person truly begins to understand the "psychology of trouble" and to apply it, he naturally cuts down on his automobile accidents and on his other troubles because he no longer fears them. As he eliminates the fear, so does he stop attracting those troubles. Take a radio, for instance. You know that you tune in to the station that you wish to listen to by turning the dial from one station to another. So it is with us. If we tune in "station trouble," what can we expect? If you drive your car expecting to have an accident any minute, naturally the fear will bring about this very thing. On the other hand, if you become familiar with the use and practice of the "psychology of trouble," you will eliminate those fears and thereby eliminate the troubles themselves.

Another very common difficulty, disappointment, or discouragement is that which occurs between husband and wife. Whenever both husband and wife understand the "psychology of trouble," their married life naturally runs much smoother and the marriage relationship is much more enjoyable and there really is no trouble. After all, the "psychology of trouble" says that it will bring you something bigger and better. When the husband and wife understand this, their troubles and difficulties will only bring them closer together. Even if only one of them were to understand this, it would be better than if neither had understood it. One of the finest examples of difficulties between husband and wife is taken from the famous lecture "Acres of Diamonds" by Russell H. Conwell. One reason that I have adopted this story from "Acres of Diamonds" is that every man or woman who reads this "psychology of trouble" should be familiar with this lecture which was delivered by Conwell 5,700 times.

Conwell tells of a husband and a wife having a quarrel. This couple lived on a farm. The wife chased the husband out of the house with a broom. He went to find refuge in a place near the brook which was running through the farm. Comfortably seated on a sawed-off tree stump, he began dreamingly to gaze into the water of the brook. He noticed a small unusual fish darting back and forth and proceeded to catch it. He then sent it to a fish company who in return sent him a letter and a check for five dollars. In the letter, the company explained that they could use all the fish of this type and that he would receive five dollars each for them. However, he could not find anymore in the brook. He went to his minister and told him of his predicament. The minister, who happened to have a book on the breeding of fish, gave it to him. He proceeded to learn how to breed fish and did it to such an extent that he developed a fishery on the very brook of the farm that he loved. The story goes on to tell how the couple later moved their fishery to the Hudson River and the man became an expert in the United States Department for the development of fisheries. Now, how did all of this come about? Was it not due to the fact that the husband and the wife had quarreled? The quarrel was really responsible for the finding of wealth and position for this couple.

Understanding the "psychology of trouble" puts more joy into the married relationship than anything I know. Two people may have arguments and quarrels, but there is usually a lot of good inherent in these quarrels, particularly so if one of them understands the "psychology of trouble." If married people would ask themselves "What is this trouble trying to teach me?", they would find that they would do away with heartaches, disappointments, and misunderstandings. Most married people are afraid of arguments. Due to this fear in their hearts, they unconsciously attract troubles to themselves. When they know and understand that there is something bigger and better coming their way, that there is some good coming from this trouble or argument, there will never again be any serious trouble between these married couples. They will develop confidence, they will gain faith, they will go about their business and not attract difficulties to themselves.

Please do not think that I advocate arguments between husband and wife in order to find some good. Do not think that I advocate accidents so that some good may come your way. Do not think that I advocate that you should be careless on your job so that you will be fired and you will get a better job as a result. I do not believe in fatalism and do not say that everything happens for the best, but I do say: Let it happen if it must . . . and when it does, I will be able to see the lesson in the trouble . . . I will be able to see the good in it . . . and I will use this good to my advantage . . . that I will be able to feel that there is something bigger and better coming my way . . . so that I will have confidence . . . I will have faith . . . and I will not attract trouble to myself. Remember that "He whosoever doeth good, what wrong can come to him?" I am appealing to the thousands who live good, clean, moral lives and do no wrong to anyone, and yet are completely surrounded by some kind of trouble that is unnecessary.

It seems that every married couple has some trouble. Many men and many women have refused to marry because they have not seen a truly happily married couple. The reason that many married couples are not happier than they are, is that they are so afraid of trouble that they are constantly attracting it to themselves. However, if husbands and wives understood the "psychology of trouble," they would live an altogether different kind of life. They would really be happily married and as one man said, "I love my wife today after twenty years of married life more than I did when I first married her." This may be the exception to the rule, but it *should not be the exception* and *will not be the exception* when more people understand the "psychology of trouble." Look for the lesson in your so-called trouble if you want to have more joy out of your married life. As one man said, "Heaven is right here on earth, but most of us have not taken advantage of it." The real road to a "heaven on earth," as we see it, is a real understanding that our troubles do not come into our lives to tear us down and make us weaker, but to build us up and make us stronger; and as long as that is true, troubles will not harm us. Troubles are not our enemies, but our friends. Make a friend of trouble and it will no longer spoil your life.

Young people in courtship are confronted with plenty of disappointments and problems at different times. If two people who are in love will understand and apply the "psychology of trouble," there will never be any real heartaches for either one. The disappointed lover should remember that whenever something happens between them, it will do one of two things: First, after the argument is over, it will bring them closer together; second, if it breaks them up, it is only because that person was not the right one after all. Someone finer and better, someone who will contribute to the overall happiness of the relationship is coming his or her way.

I have given advice in many cases where engaged couples seemed to be breaking apart and in every case, either of the two things described above happened. Although one will be tested at a time when the truth of these statements may be hard to believe, yet after it is all over, you will find the "psychology of trouble" is right. I have heard many reports on many cases where either one or the other says, "I am glad that I did not marry so and so."

A young lady had an argument with a young man with whom she had been going for over four years. This argument broke up the engagement. The young lady was quite upset. All her friends knew of this breakup. Now it meant that she had to stay at home and wait until someone else would came along. She was quite sick about the whole matter. In explaining the "psychology of trouble" to her, she said that it wasn't possible that something bigger and better was coming out of the entire affair. In talking with her the first time, she felt as though it was the end of everything for her. However, the following week, she was a changed young woman. She had made up with her fiancé and was happy again. This was her story: "The reason that this friend of mine and I could not marry was that he loved to play cards. For four years he had been putting off the marriage. Finally, we had this argument and we decided it was all over. But now, he has agreed to give me his pay envelope and I am going to give him his spending money and money for board, and within a year's time, we will be able to marry." She went on to say, "When I first heard the 'psychology of trouble,' I thought it was a lot of fancy Pollyanna material. But now, I see that it is true, that it will either bring you closer together, or someone finer and better will be coming your way."

A young man was going with a very lovely young lady. He thrilled to her very presence. He worshipped the very ground that she walked on. All he could do was think and talk about his beloved. This young lady, however, refused to see him and to have anything more to do with him. She thus broke up the courtship, leaving the young man heartsick. All he could think of was the loss of the one whom he loved so dearly. In learning of the "psychology of trouble," he said that it could not be possible that someone finer and better could come along. He became so disappointed that he went home sick and was in bed for two weeks. Finally, he recovered. Six months later, he reported to me again. This time he was thrilled and jubilant again. Why?—because he had actually found someone who was finer and better than the previous lady. He said, "I never thought that could be possible."

The "psychology of trouble" is not easy to apply especially when one is steeped in trouble. As one begins to see its workings clearly, one realizes that there is no greater truth than the "psychology of trouble." No, troubles do not come into our lives to tear us down and make us weaker, but instead to build us up and make us stronger. In order that you may properly test the truth of the "psychology of trouble," make a list of five or ten of the troubles or disappointments that may have happened to you in the past. Analyze them carefully. Look for the lesson in each of them. Test out every one of these stories in this lesson with your own personal experiences, or that of your friends and relatives. You will see in every case that your disappointment was only temporary and that something bigger and better did come about, that something finer and superior had come to you, as a result of this temporary disappointment.

In business, stories that illustrate the "psychology of trouble" are so numerous that volume after volume has been written showing how all great businessmen have overcome disappointment after disappointment until they reached the highest position of wealth and standing. A good example is the story of Barnum, of the famous Barnum and Bailey Circus. Barnum built a circus in a building and this building burned down. He went to his friends and creditors and borrowed money to build another circus, this time bigger and better than the one before. The second circus burned down. Again, he went to his friends and creditors, raised funds, and built an even bigger and better circus. The third circus burned down. Keep in mind that all this happened at a time before there was fire insurance. Needless to say, after these three fires, Barnum was unable to obtain help from his friends and creditors who believed it was useless. Jumbo the elephant was all that Barnum had left from the circus. He said to himself, "All right, I can't afford a building anymore, but I can buy a tent. I will show Jumbo the elephant in a tent to the people of New York and when the people of New York have seen him, I will take him to Albany; and when the people of Albany have seen him, I will take him to Rochester; and when the people of Rochester have seen him, I will take him to Buffalo." That is the way the traveling circus came into being in the United States. Barnum made more money with the traveling circus under the tent than he could ever have made in one place. It was only after three fires that the big lesson that was coming Barnum's way finally came to him. It was only when he could no longer obtain any outside help, and when he depended on his own mind and on his own creative powers, that he finally grasped the one thing that was to make him a millionaire many times over!

If you are in business, apply the "psychology of trouble." It will save you lots of heartaches, disappointments, and troubles. So many times, a person may be in business and is getting along very well, and then competition comes along and deprives him of everything that he has ever owned. To a person who does not understand the "psychology of trouble," this competition may be interpreted to mean that he is being punished, that the competition will take away or even destroy his business. The "psychology of trouble" says that something bigger and better is coming his way and the business person who understands this is not afraid of competition, but it makes him a more alert business individual; and instead of the competition destroying the business, it makes it a bigger and better one. It all depends on his knowledge of the "psychology of trouble." If he does not have this knowledge, he is filled with fear. Having this knowledge, he knows that something bigger and better is on the way and that something is going to happen to build him up and make him stronger and is not intended to tear him down and make him weaker.

Many or most great businessmen were so determined that nothing could stop them, probably unconsciously, that they applied the "psychology of trouble." They felt inwardly that something bigger and better was coming their way. So, if you are in business, or if you have failed in business once or twice, or if your business is not moving along as smoothly as you want, here is your chance to apply the "psychology of trouble" and discover what it is that is coming your way to make you bigger and stronger.

With physical defects, we may also apply the "psychology of trouble." In many examples of great outstanding characters, physical defects have played an outstanding role. A physical defect will do either one of two things—tear a person down and destroy his confidence and cause that person to become dependent on society or make him strong so as to become outstanding in his work. Helen Keller, often referred to as the eighth wonder of the world, was deaf, blind, and mute. Yet, she graduated from college, wrote books, lectured, and was as well informed as any person of normal reasoning, and in many ways, superior. Thomas Edison, as you probably know, was deaf, but he invented the phonograph. Steinmetz, referred to as the electrical wizard of the world, was hunchbacked and crippled. Theodore Roosevelt, as a child, was an invalid, and yet he became a giant of power, physically as well as mentally. So many fine and noble characters have been handicapped physically, and yet, unconsciously, apply the "psychology of trouble" and have risen to the top. There is only one thing to do with handicaps, either with physical or otherwise, and that is *to cash in on them.*

One example of a physical defect that I always like to tell is that of a man who desired to become an orator. This man was unable to speak clearly because of his stammer. He finally overcame his speech difficulty by practicing with pebbles in his mouth. He then felt that without the speech defect he would be able to speak to the assembly. The assembly in ancient Greece corresponded to our present Congress. When he went there to speak, the assembly made so much noise that they would not listen to him. He decided that the next thing to do would be to develop a strong and powerful voice. He practiced day and night in order to strengthen his voice. He practiced near the sea so that the sound of the sea would resemble the noise of the assembly, practicing so that his voice could be heard over the noise of the waves. After developing a strong, clear voice, he went again before the assembly. This time, although he was able to speak above the noise, the assembly once again did not listen to him.

The man gave up. He said there was nothing for him to do. He had overcome his speech defect, developed a very strong voice, and yet he was not heard. One day, as he was seated despondent and discouraged because he could not realize his dream, a friend of his, Satyrus by name, approached him and inquired as to what was troubling him and why he was so downhearted. After hearing of his friend's disappointment, Satyrus responded: "Let me hear the last speech that you made, that the assembly would not listen to." Satyrus, an actor by profession, told him what was wrong with the speech. The man corrected the fault and proceeded to appear before the assembly for the third time. This time, the assembly listened to him!

Today, after 2,000 years, we still hear of Demosthenes, the great Greek orator who spoke with pebbles in his mouth. His name lives to this day. In his day there were thousands who spoke clearly. Why did they not become orators? Notice that each time Demosthenes failed, there was something bigger and better coming his way. The "psychology of trouble" always works, once you understand how to use it. The defect, the failure of the assembly to listen, was not sent to Demosthenes to make him weaker and tear him down, but was sent to make him stronger and build him up. Apply the "psychology of trouble" to your own life and you must succeed!

Physical defects and sickness, both have their "psychology of trouble." There was a man who at eighteen years of age was so handicapped that he could not dress himself, and yet, at thirty-five years of age, was a doctor and had opened an institution for the curing of handicapped children. His parents must have thought that they had been cursed with a handicapped child only to realize later that all along there was something very, very great coming to them. The son who was to help thousands and thousands of other handicapped children had a career based upon his own handicap.

Physical defects and sickness, both have their "psychology of trouble." If you become sick and do not understand the "psychology of trouble," you may repeat the same sickness over and over again. If you do understand the "psychology of trouble," a slight cold does not turn into a fever or something that requires you to go to bed. I have found from experience that when a person has a dependable medical doctor, this person is usually healthy. He worries less about illness than a person who doesn't have a dependable physician. He feels that if anything goes wrong, his doctor will fix him up, so he no longer worries about colds, etc. The same is true about the "psychology of trouble." When a person understands it, he knows that he has the secret of dealing with trouble and therefore he is not likely to attract many troubles to himself.

Oftentimes people who are ill find a cure for their own illness. Sometimes this leads to the development of patent medicines that are marketed to the general public for the same illness. The knowledge gained by the ill person is passed on to help others. The knowledge gained due to the illness not only helps others, but makes a fortune for the person who discovers it as well. Had the original person not been ill, he would not have discovered a medicine that would relieve thousands.

One young lady was troubled with a certain sickness. As a result of this sickness, she had overcome another sickness which had troubled her for years, yet had allowed her to walk and work. If it had not been for the second sickness, she would still be suffering from the first. Here, again, is the "psychology of trouble." Very often doctors tell us of cases where patients come to them with one kind of illness and say nothing to them about a more serious ailment. Then the doctor, as a result of the treatment of the visible illness, also cures the one that is not apparent. It is easy to see the "psychology of trouble" in these cases. Always look for the "psychology of trouble" in the case of illness as well as in any other trouble or difficulty. You will find it. If not right away, it will come to you and then the lesson will become quite clear.

Every time you have trouble, it makes you think. Every time you think, you create. You become a little "creator." You will remember that God is often spoken of as the Great Creator. Remember, the Master said,

> *If I am not doing the works of my Father, then do not believe me; but if I do them, even though you do not believe me, believe the works, that you may know and understand that the Father is in me and I am in the Father.*
>
> [John 10:37,38]

What He means is that we are all little creators as God is the Great Creator. Your troubles make you a creator, building you always in the image of the Father.

It is not true, however, that one must have troubles in order to become a "great creator." All through the ages, we have been taught that "Adversity is man's best teacher" and . . . so we believe that one must have troubles before one can learn the ways of life. Throughout the centuries, the idea that "everybody has had his trouble" has been placed in our minds because man has not yet learned to analyze his successes. When we do a thing well, we do not ask why. When everything goes right, we never ask why. When we are healthy and strong, we never ask why. As soon as something goes wrong, as soon as we are ill, as soon as difficulty or disappointment confronts us, we then begin to ask the question "Why?"

Psychologists today are trying to show the world that it is not true that everyone must have troubles. This is a result of wrong education or a development that people must go through. Here too, there is something bigger and better coming to people of the world as a whole. You are one of the first ones in this world to enjoy the benefits. Before long, thousands and thousands of people will become acquainted with the "psychology of trouble."

First of all, if you understand the "psychology of trouble," you will automatically not attract so many troubles to yourself. You will not look for them. You will know that it is natural for you not to have any. You do not have to knock on wood every time something goes well. It should be so. *It is natural, that everything should go just right.* God makes the world turn just right—the sun and the stars and the moon, the day and the night. God has things work just right for us. However, we—through wrong thinking and foolish ideas—interfere with this perfection and make life otherwise. If difficulty, disappointment, and trouble come your way, you will have faith. You will know how to handle your trouble as you know how to handle the alphabet to make words. You will learn from now on to analyze your successes as well as your failures and disappointments. You will become a creator, the way God originally intended his children to create.

Before: TROUBLES - - - -THINK - - - - CREATOR
Now: SUCCESSES - - - THINK - - - - CREATOR

Appendix 3

Mental Millionaire Progress Report

Chart Your Progress

Directions: Plot your progress by placing a dot on the point at which you have mastered the lesson. Next, connect the dots. This, then, becomes your "Positive Mental Attitude—EKG" chart.

Lessons	10%	20%	30%	40%	50%	60%	70%	80%	90%	100%
1. Mental Pictures										
2. Self-Confidence										
3. Dealing with People										
4. Finances										
5. Trouble										
6. Control Your Nerves										
7. Imagination										
8. Success										
9. Happiness										
10. Mind over Body										
11. Good Health										
12. Secret of Youth										
13. Dealing with Children										
14. Power of Creation										
15. Getting What You Want—1										
16. Getting What You Want—2										
17. Problem Solving										
18. Why Are We Here?										
19. Mental Millionaire										
20. Power of Grace										

www.ingramcontent.com/pod-product-compliance
Lightning Source LLC
Chambersburg PA
CBHW052008070526
44584CB00016B/1672